American Tempest

American Tempest

How the Boston Tea Party Sparked a Revolution

HARLOW GILES UNGER

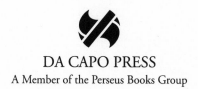

DA CAPO PRESS
A Member of the Perseus Books Group

Designed by Trish Wilkinson
Set in 11.5 point Adobe Garamond Pro

Library of Congress Cataloging-in-Publication Data

Unger, Harlow G., 1931–
    American tempest : how the Boston Tea Party sparked a revolution / Harlow Giles Unger. — 1st Da Capo Press ed.
        p.   cm.
    Includes bibliographical references and index.
    ISBN 978-0-306-81962-9 (hardcover : alk. paper) 1. Boston Tea Party, 1773.
2. United States—History—Revolution, 1775–1783—Causes. I. Title.
E215.7.U64 2011
973.3—dc22   2010047734

First Da Capo Press edition 2011

Published by Da Capo Press
A Member of the Perseus Books Group
www.dacapopress.com

Da Capo Press books are available at special discounts for bulk purchases in the U.S. by corporations, institutions, and other organizations. For more information, please contact the Special Markets Department at the Perseus Books Group, 2300 Chestnut Street, Suite 200, Philadelphia, PA 19103, or call (800) 810-4145, ext. 5000, or e-mail special .markets@perseusbooks.com.

10 9 8 7 6 5 4 3 2 1

To Bob Pigeon and Lissa Warren

There is nothing so easy as to persuade people that they are badly governed.

—THOMAS HUTCHINSON,
GOVERNOR OF MASSACHUSETTS

Contents

List of Illustrations

Maps

Illustrations

Acknowledgments

My deepest thanks to the wonderful staff at my publisher, Da Capo Press of the Perseus Books Group. All work incredibly hard behind the scenes and seldom receive the public acknowledgment they deserve for the beautiful books they produce and market. I owe a great debt of thanks to Publisher John Radziewicz, who has championed the publication of this and other books on American history. Special thanks, too, to Lissa Warren, the brilliant director of publicity, whose tireless efforts I believe do more to promote the study of American history than many schools and colleges. Among other essential contributors to this and other Da Capo books are Kevin Hanover, director of marketing, and the wonderful sales force of the Perseus Books Group; marketing executive Sean Maher, editor Jonathan Crowe; the incredibly skilled—and patient—Cisca L. Schreefel, associate director of editorial services and project editor for this book; copy editor Josephine Mariea; proofreader Anna Kaltenbach; and indexer Robie Grant.

Finally, my most sincere thanks to my wonderful editor Robert Pigeon, executive editor at Da Capo Press, for the time, energy, passion, and skills he contributed to this book, and to my literary agent Edward W. Knappman of New England Publishing Associates, for his enduring faith in my work.

Author's Note: Spellings and grammar in the eighteenth-century letters and manuscripts cited in this book have, where appropriate, been modernized to clarify syntax without altering the intent of the original authors. The original spellings may be found in the works cited in the endnotes and bibliography.

Introduction

ostonians had just stepped out of their homes to go to work when they spotted the notices on fence posts and trees: "Friends! Brethren! Countrymen! That worst of plagues, the detestable tea is now arrived. . . . The hour of destruction or manly opposition to the machinations of tyranny stare you in the face."[1]

It was Monday morning at nine, November 29, 1773, when the first church bell tolled, then a second, and another—until every church tower in the city rocked in the fearful crescendo. All but paralyzed with fear by the din, neighbors glanced at each other, then began trotting down the narrow alleys to the waterfront. Shopkeepers who had just opened for business shuttered their doors and joined the flow of people—hundreds, at first, then thousands, from all directions swarming into the square in front of Faneuil Hall. All tried forcing their way in—rich, poor . . . merchants, craftsmen, farmers, shipfitters, seamen, laborers . . . beggars, thieves, thugs . . . men and boys . . . clubs, rifles, pistols, and a variety of missiles in hand, ready to shatter windows of the capitol or fire at the gods in heaven. They called for the blood of those they hated—British officials, those who supported British rule, those who deprived them of what they perceived as liberty. They called for the overthrow of a government that had fostered their prosperity for generations and protected them from enemy attacks by

1

hostile Indians, French troops, and Spanish conquistadores for a century and a half.

Massachusetts Chief Justice Peter Oliver puzzled over the tempest swirling around him: "For a colony which had been nursed in its infancy with the most tender care and attention, which has been indulged with every gratification that the most forward child could wish for . . . to plunge into an unnatural rebellion . . . must strike some with a degree of astonishment. By adverting to the historic page, we shall find no previous revolt . . . but what originated from severe oppressions."[2]

The cause of the ruckus was indeed astonishing: a three-penny-*per-pound* tax on British tea, which was nothing more than a "social beverage" largely consumed by idle women as "a sign of politeness and hospitality . . . a mark of civility and welcome." But men seldom drank it, and it ranked below ale or rum among the beverages that Americans consumed most. Indeed, only about one-third of the population drank as many as two cups a day, and the tax had no effect on consumption. Eminently affordable by almost every American, tea had first appeared in America as an all-purpose elixir for "headaches, giddiness, and heaviness . . . colds, dropsies, and scurvies—and it expelleth infection . . . prevents and cures agues, surfeits and fevers."[3]

Although the largest, wealthiest merchant groups routinely paid whatever duties the government demanded and absorbed the tiny extra costs, second-tier and third-tier merchants on the edge of failure evaded duties and tried to gain a competitive edge by buying low-cost, smuggled Dutch tea that they could sell at prices well below those of duties English teas. The British government, however, badly needed to collect those duties. It had accumulated debts of more than £1 million in the French and Indian War in the north and west, and Parliament was determined to step up tax enforcement to force Americans to assume more of the costs of their own defense.

Boston's mid-level merchants objected and, as Massachusetts Royal Governor Thomas Hutchinson put it, "From so small a spark, a great fire seems to have been kindled."[4] The dissenting merchants responded to the increased taxes by organizing waterfront workers into a raging mob that surged through the streets, taking control of the town and its government.

The mob brooked no dissent, burning homes of the most outspoken opponents and sending the dreaded tumbrel, "in imitation of the Inquisition coach," to the doors of citizens who dared voice support for the established government. The squeaking wooden tipcart arrived at dawn, its drivers breaking down doors and dragging shrieking victims from their beds for transport to the "Liberty Tree." A jeering mob awaited to strip them, swab them in scalding tar, and dress them in chicken feathers before hanging them by the waist from a branch to be scorned, beaten, and humiliated.[5]

"The tarring and feathering and riots reigned uncontrolled," Chief Justice Peter Oliver recalled. "The liberty of the press was restrained by the very men who had been halloowing for liberty. . . . Those printers who were inclined to support government were threatened."[6] After the mob burned down the home of a merchant who had paid the required duties on imported tea, a churchman at the conflagration assured the merchant's frightened neighbors "that it was all right, it being in a good cause."[7]

Oliver explained that "all this struggle and uproar arose from the selfish designs of the merchants." He called them "mock patriots who disguised their private views by mouthing it for liberty . . . [but] who will sacrifice everything for money."[8]

The struggle and uproar climaxed on Thursday, December 16, 1773, with the legendary "Boston Tea Party," when an estimated six to seven dozen men, many amateurishly disguised as Indians—who were then a symbol of freedom—dumped at least £10,000 of tea (about $1 million today) into Boston harbor. Whatever the motives of its perpetrators, they unleashed social, political, and economic forces they would never again be able to control.

The Boston Tea Party provoked a reign of terror in Boston and other American cities, with Americans inflicting unimaginable barbarities on each other. Mobs dumped tea and burned tea ships in New York; Philadelphia; Charleston, South Carolina; and elsewhere—and Boston staged a second tea party a few months after the first one. The turmoil stripped tens of thousands of Americans of their dignity, homes, properties, and birthrights—all in the name of liberty and independence. Nearly 100,000 Americans left the land of their forefathers forever in what was history's largest exodus of Americans *from America,* and untold thousands who refused to leave their native land fled westward into the dangerous wilderness to start life anew under new identities.

Even in the face of such horrors, John Adams saw a grander picture, calling the Boston Tea Party nothing short of "magnificent" and insisting it displayed "a dignity, a majesty, a sublimity. . . . This destruction of the tea is so bold, so daring, so firm, intrepid and inflexible, and it must have so important consequences, and so lasting, that I cannot but consider it as an epocha [sic] in History."[9]

Ironically, few, if any, Americans today—even those who call themselves Tea Party Patriots—know the true and entire story of the original Tea Party and the Patriots who staged it. Their names are long forgotten; no monument lists them or describes what they did and why. Before the original Tea Party Patriots disembarked, they swore never to reveal each other's names, although British authorities accused John Hancock, Sam Adams, James Otis—and even fat little John Adams—of dumping some of the tea. Although the names of Tea Party Patriots are of some interest, what John Adams called the "important consequences" of the Tea Party had far more impact on American history—socially, politically, and economically. One social consequence, for example, was a shortage of tea that helped transform Americans into a nation of coffee drinkers. However, the political and economic consequences went far beyond culinary tastes and also affected the minds, hearts, souls, and lives of almost every American then and now. These included, among others, a declaration of independence, a bloody revolution, and the modern world's first experiment in self-government.

What a party! What a teapot! And what a tempest!

Chapter 1

"Rally, Mohawks!"

*T*housands had pushed into the Old South Meeting House, "turning the House of God into a den of thieves," according to Massachusetts Chief Justice Peter Oliver. "Thus assembled, they whiled away the time hissing and clapping, cursing and swearing until it grew near darkness and then the signal was given to act their deeds of darkness."[1]

A burst of blood-curdling war whoops from without silenced the huge congregation for a moment.

"Rally, Mohawks!" came a cry from the rear—and again the terrifying war whoops from beyond. From the pulpit, moderator Samuel Adams called out, "This meeting can do no more to save the country."[2] And the doors of the church burst open, spilling congregants onto the stony parvis in the icy moonlit air.

"Boston harbor a tea-pot tonight!" someone shouted.

"Hurrah for Griffin's Wharf!" answered another.

"The Mohawks are come!" a third voice called.[3]

Fifty or more men stood huddled in the shadows of the buildings opposite the church—blankets draped over their heads and shoulders, their faces smeared with lamp-black. Poised as Indians, they wore tomahawks, knives, or pistols in their belts and carried an axe or hatchet in their hands. Together, they represented the first—the original—Tea Party Patriots and would redound through history as a collective symbol against government taxation without the consent of the taxed.

As the throng burst from the church, the Mohawks signaled to them to follow in silence along Milk Street, then a sharp right toward the waterfront, flowing like molten lava—steadily, relentlessly—until it reached Fort Hill. Other "Indians" stepped into the line of march, "one after another, as if by accident, so as not to excite suspicion."

Three ships lay tied to the pier as the procession approached Griffin's Wharf. Armed guards protected the entrance, but stood away as the Indians approached. The crowd of followers halted on a rise above the wharf to watch the Indians as they boarded the ships. Like a swarm of locusts, the Indians spread across the decks, with some attaching blocks and tackles to lift chests from the holds. Chest after chest rose from the darkness of the ship's bowels onto the decks, where axes and hatchets split their seams so expertly that spectators barely heard a sound. "We resembled devils from the bottomless pit rather than men," recalled Joshua Wyeth, a sixteen-year-old blacksmith at the Tea Party. "Many of [us] were apprentices and journeymen, not a few, as was the case with myself, living with Tory masters.

> We boarded the ship . . . and our leader in a very stern and resolute manner, ordered the captain and crew to open the hatchways and hand us the hoisting tackle and ropes, assuring them that no harm was intended them. . . . Some of our number jumped into the hold and passed the chests to the tackle. As they were hauled on deck, others knocked them open with axes, and others raised them to the railing and discharged their contents overboard. . . . We were merry . . . at the idea of making so large a cup of tea for the fishes.[4]

A reporter from the *Massachusetts Gazette* was also on the scene:

> They applied themselves so dexterously to the destruction of this commodity that, in the space of three hours, they broke up three hundred and forty-two chests, which was the whole number in these vessels, and discharged their contents. . . . When the tide rose, it floated the broken chests and the tea insomuch that the surface of the water was filled there-

with a considerable way from the south part of the town to Dorchester Neck and lodged on the shores [see map 2, page 82]. . . . The town was very quiet during the whole evening and the night following. Those who were from the country went home with a merry heart, and the next day joy appeared in almost every countenance, some on account of the destruction of the tea, others on account of the quietness with which it was effected.[5]

The Tea Party left government officials irate, with Chief Justice Peter Oliver condemning it as a "villainous act." Tea Party leaders, he said, had "assembled the rabble . . . to perpetrate the most atrocious acts of treason and rebellion."[6]

One of the brilliant minds of his native Boston, Justice Oliver pointed out that few, if any, of the men who dumped the tea into Boston harbor that night could even explain their irrational behavior. None consumed as much tea as he did ale, rum, or whiskey; few had any objections to others consuming tea, including their wives; and most bore no malice toward the East India Company, which owned the tea. Moderators at the church who inspired the assault on the tea ships at Griffin's Wharf had railed against taxation, yet the tax on tea was negligible—a mere three-pence *per pound*, or slightly more than *one-tenth of one penny* for a nine-pence cup of a beverage consumed largely by women as "a sign of politeness and hospitality . . . a mark of civility and welcome." On the surface, the Tea Party seemed a senseless, wanton act of vandalism—beyond the ludicrous, drawing the disbelief of most Americans, the ill will of many others, and the wrath of government.

"Had they been prudent enough to have poured it into fresh water instead of salt water," Oliver sneered, "they and their wives and their children and their little ones might have regaled upon it at free cost for a twelve month. But now the fish had the whole regale to themselves. Whether it suited the constitution of a fish is not said, but it is said that some of the inhabitants of Boston would not eat of fish caught in the harbor, because they had drank of the East India Company tea."

To Samuel Adams and other organizers of the Tea Party, however, the tea had become a symbol of property, and the tax on it represented nothing less than confiscation of that property from its rightful owners or purchasers. In fact, the Tea Tax, small as it was, marked the fourth time in forty years that Parliament had tried to tax Americans without their consent. They began with the Molasses Act of 1733, then added the Grenville acts in 1764, the Stamp Act of 1765, and, finally, the Townshend Acts of 1767, which included the notorious Tea Tax that would irritate Americans for more than eight years and provoke the Boston Massacre in 1770, the Boston Tea Party in 1773, and the American Revolution in 1775.

"I truly can have no property which another can by right take from me when he pleases," Samuel Adams thundered. "If our trade may be taxed, why not out lands? Why not the produce of our lands and everything we possess or make use of?"[7]

Chief Justice Oliver, however, dismissed Adams's complaints, insisting that personal ambitions lay behind the carping of Adams and other organizers of the tax protests.

"Toward the latter end of the year 1760," Oliver explained, "the chief justice of the province of Massachusetts died, and a mentally unbalanced, but politically ambitious young lawyer, James Otis, Jr., swore *that if* his father was not appointed justice of the superior court [to replace the deceased jurist], *he would do all the mischief he could to the government [and] would set the province in a flame if he died in the attempt.*"[8] Oliver's brother-in-law Thomas Hutchinson, a phenomenally prosperous Boston merchant who later became Massachusetts royal governor, agreed that Otis provided the "spark" that kindled the conflagration that eventually engulfed Boston.

At the time of Otis's outburst, Hutchinson was lieutenant governor of Massachusetts, and the death of the chief justice had interrupted a critical trial with constitutional ramifications. By seniority and years of service in the Massachusetts House of Representatives, Otis's father, Colonel James Otis, Sr., deserved the higher post. Indeed, two former royal governors had promised him the job as a reward for service as militia commander in the war against the French and for twenty-five years of service as judge in Barnstable, Massachusetts. Elected Speaker of the House of Representatives, Otis was both the logical and the most popular choice, but the new royal governor, Sir Francis Bernard, rejected him because of what he said was a clear conflict of interest: His son, James Otis, Jr., was one of the lawyers representing a group of Salem merchants opposing the crown. Instead, Bernard appointed Hutchinson rather than the elder Otis, and according to Oliver, "the two Otises now exerted themselves, *totis viribus* [with all one's might], to revenge their disappointment in Mr. Hutchinson's destruction."[9]

Bernard's choice of Hutchinson set off a storm of protests. Although a brilliant graduate of Harvard College, Hutchinson was one of Boston's leading merchants and faced no less a conflict of interest in judging a group of Salem merchants than the elder Otis. In addition, Hutchinson was not even a lawyer and had no legal training. Even Hutchinson himself puzzled over Bernard's decision to appoint him, given Bernard's own background in the law. Hutchinson's deficiencies became evident when he took his seat on the bench and faced the brilliant arguments of the younger Otis—a consummate lawyer who attacked with a vengeance. He did not disguise his intent to humiliate the great merchant, who, Otis believed, was more responsible than Bernard for crippling his father's career and, indeed, damaging the older man emotionally.

"Otis was a flame of fire," according to John Adams. "He demonstrated the illegality, the unconstitutionality, the iniquity and inhumanity" of the crown's case so cogently "that every man appeared to me to go away ready to take arms against it. No harangue of Demosthenes or Cicero ever had such effects." Adams was a young lawyer then and had come to observe what he and many of his colleagues considered one of the most important cases in colonial history. "American independence," Adams enthused, "was then and there born; the seeds of patriots and heroes were then and there sown."[10]

At the heart of the case was whether a customs official had the right to issue a blanket search warrant, or "writ of assistance," and, without warning, "search in all suspected places" for smuggled goods—on a merchant's ship, in his barns, in any and every room of his home and anywhere on the merchant's property he chose. Otis called writs "against the fundamental principles of law," arguing that "every man is an independent sovereign. . . . His right to his life, his liberty, no created being could rightfully contest. Nor is his right to property less contestable."[11]

James Otis, Jr. A young Boston lawyer, his irrational hatred for Chief Justice Thomas Hutchinson turned him into a revolutionary. A beating administered by Boston's Customs Commissioner left him insane for the rest of his life. (LIBRARY OF CONGRESS)

The crown, however, did not dispute man's right to property—only his right to property that he smuggled to America without paying import duties.

The roots of the dispute stretched back three decades to 1733, when Britain passed the Molasses Act—the first of a series of ill-advised tax laws that would eventually incite Americans to rebellion. The Molasses Act of 1733 added a six-pence-a-gallon duty on foreign molasses, which American distillers claimed would all but destroy their industry, drive many of them into bankruptcy, and put thousands of their employees out of work. It was not the first time Parliament had interfered in American trade, but it was the first time Parliament had enacted a tax that seemed to limit the growth of a colonial industry. The Navigation Act of 1660, for example, had restricted the carrying trade in and out of the American colonies to

British or American ships, but the restriction spurred the growth of an enormous American ship-building industry that not only eclipsed England's shipbuilders but made it the finest such industry in the world. New England's huge, virgin forests yielded seemingly endless supplies of the finest oak for ships' hulls and incomparably strong and flexible white pines for use as masts. Massachusetts shipbuilders built better quality ships at half the price of comparable English ships, and because of the nearness of forests to the sea, they built them in one-third the time. By 1700 Massachusetts shipyards alone were launching 140 ships a year, and by mid-century, American shipyards as a group had built more than 30 percent of all the ships sailing under the British flag.

And because Boston lay in a protected harbor closer to Britain than any other large American seaport, it rapidly became America's richest, most important shipping center. It boasted other advantages as well. For one thing, it lay on the edge of the infinitely rich New England fishing and whaling grounds. For another, its unusual contour allowed far more wharves to be constructed than in a conventional port city lying in a straight line along the water's edge. Eighteenth-century Boston was almost an island—its only tie to the mainland a narrow little strip of land called Boston Neck, which reached across an expanse of tidal marshes and mud flats that would eventually be filled and renamed Back Bay (see map 1, page 12). Seen from above, the town lay in the water like a fallen bird, its stubby wings outspread, one of them stretching into the Charles River on the northwest and the other reaching into the harbor pointing the way to the open sea. Its head—the North End—lay in the middle of the water, beneath Charlestown. Its multiform shape gave it an enormously long shoreline that permitted construction of endless numbers of wharves and attracted more merchants than conventional ports, along with thousands of waterfront workers from Europe, England, Scotland, Ireland, and elsewhere.

At high tide the Charles River estuary flooded the mud flats and salt marshes to the west of the city and formed the Back Bay. On the east, or harbor side, endless finger piers reached into the water, side by side, embracing hundreds of sailing ships that glided in and out of the harbor each day. After viewing the many ships, the shops, and the opulent mansions of Boston's merchants, Swedish botanist Peter Kalm, who came to

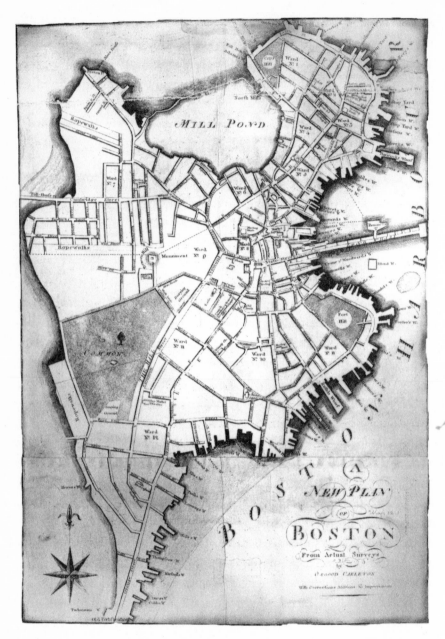

Town of Boston. It was a virtual island at the time of the Boston Tea Party. Griffin's Wharf, the site of the Tea Party, protrudes beneath Fort Hill, between Gardner's Wharf and Russel's Wharf. (BOSTONIAN SOCIETY)

America in 1748 on a natural history survey, remarked, "They outdo London." Later, he lauded the city's "grandeur and perfection. . . . Its fine appearance, good regulations, trade, riches, and power are by no means inferior to those of any, even the most ancient towns of Europe."[12]

Unlike Britain, where class barriers frustrated the ambitions of those seeking wealth, the colonies offered unimagined wealth to almost any talented, imaginative, hard-working man, regardless of social or economic class—provided, of course, he fit into community racial and religious norms. Many of Boston's wealthiest merchants began in small, specialized shops—books, in the case of Thomas Hancock. Books were a good choice in a colony that, from its beginnings, made education and the teaching of literacy compulsory and created a population that depended on reading as a major leisure activity. Besides the Scriptures, every bookseller carried tracts and sermons of every minister of note—sold in clumsy, uncut, unbound sheets. Recognizing the need for bookbinding facilities in Boston's growing printing and publishing industry, Thomas Hancock learned bookbinding, became a master bookbinder, and solicited bookbinding orders from Boston's printers and booksellers, who were elated to turn the jumble of unprinted sheets into rows of neatly shelved, easy-to-find, bound books. Hancock accepted payment in stocks of stationery and printed materials as well as cash. By the end of six months, he had accumulated enough to expand his shop to include stationery—writing paper, quills, sealing wax, inkhorns—even spectacles—along with an enormous array of books: "Bibles large and small, Testaments, Psalters, Psalm Books with tunes or without, Singing-books, School-books . . . Books on Divinity, Philosophy, History, Navigation, Physics, Mathematics, Poetry. . . ."

Only one constraint slowed Boston merchants' breathtaking race to riches: a shortage of cash. Most New Englanders did business by barter, with some trading their labor or handiwork for food, lodging, and other necessities. Others hunted, fished and farmed to survive. Merchants routinely accepted produce, livestock, pelts, whiskey, and other goods as currency. Although many small merchants fell by the economic wayside, bolder—and luckier—merchants gambled every penny they had on growth, expanding into general stores with a wide variety of cloth (calico, chintz, muslin, cotton, buckram, taffetas, damasks, and silks), thread, fans, girdles, "and sundry other sorts of Haberdashery," according to an advertisement in the *Boston News-Letter*. The ad also listed "Silk Shoes, Men's and Women's Hose, millinery, compasses, hour glasses, leather, cutlery, and such staples as sugar, tea and corn."[13] The most successful merchants organized their stores into departments; some offered volume discounts, and all tried stocking their shelves according to seasonal needs, selling off one season's goods before the new season began, to avoid accumulating shopworn inventories. Their advertisements were clever for that era:

> Excellent Bohea Tea, imported in the last ship from London:
> sold by Tho. Hancock.
> N.B. If it don't suit the ladies' taste, they may return the tea and receive their money again.[14]

The women's dress department was usually the largest, with cloth, ribbons, knee and shoe buckles, hats, fans, and other items. Hardware departments, with brass compasses, fire steels, larding pins, swords, and so forth, provided about 10 percent of total sales. Rum and similar provisions also contributed about 10 percent of sales, whereas coal and ships' stores accounted for just over 1 percent in the early eighteenth century and tea somewhat less than 1 percent. Americans had yet to discover the pleasures and pomp of tea and tea parties.

Few shoppers could not find what they needed at the House of Hancock, the House of Hutchinson, or the other great merchant houses. Flocks of city and country folk filled Boston's general stores store each day, and as sales increased, some merchants bought larger quantities at lower costs and expanded into wholesaling, supplying shopkeepers, farms, and merchants in smaller towns. The largest houses—like the House of Hutchinson and House of Hancock—also supplied the government and the military, which forced them to extend credit and drew them into banking.

The leap into merchant banking propelled them into still-larger enterprises such as "commodity barter"—the exchange of shiploads of commodities with merchants in other colonies and overseas without exchanging cash—or paying any taxes. In effect, each colony was an independent nation, and none trusted the value of the other's paper money. Merchants in different colonies paid each other with either specie—gold or silver coins—or "commodity money." In one transaction, a Rhode Island arms merchant wrote to Thomas Hancock that he was "bound to Boston in order to buy two hundred small arms for our force and two hundred blankets for them, and as our currency will not pass at Boston, I prepare to pay for the above articles in molasses."[15]

When the values of commodities in both ends of a trade were unequal, one merchant simply gave the other "change" in the form of nonperishable staples, such as gunpowder, molasses, corn, rum, or, more commonly, salted fish.

Each expansion opened other opportunities. Commodity trading, for example, grew into two-way international trade and even more profitable triangular trade, which involved huge, complex three-way trades between three continents—again, all tax-free. Reinvested profits on the first trade added to the profits on the second, and when the accumulated profits were reinvested carefully in a third trade, all the seamen, ships' officers, and, of course, the merchant often garnered undreamed-of riches when their ship unloaded its last cargo at the end of its last leg . . . as long as the ship didn't fall prey to a storm or pirates.

All too often, one leg of a triangular trade involved the purchase of slaves in Africa and their shipment to the West Indies or the American South for resale in barter deals for molasses, sugar, rum, or tobacco. In two-way trade, a New England merchant, for example, might sell salted fish to a French West Indies trader for molasses that his ship brought home to New England for distillation into rum. In a triangular trade, he might take his initial cargo to Africa, trade it for slaves, whom he carried to the West Indies and traded for molasses for the New England distillery. To cut costs of international trade, the largest merchant houses bought and operated their own ships.

The most successful merchant-bankers took advantage of every profit opportunity—especially the huge, rough-and-tumble London market for whale oil and whale "bone," which was actually cartilage. The former was essential for both illumination and lubrication, and manufacturers used whale bone to make corset stays, cap stiffeners, buggy whips, and similar items. The first boats to arrive in England from America with spring supplies each year made the most money, and the most successful merchants always found ways to be first. Although some merchants waited for whalers to bring their catch to Boston for processing and subsequent transport to London, Thomas Hancock sent his ships to isolated whaling settlements along the shores of northern New England and Newfoundland nearer the hunting grounds and closer to England. There, his agents traded badly needed items such as clothing, tools, foodstuffs, and rum for processed oil and bone, which they then carried directly to London before other whalers had even off-loaded their catch in Boston. Once in London, the sailors, who earned a percentage of the proceeds for each load, jumped onto the piers and drove bidding for their cargoes to fever pitch by spreading rumors that theirs might be the last oil cargo to reach port for months. London agents earned 3 percent of the proceeds whereas captains and crews earned 89 percent—either to pocket or to buy goods to bring back to Boston to resell for even more money.

As they prospered from whale oil transactions, some Boston merchants bought or built their own fleets. By 1732 the House of Hancock owned more than a dozen ships. Whenever overproduction of a commodity sent prices too low to be profitable, Hancock simply dropped out of that particular trade and looked elsewhere for profit opportunities. One year he bought twenty thousand acres of timberland in Connecticut, Massachusetts, and Maine to convert into lumber. In Boston he bought some rental properties and a three-eighths share in Clarke's Wharf, the city's longest and busiest finger pier after Long Wharf. Renamed Hancock Wharf, it stretched into the harbor from Fish Street, where Paul Revere sold silverware, copper engravings, carved picture frames, music sheets, surgical instruments, dental plates, and his own crude drawings.

With wealth came power, of course, and, in 1740, a year after building and moving into his palatial home on Beacon Hill overlooking Boston, Hancock joined the town's other great merchants—Thomas Hutchinson, Andrew Oliver, Thomas Cushing, Richard Clarke, and brewer Samuel Adams, Sr.—on both the Governor's Council and as one of five selectmen who ruled the town of Boston as both legislators and executives with control over the city's finances and commerce. As with elections to the General Court (the provincial legislature), Boston limited voting for selectmen to the town's six hundred–odd "freeholders"—the wealthiest, most influential white, propertied males who made up about 4 percent of the population.

As leaders in both business *and* politics, however, selectmen held in their hands the destinies of thousands of farmers, craftsmen, shopkeepers, and small merchants who depended on Boston's giant merchant-banking houses as a central market to buy supplies and sell goods and services. All had worked together in the friendliest fashion for more than a century— until 1740, when an acute shortage of British currency combined with an economic slump to leave New England farmers, craftsmen, and shop- keepers with too little cash to buy supplies from the big merchant houses. Forced to barter, farmers often found themselves at the mercy of Boston's merchants, who drove produce prices lower by pitting one farmer against another—and soon threatened the survival of many local farms.

In 1740 Samuel Adams, Sr., the owner of the town's largest brewery, came up with a scheme to establish a "land bank" to print paper currency of its own and lend it to farmers against the value of their lands, or "real estate." As producer of New England's most popular beverage, he had an interest in seeing that farmers who came to town to sell produce could fill their pockets with enough cash to fill their carts with barrels of beer to take home. As Sam Adams's Land Bank paper gained currency, farmers gained the upper hand in the marketplace, forcing merchants to accept the paper or see suppliers and customers turn to merchants who would. Within a year of its appearance, Land Bank paper began undermining the value of British currency, and Boston's leading merchant bankers—the Hutchin- sons, Olivers, and Clarkes along with Royal Governor Jonathan Belcher, who was also a merchant—appealed to Parliament to outlaw local cur- rency in New England. Farmers descended on Boston to protest, threat- ening merchants who refused to accept land bank currency.

"They are grown so brassy and hardy as to be now combining in a body to raise a rebellion," Belcher complained. Believing the mobs of farmers were "ripe for tumult and disorder," Belcher ordered sheriffs to jail mob leaders and break up demonstrations—with rifle butts if neces- sary. Although the farmers dispersed, they voted Samuel Adams and other members of the Land Bank party onto the Executive Council. Gov- ernor Belcher vetoed their election and Parliament outlawed the Land

Bank, converting the Samuel Adams family into bitter foes of British rule in America.

Declared "criminals" and criminally liable for all outstanding Land Bank paper at face value, Adams and his partners became the targets of speculators and charlatans who scoured the farmlands, buying up Land Bank currency at huge discounts, then presenting them to Adams and other Land Bank directors in Boston for payment at face value. The run on Land Bank assets all but bankrupted Adams and created a lasting division between Boston's merchant-aristocrats and the rest of the economic community—farmers, shopkeepers, small merchant houses, and, most especially, Samuel Adams.

The split—and the bitterness it engendered—reached down into the next generation, when Harvard demoted Samuel Adams's son, Samuel Adams, Jr., from the fifth-highest rank in his class to the bottom. Harvard's humiliating system of "gradation" ranked students according to family social and economic standing. Although all acquired the title "Sir" as upperclassmen and alumni, they sat, walked, ate, and slept according to family rank while still in school. The son of a Massachusetts governor or Harvard president stood, marched, or sat at the head of his class in processions, in church, in recitation rooms, and at meals. Next in rank came sons of former governors, trustees, large landowners, major contributors, clergymen, and so on. Sons of farmers ranked last, with Sam Adams, Jr., ranking even lower after the Land Bank fiasco. His father's plight forced the young man to find work to help pay costs of attending college and sparked what became both a lifelong loathing of Hutchinson and other merchant-aristocrats and a deep hatred for British authority. According to Chief Justice Peter Oliver, Sam Adams was ready to commit any "crime" to overthrow the government. "When asked to draw the picture of the devil," Oliver recounted, "a celebrated painter responded he would ask Sam Adams to sit for him."[16]

Chapter 2

The Saints of Boston

hen, as now, war—or preparations for war—promised enormous riches for merchants large enough to supply the military needs of warring nations. War had been a virtual constant somewhere in the American colonial world since 1613—in New England, Canada, Ohio, along the Mississippi River, in the Floridas or West Indies, and along the South American coast. It had usually been a three-way affair between England, France, and Spain—with Indian tribes joining one side or the other, depending on which of the white forces seemed strongest and likeliest to serve Indian interests with guns, land, and liquor.

Thomas Hancock had lived on Beacon Hill only a few months when British King George II declared war on Spain after British captain Robert Jenkins claimed that the Spanish had seized his ship eight years earlier and cut off his ear—and he displayed what looked like an ear to a committee of Parliament. In fact, the British had been raiding Spain's forests in Central America and Florida for a decade, and Jenkins's ear provided an excuse for England to seize the territories. In January 1740 James Edward Oglethorpe, founder of Georgia, invaded Florida, and Massachusetts Governor Jonathan Belcher organized an expedition to raid Spanish cities in the Caribbean. A thousand New Englanders, eager for plunder, signed up—a huge number for a city of only fifteen thousand—and Belcher, who had built a fortune as a merchant before securing the governorship, turned to his selectman-merchant friends to supply troops with beef, pork, clothing, tents, and other basics.

Boston's merchants found other ways to profit from the conflict by arming their own ships and obtaining government licenses, or "letters of marque," to seize and plunder enemy merchant vessels on the high seas. Such letters of marque distinguished privateers from pirate vessels, in that they complemented their nation's navies by attacking enemy cargo ships. As compensation, privateers kept the goods and ships they seized and sold them on the open market. Members of some of the colony's most renowned families joined the treasure hunt, including Colonel Josiah Quincy and his brother Edmund, neighbors of lawyer John Adams in Braintree (now Quincy), Massachusetts. The first Quincys had arrived in Boston in 1633 and could trace their family to the Baron de Quincy, one of the noblemen who forced King John to sign the Magna Carta. Josiah and Edmund moved to Boston and built just one privateer, but it returned from its first and only voyage with a Spanish vessel in tow containing a lifetime of riches—161 chests of silver, two chests of gold, and untold amounts of jewelry, silverware, and other valuables.[1] The Quincys never went to sea again.

As Spain and England spilled their treasures into the ocean in the War of Jenkins's Ear, much of it washed ashore onto Boston's docks and into the pockets of the town's great merchants. In March 1744 the French joined Spain and enlarged the conflict—and the profits of Boston's merchants. A new royal governor in Massachusetts, William Shirley, believed that Boston's safety depended on capturing the French fortress at Louisbourg on Cape Breton Island. He organized the largest military expedition ever undertaken in the colonies—a fleet of about one hundred vessels—to carry four thousand New England militiamen and their British commanders to Canada. On the recommendation of his predecessor, he appointed Thomas Hancock to round up the ships and supply the entire expeditionary force with food, clothing, arms, ammunition, and all other materials for as long as the force remained in Canada. Although Britain ceded Louisbourg back to the French at the end of the conflict, the Louisbourg

Thomas Hancock. Founder of the House of Hancock, he was one of the great enterpreneurs in colonial America. He was the uncle of the patriot John Hancock. From a portrait by John Singleton Copley in the Fogg Museum of Art at Harvard University. (COURTESY OF THE HARVARD PORTRAIT COLLECTION, PRESIDENT AND FELLOWS OF HARVARD COLLEGE. GIFT OF JOHN HANCOCK TO HARVARD COLLEGE, 1766. PHOTO BY DAVID MATTHEWS. IMAGE COPYRIGHT, PRESIDENT AND FELLOWS OF HARVARD COLLEGE, HARVARD UNIVERSITY.)

expedition earned Hancock almost £100,000 and made him Boston's—and possibly America's—richest man.

With his wealth and political and social prominence came social responsibility—*noblesse oblige*, as British aristocrats called it—and Thomas Hancock personally undertook, at his own expense, the care and maintenance of the entire Boston Common—the forty-five-acre park that stretched from his front door down Beacon Hill. He had the Frog Pond cleaned regularly to prevent stagnation, planted a grove of elm trees to shade the park, and continually saw to the upkeep of all public areas. Like other prominent Boston merchants—Hutchinson, Oliver, and a few others—he also made generous gifts to the Church, and together they earned the collective epithet "The Saints of Boston."

The Molasses Act of 1733, however, had already turned many lesser saints into sinners. Rum, by then, had become New England's most popular drink, and New England distillers imported the vast majority of molasses to make their rum from the French and Spanish sugar islands of the Caribbean. Although sugar cane grew in the British West Indies, output was small, and the molasses they produced was 25 to 40 percent more costly than that of the foreign sugar islands. Rhode Island's thirty distilleries imported nearly 900,000 gallons of molasses a year, of which 725,000 came from foreign islands; the sixty distilleries in Massachusetts produced 2.7 million gallons of rum a year and imported about 1 million gallons of molasses annually—only 30,000 of it from the British West Indies. By adding a six-pence-a-gallon duty on foreign molasses, the Molasses Act threatened to drive production costs and the price of rum beyond the reach of most New England consumers and cripple an industry on which thousands of American shipfitters, sailors, longshoremen, coopers, distillery workers, merchants, tavern keepers, wine shops, and their employees depended. The *Boston Evening Post* charged Parliament with passing the act merely to allow "a few pampered Creolians to roll in their gilded equipages thro' the streets of London" at the expense of two million American subjects.[2] Some physicians and blue-nosed church ladies, however, hailed the Molasses Act, citing the dangers to physical and moral health and the benefits of tea. Some ministers joined in railing against demon rum and, unaware of the historic irony of their words, urged congregants to hold tea parties instead, and, little by little, many Americans began consuming tea in increasing quantities.

Faced with a collapse of the rum trade and the distilling industry, distillers, merchants, and shipping firms combined to smuggle molasses from foreign sugar islands. Taking advantage of hidden coves along the long, isolated stretches of New England coastline, shippers landed hundreds of cargoes out of sight of customs officials—and, therefore, duty-free. It was the first time that so many otherwise loyal British subjects in America had turned against their king's government.

"It is a defrauding of the King of those dues which the law hath granted to him," Peter Oliver growled, "which fraud is equal in criminality to the injuring of a private person."[3]

But unpredictable waves and currents often sent ships crashing into the rocks, spilling cargoes into the sea. However, with merchants sitting in some of the highest government posts, it was not difficult for them to reduce their losses by bribing underpaid customs officials to declare shiploads of molasses and other dutiable goods as nondutiable "ships' stores" or "for personal use by owner." With armies of burly waterfront workers in their employ, merchant-bankers easily convinced reluctant customs officers that accepting bribes provided both financial security and physical security for their persons, families, and properties. Within a few years, even admiralty judges, who had the last words in deciding whether or not a cargo was dutiable, found many financial advantages to overruling the customs service in favor of Boston's merchant-bankers.

There were also social and political advantages to letting ships slip in and out of Boston harbor without official interference. Boston's leading merchants were political and social leaders who could advance the careers of lesser figures in government—or leave them hopelessly mired in subsistence posts.

Together, the city's merchant-bankers *were* Boston: Thomas Hutchinson, Sr. was a member of the Massachusetts Executive Council, or upper house of the General Court; his son, Thomas, Jr., was a Boston selectman and member of the lower house. The Hutchinsons were direct descendants of Anne Hutchinson, the religious leader who arrived from England in 1634, only fourteen years after the founding of the Massachusetts Bay Colony. Daniel Oliver had married royal governor Jonathan Belcher's daughter and, together with James Bowdoin, another prominent merchant, served on the governor's Executive Council and as a Boston selectman. Bowdoin also served in the upper house of the General Court. Oliver traced his American roots back to the earliest days of the seventeenth century, whereas Bowdoin's father had been among the French Huguenots who fled France for America in the late seventeenth century after Louis XIV revoked the Edict of Nantes and banned Protestantism in France. Thomas Hancock's grandfather Nathaniel was a minister and one of the early settlers of Cambridge, Massachusetts. Collectively, Boston's "saints" lived in the city's most opulent mansions; they owned and occupied the front pews of the Old South Meeting House and sustained it and other Boston institutions financially.

And, with the exception of the minister's son Thomas Hancock, they were all men of Harvard, the educational and social institution that conferred the only equivalent of noble rank that America had to offer.

Founded as a divinity school in 1636, Harvard had broadened its curriculum in the late seventeenth century to adapt to the needs of American mercantile society. Although textbooks were in Latin—and every student admitted to Harvard could read, write, and converse fluently in Latin—the curriculum included Greek and Hebrew along with logic, rhetoric, ethics, metaphysics, and the *belles lettres*—mostly English prose and poetry of the Elizabethan and Jacobean eras. Harvard emphasized the study of Greek and Hebrew to permit students to read original texts of the Scriptures, including the Aramaic books of the Old Testament and the Syriac New Testament. Some students studied French—the mark of a "Gentleman's Education"—with a private tutor. The Harvard day began with prayers at five, followed by a *bever*, or light breakfast, then a study hour at seven and the day's first lecture (in Latin) at eight—often lasting three hours. Students ate dinner at eleven, followed by a recreation hour and three hours with a tutor, who reviewed the morning lecture and quizzed students until they had ingested the subject matter. Evening prayers followed at five, then supper and a few hours of recreation—smoking, chatting, and, finally, sleep— usually at about nine.

But above all, Harvard, as the oldest of America's only three colleges,* taught its sons to lead "their country," which was synonymous with the Massachusetts Bay Colony in an age when each of the colonies were independent "countries." From the day they entered Harvard, incoming freshmen addressed upperclassmen as "Sir"—Sir Hutchinson, Sir Oliver, Sir Bowdoin, Sir Hancock. And at commencement exercises, the entire student body—about one hundred strong at the time—sang this hymn with fervor and confidence in the truths it revealed:

> Thus saith the Lord,
> From henceforth, behold:
> All nations shall call thee blessed;
> For thy Rulers shall be of thine own kindred;
> Your Nobles shall be of yourselves,
> And thy governor shall proceed from the midst of thee.[4]

And as Harvard—and, presumably, God—had ordained, Jonathan Belcher, born in Cambridge, the son of a prosperous merchant, graduated from Harvard, amassed a fortune in his father's business, and won appointment as royal governor of *both* Massachusetts *and* New Hampshire in 1730. Three years later, he simply turned his official eyes away when his father and other merchants—his "kindred"—ignored the Molasses Act and began smuggling molasses and other dutiable goods into Massachusetts and New Hampshire.

During Belcher's reign as governor, New England merchants smuggled an estimated 1.5 million gallons of molasses a year, on which they should have paid £37,500 in duties. The merchants argued disingenuously that the duties would have doubled retail prices of rum and left colonists unable to afford a drop of their favorite drink. In truth, only greed lay behind their objection to paying the duty on molasses, for they were able to distill a 16-pence gallon of molasses into a gallon of rum to

---

*The College of William and Mary was founded in 1693 and Yale College in 1701—both as divinity schools.

Harvard College. Engraving of the college buildings in the eighteenth century, when John Hancock, Samuel Adams, and other Tea Party Patriots attended. Hancock lived in Massachusetts Hall on the right. Founded in 1636, Harvard was America's first college. Its original buildings burned and were replaced by Harvard Hall in 1675 (left), Stoughton Hall in 1699 (center), and Massachusetts Hall in 1720. (LIBRARY OF CONGRESS)

sell at 192 pence—a gross profit of 1,200 percent! The six-pence-per-gallon duty would have cut profits to 1,161.5 percent!

In all, New England merchants paid about £100,000 a year for molasses and earned gross revenues of about £1.2 million, on which they refused to pay a mere 3 percent—£37,500—in taxes. Although merchants in England routinely paid duties on imports, decades of unfettered free enterprise had left American colonists convinced of their "natural" right to import cheap, duty-free molasses—and any other commodity, for that matter—from the French, Spanish, and Dutch West Indies, even if doing so undermined the economic future of their fellow countrymen in the British West Indies. For Boston merchants, duties, no matter how small, on molasses, tea, or any other commodity that they purchased in the marketplace, represented confiscation of part of their own private property and an infringement on their liberties. Taxes suddenly emerged as a central, incendiary issue in their relationship with the government of their motherland.

In addition to reducing the flow of British government revenues, however, smuggling took on a darker complexion in 1754, when the first sparks of war set the wilderness of western Pennsylvania aflame, and some merchants hoped to ensure the survival of their businesses after the war by secretly supplying both sides during the war. A westward migration across the Appalachian Mountains into what Britain claimed as its Ohio Territory brought French troops streaming down from Canada to fortify the area and reaffirm French claims to sovereignty over what they deemed a part of French Louisiana. Virginia's royal governor ordered twenty-one-year-old Lieutenant Colonel George Washington to lead a force of militiamen to reassert Britain's (and Virginia's) claims at the Forks of the Ohio (now Pittsburgh), where the Allegheny and Monongahela Rivers meet and where the French had built a rudimentary fortification they would later expand into Fort Du Quesne. By mid-May, Washington and his force reached a point sixty miles south of the French fort and made camp. On May 27, a scout reported fifty French troops only six miles away, and Washington set out to attack with forty troops and a contingent of friendly Indians. "We were advanced pretty near to them, when they discovered us," he said later.

> I ordered my company to fire . . . the action only lasted a quarter of an hour before the enemy was routed. We killed . . . the commander of the party, as also nine others. . . . The Indians *scalped* the dead and took away part of their arms.[5]

With his order to fire, Washington's men unwittingly fired the first shots of what would explode into the planet's first world war. Called at the time the "Great War for Empire," it would spill the blood of millions across four continents and the seas in between, as seven nations vied for control of the world's wealth over seven years—and Boston's merchants vied for as large a share of that wealth as they could earn or steal.

"They are a set of brave, hardy dogs," Peter Oliver said of the merchants he had known as boys in Harvard. "They will sacrifice everything for money."[6]

Indeed, many were ready to sacrifice their honor as human beings—and the blood of innocents—by disguising their struggle for wealth as a quest for liberty for the common man.

Chapter 3

Mr. Cockle:
The Governor's Creature

Instead of retreating eastward to the safety of British-controlled Fort Cumberland after his attack on the French, young George Washington allowed bravado to govern his judgment and intellect, and he remained at his temporary encampment—scoffing at the 1,100 French troops at Fort Du Quesne. "If the whole detachment of French behave with no more resolution than this chosen party did," he boasted, "I flatter myself we shall have no great trouble in driving them to . . . Montreal."[1]

At dawn on July 3, the crack of a musket shot pierced the chatter of heavy rain over Washington's camp, followed by the cry of a wounded sentry. A chorus of Indian war whoops heralded the emergence of three columns of French troops, who raked the camp with musket fire. When the firing stopped, thirty Virginians lay dead and seventy wounded; Washington had little choice but to accept French demands that he surrender all his arms in exchange for safe passage home for himself and his troops.

For the moment, the West remained in French hands, and British authorities, sensing an expansion of North American hostilities with the French, urged royal governors in America to make joint preparations for war. Delegates from New England, New York, Pennsylvania, and Maryland met in Albany, New York, where Benjamin Franklin, a Pennsylvania delegate, stunned the conference by proposing that the colonies unite politically. With strong support from Massachusetts merchant-banker Thomas Hutchinson, Jr., the delegates approved a plan that would unite all the colonies except Georgia and Nova Scotia under a crown-appointed president general and a grand council, or legislature, to be elected by colonial assemblies. However, the plan met with a curt rejection by the home government in Britain and all the royal governors in America, thus postponing all prospects of union for a generation.

The following spring, a British convoy sailed into Chesapeake Bay with a contingent of professional British troops under General Edward Braddock, who planned to combine his force with provincial militia to drive the French from the Ohio Valley. From the first, however, everything that could go wrong for Braddock did. Maryland failed to send wagons to carry supplies; Pennsylvania failed to send horses; and Maryland, Pennsylvania, and Virginia all failed to raise their complements of troops to supplement British regulars. Even the Indians who had pledged to support the English failed to appear.

"I am almost in despair," Braddock lamented, "from the . . . sloth and ignorance . . . of the people and the disunion of the several colonies."[2]

Nonetheless, Braddock ordered his troops to march westward across the Appalachians to Fort Du Quesne, "confident they would never be attacked,"[3] according to Washington, who joined Braddock as an aide. Suddenly, the crackle of shots and blood-curdling whoops engulfed the woods just east of the French fort. A mob of half-naked French and Indians materialized among the trees above the British right column, fired a staccato of shots, then disappeared into the forest. Dozens of British troops fell dead and wounded. Before stunned survivors could reform their lines to return fire, the French and Indians had vanished. The British fired at trees, only to hear war whoops build to a deafening crescendo at the rear. Before they could turn, another band of Indians had emerged, fired, and vanished. In and out they sprang, left, right, front, rear . . . appearing, disappearing, reappearing. They were everywhere, nowhere, never forming lines to fight by European rules of linear warfare.

Confusion and terror gripped the British ranks. Officers on horseback charged back and forth, their mounts shifting right, left, and whinnying in blood-curdling dissonance with Indian war cries. All-too-easy targets on the open ground, troops, officers, and horses toppled like toys. Washington felt musket balls slice through his hat and uniform as he tried in vain to rally troops; shots felled two of his horses but left him uninjured, and he remounted horses of dead riders. Braddock was less fortunate. A ball shattered his arm, smashed through his rib cage and lodged in his lungs. One by one, other officers fell onto the blood-soaked ground as they tried to rally troops. The slaughter lasted three hours; 977 of the 1,459 British troops lay dead or wounded. Twenty-six of the eighty-six officers were killed; thirty-seven others, including Braddock, suffered wounds. Braddock died five days later. French casualties amounted to seventeen dead or wounded; the Indians lost about one hundred warriors.

As they ran out of ammunition, British survivors dropped their weapons, ran to the river and thrashed their way to safety on the opposite bank. Instead of pursuing, the Indians remained on the battleground, hopping about the dead and wounded—like vultures—plundering wagons and bodies, methodically scalping, ignoring shrieks of the wounded as they sliced and ripped hides off living heads as well as dead. Washington used his knowledge of the western wilderness to lead the three hundred-odd survivors back to the safety of British-held Fort Cumberland. Although Americans hailed Washington for his heroism in leading survivors to safety, British military commanders puzzled over the depth of the military supplies in the hands of the French and Indians in so isolated an outpost as Fort Du Quesne. With British ships in control of the Atlantic, the only sources of arms in North America were New England's merchants. Although British authorities called such traffic treasonous, the merchants viewed all cash customers alike and bristled at government attempts to restrict their freedom to buy from and sell to whomever they pleased.

The humiliation of English troops in the West encouraged the French to expand the war against their ancient enemy and, by 1757, what had been a regional struggle called the French and Indian War expanded, with France, England, and five other nations at war across the face of the earth for domination of territories in Europe, Africa, and Asia as well as the Americas. In North America, a twelve thousand–man French army swept southward along Lake Champlain in New York, capturing Lake George to the south and threatening to sweep across the entire northern half of New York. Again, the French forces surprised the British military by the endless reserves of military supplies and other essentials at their command in a wilderness far removed from the French homeland by a vast ocean controlled by the British navy. In the ensuing months, the British replotted their strategy in North America, relegating ill-trained amateur soldiers of the American militia to secondary roles and sending only professional, regular army troops into battle.

To try to cut the flow of supplies from the British colonies to French Canada, the British launched a massive attack from the south, recapturing Lake George and Lake Champlain and cutting the links between New York's productive farmlands and Montreal. Meanwhile, a British fleet of thirty-three ships with ten thousand regulars aboard sailed to attack Cape Breton Island and the huge fortress of Louisbourg, which guarded the entrance to the St. Lawrence River Valley and the flow of arms, ammunition, and other essentials to French forces and the French population in Quebec. With Louisbourg in British hands, the French would have to surrender all of New France.

When the huge British invasion force landed on June 8, 1757, the French had only 4,500 troops and twelve fighting ships to defend the massive fortress. At the end of two weeks, British attackers had overrun the fort's outer defenses and trapped the remaining French troops inside. On August 1, the French raised the flag of surrender.

In the West, meanwhile, English Brigadier General John Forbes was leading two thousand British regulars and two thousand Virginia militiamen toward Fort Du Quesne to avenge the massacre of General Braddock and his men and force the French out of the Ohio Territory. By the time they came within sight of Fort Du Quesne, however, its French occupants had set it ablaze and fled. The British would rebuild the fort and rename it Fort Pitt.

As the British combed through the detritus of Louisbourg's previous inhabitants, they made a shocking discovery: Most of the French army's supplies—clothes, tents, and other accouterments, along with considerable amounts of arms and ammunition—were British, smuggled to Newfoundland by American merchant ships sailing from Boston, Rhode Island, and New York. A subsequent investigation found that as many as forty American ships had smuggled supplies to French forces at Louisbourg before it fell—and were still carrying goods to French military authorities in Newfoundland.

"An illegal trade is carried on between Rhode Island and the French settlements . . . for supplying His Majesty's enemies," declared the captain of a British privateer charged with capturing cargo ships bound for French Canadian ports.[4]

Infuriated by the findings, Major General Jeffrey Amherst wrote angry notes to the governors of Massachusetts, Connecticut, and Rhode Island, singling out the last as "one of the principal colonies upon which they [the French] depend. . . . Several of the merchants of Newport," he declared, "are deeply concerned in this iniquitous trade, which is not only infamous in itself by supporting the avowed enemies of the king, but occasions great difficulty in procuring necessary supplies for carrying on His Majesty's service."[5]

In Britain, the king's intimates raged at New England merchants' refusal to put British interests or patriotism ahead of their lust for money. Colonel William Byrd, a king's councilor with a penchant for lyricism, put it this way: "The Saints of New England have a great dexterity at palliating a perjury so well as to leave no taste of it in the mouth, nor can any people like them slip through a penal statute."[6]

With British warships guarding the entrance to the St. Lawrence River Valley, French defeat became inevitable, but British military commanders feared that if smugglers continued to supply French forces in Canada, they would stall British victory and force Britain to pay a heavy price in men and materials. At their urging, William Pitt, the Earl of Chatham, who was responsible for British foreign and military affairs, sent a circular letter to the royal governors, warning of

> an illegal and most pernicious trade, carried on by the King's subjects in North America . . . by which the enemy is . . . supplied with provisions

and other necessities whereby they are . . . enabled to sustain and protract this long and expensive war. . . . It is His Majesty's express will and pleasure that you do forthwith make the strictest and most diligent enquiry into the state of this dangerous and ignominious trade.

Pitt's letter went on to demand that colonials "desist from the infamous and traitorous practices of supplying the enemy with provisions and military stores during a war undertaken at their request and for their immediate protection."[7] Parliament backed Pitt's demands by passing an act allowing customs officers to obtain writs of assistance to search and seize without specifying in advance what they were searching for, what they might seize, or where they would search. With writs of assistance, customs officials would, for the first time, have powers to collect duties and other taxes—and, indeed, end most of the trade. In effect, the writs threatened to drive many if not most Massachusetts merchants out of business by forcing them to pay duties on goods they had long smuggled tax-free into port, then up the St. Lawrence River.

In 1759 British troops forced the French to evacuate the last of their forts in the West and retreat into Upper Canada (now Ontario) and Quebec. To the south, 11,000 troops under Amherst sat on the banks of the St. Lawrence River opposite Montreal. From the east, a fleet of twenty-one British ships of the line, twenty-two frigates and sloops, and nearly one hundred transports sailed up the St. Lawrence toward Quebec with an army of about 7,500 under the command of Major General James Wolfe. The French defenders numbered about 15,000 but offered no resistance as the British landed at the foot of the cliffs beneath Quebec city. On the evening of September 12, Wolfe sent his light infantry scaling the cliffs. By seven the next morning, they had reached the top and the Plains of Abraham, initially catching the French by surprise. By nine, the two sides had lined up against each other in traditional linear warfare. After several days of furious exchanges, the French retreated, and on September 18, 1759, the city of Quebec surrendered to the British. British forces captured Montreal the following summer, effectively ending the North American segment of the Seven Years' War and giving Britain control of Canada and the rest of North America east of the Mississippi River. Although the Seven Years' War would rage on in Europe, Africa, Asia, and the high seas until 1763, peace returned to North America, where British authorities pieced together the events that had hindered their victory.

Clearly, many merchants in Massachusetts had prolonged the war by smuggling essential goods to French forces, not only undermining the British military effort but depriving the British treasury of revenues to help pay for the war. A British vice-admiral, for example, found almost one hundred vessels flying British colors in the French West Indies, where they were purchasing molasses that they planned to smuggle to New England distillers, who had paid for it with contraband war materiel for French forces. Aside from trading with the enemy, the New England merchants were depriving the British government of revenues by smuggling in French molasses duty-free and, at the same time, threatening the future of British sugar cane growers in the British West Indies.

"So pernicious is this illicit trade," Justice Peter Oliver railed, "that it . . . wrongs the society of those dues which are the resources for its support and injures the fair dealer by lessening his abilities to aid society and maintain his private family."[8] New England merchants disagreed vehemently, however—idealizing what Oliver called "illicit trade" as legitimate free trade and a basic right of free men.

When Sir Francis Bernard accepted the governorship of Massachusetts in 1760, he ignited the first embers of revolution by assuring William Pitt that he would crush the smugglers. A former governor of New Jersey, Bernard arrived in Boston and made a show of appointing one of his personal aides, James Cockle, as customs inspector in Salem, which harbored much of the molasses smuggling trade. Bernard then ordered importers of French molasses either to pay duties on their cargoes or switch to duty-free molasses from the British West Indies. Within months, shippers apparently stopped smuggling French molasses into Salem and imported only duty-free British molasses. The strategy boded well for the economy of the British West Indies but reduced customs collections in Salem to near zero—and attracted the attention of John Temple, the surveyor-general of Massachusetts customs. To his astonishment, Salem merchants were importing more cane from the English island of Anguilla in just a few weeks than that island's entire annual crop.

"It was known that the island did not grow as many sugar canes as to afford cargo for one vessel," Thomas Hutchinson explained. In fact, he said, the Salem merchants had continued importing French molasses, paying Cockle sizable sums to relabel the cargo as duty-free British molasses. A subsequent investigation proved that Governor Bernard had engineered the scheme. Before coming to America, one of his predecessor governors had explained the financial benefits that accrued to permissive royal governors, and Bernard arrived in Boston prepared to make Massachusetts merchants pay him dearly for the right to continue their smuggling trade.

Within weeks of Cockle's appointment, every ship coming into Salem with dutiable goods paid Cockle (and Bernard) substantial bribes for labeling a cargo as entirely or partially duty-free. According to an affidavit filed at the Salem Custom House, Cockle accepted "casks of wine, boxes of fruit, etc., which was a gratuity for allowing . . . vessels to be entered with salt or ballast only, and passing over unnoticed such prohibited cargoes as wine, fruit, etc . . . part of which the said James Cockle used to share with Governor Bernard."[9]

When a smuggler offered a bribe that did not meet Bernard's expectations, the governor ordered Cockle to seize the ship and, under admiralty proceedings, often recovered triple damages from forfeiture of the ship and its cargo. One-third of the award went to the "informer"—in this case Cockle, who shared his proceeds with Bernard—one-third to the province (Bernard pocketed much of the award), and one-third to the crown.

"The governor," Hutchinson wrote later, "was very active in promoting seizures for illicit trade, which he made profitable by his share in the forfeitures. The collector in Salem [Cockle] was the Governor's creature."[10]

When confronted, Cockle tried bribing the surveyor-general, who summarily fired him. "This raised a great clamor, a great share of which was against the governor," according to Hutchinson. Bernard not only denied participating in Cockle's schemes, he denied that they were, in fact, corrupt. "If conniving at foreign sugar and molasses, and Portugal wines and fruit is to be reckoned corruption," he scoffed, "there was never, I believe, an uncorrupt customs house officer in America."[11]

Exposure of the Cockle-Bernard scheme left Bernard all but impotent as governor—a target for merchant jokes and laughter. By participating in merchant smuggling, he had crossed a line as fateful as the Rubicon—a line that neither he nor the British government would ever be able to re-establish. Bernard was, after all, the king's own representative, and Boston merchants naturally assumed that the king himself had agreed to ignore smuggling in favor of fostering the local colonial economy.

"I do not know that he has done more than all his predecessors used to do," Hutchinson sighed.[12]

The Cockle-Bernard scheme set off a wave of smuggling that made it the accepted, all-but-universal modus operandi in American international trade, expanding beyond West Indian molasses to include a wide range of dutiable goods from Europe—dry goods, wines, gunpowder, fruit, oil, salt, and an array of other imports, including tea. As imports of less-costly, duty-free smuggled goods increased, Massachusetts merchants amassed enormous wealth and power, and New England prospered from what amounted to free and unlimited, untaxed trade. For New England merchants—indeed, for most New Englanders—duty-free smuggling soon metamorphosed into one of the basic human rights afforded to all Americans.

The British treasury, meanwhile, suffered huge losses from the exercise of those rights, as revenues from duties plunged to a negligible £2,000—only about one-fourth of the costs of housing and paying the customs officials in America who collected them.

After firing Cockle, surveyor-general John Temple petitioned the superior court for writs of assistance, or search warrants, for the vessels in Salem harbor, and the court ordered the case sent to Boston, hoping to find an impartial jury less beholden to Salem's merchant-smugglers. Boston's chief justice, however, died before the appointed hearing date and Royal Governor Bernard incurred the wrath of Judge James Otis, the veteran jurist of Barnstable, Massachusetts. Instead of appointing Otis—the logical choice for chief justice—Bernard named Lieutenant Governor Hutchinson, Jr., with the expectation that Hutchinson would find for the Salem merchants and forbid issuance of the writs.

Forty years old by then, Hutchinson, Jr. had, like his father before him, graduated from Harvard and, after earning his M.A. in 1730, entered his father's great merchant-banking house. He had married in 1734, fathered five children—three sons and two daughters—and more than doubled the size of his father's enterprise, amassing a fortune of his own. With wealth came increased responsibilities to protect his estate and way of life by participating in public service.

Turning management of the family enterprise over to his sons Thomas III and Elisha, Hutchinson served as a Boston selectman, then representative in the colonial lower house, and, finally, Speaker of the House from 1746 to 1748. Described as "tall, slender, fair-complexioned, and fair spoken," he was both handsome and "a very good gentleman, who captivated half the pretty ladies in the colony [and] more than half the gentlemen."[13] Appointed to the bench in 1752, Hutchinson was a strong supporter of Benjamin Franklin's Plan of Union at Albany in 1754 to strengthen the colonies economically and militarily. He became lieutenant governor of Massachusetts in 1758 and held that post, along with his seat as Chief Justice of the Superior Court, when he heard the angry argument of lawyer James Otis, Jr., against John Temple's writ of assistance.

Otis's fiery tone surprised Hutchinson as well as many courtroom observers. Born in Barnstable in 1725, Otis had graduated from Harvard in 1743, studied law, and, after gaining admittance to the bar, moved to Boston in 1750. Five years later he married a merchant's daughter, and after the birth of their third child, he prepared to settle in as a member of Boston's plutocracy, serving as lawyer for his father-in-law's merchant friends. He joined the Merchants Club and the Freemasons, and his influential friends rewarded the young man by getting him appointed king's attorney then king's advocate general in the vice-admiralty court. Indeed, Governor Bernard had expected Otis to argue for the government in the writs case. Otis had, in fact, declared a few years earlier that "the authority of all acts of Parliament which concern the colonies and extend to them is ever acknowledged in all the courts of law and made the rule of all judicial proceedings in the province. . . . We know no inhabitant within the bounds of the government that ever questioned this authority."[14]

When, however, Governor Bernard failed to name Otis's father as chief justice to the superior court and named Hutchinson instead, the younger Otis resigned his government post, lashed out at Bernard and Hutchinson, and chose to represent the smuggler-merchants in their resistance to Par-

Thomas Hutchinson, Jr. Heir to a great Boston merchant-banking house, he went into the colonial government, becoming, successively, lieutenant governor, chief justice, and governor. His efforts to put down revolutionary activity in Boston eventually forced him to flee to Britain to live the rest of his life in exile. (BOSTONIAN SOCIETY)

liament. As dramatic as Otis's decision to resign from government service was Justice Hutchinson's decision to hear a case that would force him to decide between the crown, to which he had sworn allegiance, and a group of merchants to whom he was tied by family and friends.

"No acts of Parliament can establish such a writ," Otis declared, in direct contradiction to his assertion before the Massachusetts Assembly three years earlier. Calling the writs "instruments of slavery . . . and villainy," Otis warned that such writs represented "a kind of power . . . which in former periods of English history cost one king of England his head and another his throne. I have taken more pains in this cause than ever I will take again."[15]

Otis's argument non-plussed the usually implacable Hutchinson. Torn between his deep belief in individual liberty and his oath to the crown, he left the question in limbo by granting a continuance. Although his ruling seemed neutral, it proved a victory for the crown by failing to quash the writ—or halt the issuance of future writs—and Hutchinson would pay a high personal price for not ruling more decisively. In fact, Hutchinson opposed writs. As a merchant, he—like Otis—believed property sacrosanct under England's Magna Carta. As a loyal British subject, however, he believed—again, like Otis earlier—that Parliament had a constitutional right to legislate and British subjects had an obligation to obey the law. His effort to steer a neutral course between his own conflicting beliefs forced Bostonians to choose between the interests of the crown and the interests of free enterprise. In choosing, they widened the split that had been developing since the Land Bank days of the early 1740s between large merchant houses, which could afford to absorb the costs of duties, and smaller merchants, shopkeepers, and craftsmen, who depended on such low-cost smuggled goods as molasses and tea for enough profits to survive. The interest of the two had now become incompatible. Otis emerged from the case as champion of smaller merchants, winning election to the upper house of the General Court in 1763.

"He engrafted his self into the body of smugglers," Justice Peter Oliver growled, "and they embraced him so close, as a lawyer and useful pleader for them that he became incorporated with them."[16]

To protect his own smuggling operations, merchant king Thomas Hancock and his nephew/partner John Hancock were among those who embraced Otis and even recommended him to their British counterparts who needed legal representation in America.

But Otis's most avid supporter was an angry, disheveled thirty-nine-year-old, whose ragged clothes, poor grooming habits, and foul mouth repelled all but the equally ill-kempt laborers of the Boston waterfront. Claiming to despise money, Samuel Adams, Jr. had graduated from Harvard in 1740, ranked at the bottom of his class socially. He nonetheless sought and found a job at the great merchant house of Thomas Cushing, Sr., a friend of Adams's father, the brewer. Within a short time, however, Cushing dismissed young Adams for writing political tracts instead of keeping company ledgers. Adams, Sr. then gave his son some money to start a business, but Sam loaned half the money to a friend who lost it, and Sam promptly lost the rest on his own. Sam then went to work in the family brewery but ignored his job to found a political club with other young malcontents and write political diatribes in a newspaper they published. Still filled with bitterness over his father's fate in the Land Bank collapse, Adams fixed on destroying Thomas Hutchinson and the other mercantile aristocrats, but his groundless editorial attacks repelled readers, and his newspaper went bankrupt after a year.

Sam Adams's parents died in 1758, and although young Sam—by then thirty-six—inherited the brewery and the family's fine home on Purchase Street, he ran the brewery into bankruptcy and allowed the house to deteriorate. Evidently unconcerned with earning money, he married, fathered two children, and, after his wife's death, raised his children in abject poverty. Friends of his father found him a sinecure as a city tax collector to ensure his earning enough to feed his children and his slave, but within a short time, his ledgers showed a shortage of £8,000, representing tax monies he had either failed to collect or had embezzled.

Initially repelled by Adams's person, Otis only embraced his fellow Harvard alumnus after discovering Adams's skilled pen and his connections with a huge, disenfranchised, and underpaid population of shipfitters, rope makers, sail makers, caulkers, sailors, clerks, and longshoremen who worked Boston's waterfront. The waterfront workers would soon prove a natural and powerful constituency as foot soldiers for Sam Adams's political movement. Although Adams abstained from alcohol, he spent evenings roaming the city's taverns, where, according to his distant cousin John Adams, patrons "smoke tobacco till you cannot see from one end to the other. There they drink flip* I suppose, and there they choose . . . selectmen, assessors, collectors, wardens, fire-wardens, and representatives." Sam Adams patrolled the taverns to make certain that they chose the men he wanted them to choose and ensure his own ambitions for political power.

---

*"A mixture of beer and spirit sweetened with sugar and heated with a hot iron."—*The Shorter Oxford Dictionary*

Samuel Adams. A brewer's son and early leader of the American Revolution, his incompetence in business left his family business bankrupt. A master propagandist, his provocative articles in Boston's radical press helped provoke the Boston Massacre. (Library of Congress)

At the time, John Adams was a young lawyer, still in his twenties. A graduate of Harvard's class of 1755, he grew up in farm country near Braintree, Massachusetts. Descended from Henry Adams, an English farmer who emigrated to America in the early 1600s, John Adams taught school after leaving Harvard and flirted with the ministry before deciding to study law. Pledging "never to commit any meanness or injustice," he believed that the practice of law "does not dissolve the obligations of morality or of religion."[17] He gained admission to the Boston bar late in 1758 and was still building his practice and writing an occasional, thoughtful essay on public affairs for newspapers when British Prime Minister George Grenville coaxed Parliament into passing a set of tax laws to supplement the Molasses Act and add duties to a range of consumer goods, including tea. The growing popularity of tea made higher prices particularly unwelcome, and together with the other tax increases, any tax on tea threatened to incite a storm of protests.

Chapter 4

The Miserable State
of Tributary Slaves

*T*he defeat of the French and cession of New France to Britain provoked an all-but-immediate conflict with Indians in the West. When the
French army evacuated western military posts, a wave of English colonists
migrated westward, threatening to overrun tribal lands. Outraged by the
incursions, Ottawa Chief Pontiac organized western tribes and launched
a massive attack on undermanned British posts, destroying seven of the
nine British forts west of Niagara. Stiff resistance kept Fort Pitt and Detroit in British hands, but the Indians decided to await victory by attri-
tion and laid siege. Major General Jeffrey Amherst suggested breaking the
siege by sending blankets laden with small pox germs into the Indian
camps, but the British commander in the West overruled him.

Incensed by the Indian attacks and the Pennsylvania Assembly's failure
to protect white settlers, a mob of fifty-seven drunken frontiersmen from
Donegal and Paxton townships massacred twenty unarmed Conestoga Indians northwest of Lancaster. The attack incited some six hundred farmers
and frontiersmen in the area to take up arms and march to Philadelphia,
determined to seize control of Pennsylvania's government. Only the inter-
cession of Benjamin Franklin and a group of prominent Philadelphians

with some barrels of rum at the city line convinced the "Paxton Boys" to turn back and stagger home with pledges of more military aid for westerners and more equitable representation in the state legislature.

Five months later, British army regulars arrived to relieve both Fort Pitt and Detroit, and after a series of bloody encounters, Pontiac surrendered, but the campaign—along with the serio-comic adventure of the Paxton Boys—convinced British commanders that ill-trained colonial militiamen were incapable of defending frontier settlers against Indian attacks. Only a permanent, regular-army presence would permit development of the West and establishment of permanent settlements.

With Britain all but bankrupt from the war, however, the costs of maintaining a permanent army in America to defend colonists impelled Prime Minister George Grenville to try to force Americans to share the costs of their defense. The French and Indian War had left the government more than £145 million in debt, of which £1,150,000 had gone to the colonies for war costs. While colonial merchants had reaped fortunes by smuggling goods to the enemy, Parliament had crushed Englishmen with an avalanche of taxes that swept 40,000 people into debtor's prisons and provoked anti-tax riots across England. Englishmen had been paying twenty-six shillings a year per person in taxes to the government, compared to 1 shilling a year, or one-twentieth of a pound, per person in America, where the average annual income was about £100. With regional tax riots in Britain threatening to explode into a national rebellion, Grenville had no choice but to ease England's tax burden.

Formerly first lord of the treasury and chancellor of the exchequer, Grenville had become prime minister in April 1763, inheriting an annual budget that included nearly £1 million to support the king and £372,774 for American military garrisons. Described as "one of the ablest men in Great Britain,"[1] he could do little about the king's spending, but he could, at least, force colonists to pay for their own defenses. Taxes were not new in America, but, like the Molasses Act, they were indirect taxes—import duties that merchants were supposed to pay but had evaded by smuggling or by bribing customs officials.

Britain had sent ten thousand British regulars to guard western frontiers against Indian attacks, while the British navy patrolled Atlantic coastal waters and freed Americans to enjoy a prosperity that no colony had ever before experienced in world history. With land the basis of all wealth in the Americas, the crown had made millions of acres of wilderness available to every white freeman for the taking, and thousands had reaped a rich harvest of grain, lumber, pelts, furs, and ores. Grenville felt it only just that they share some of their wealth with the mother country—and the vast majority of Englishmen agreed.

The first of the Grenville tax proposals was the American Revenue Act, which aimed at strict enforcement of customs-revenue collection and a substantial increase in American contributions to British government costs. The act outraged Americans. The prospect of stricter tax collections, Governor Bernard wrote to the Board of Trade in London, "caused a greater alarm in this country than the taking of Fort William Henry [by the French] in 1757. . . . The merchants say, 'There is an end of the trade in this province . . . it is sacrificed to the West Indian planters.'"[2] A correspondent for the *Boston Evening Post* warned against "making acts and regulations oppressive to trade," while a protest in the *Pennsylvania Journal* declared, "Every man has a natural right to exchange his property with whom he chooses and where he can make the most advantage of it."[3]

The issue of so-called natural rights had been infecting western European, English, and American social and political thought periodically for more than a century, but it gained new virulence in 1762 with the appearance of Jean-Jacques Rousseau's *Le contrat social* ("The Social Contract"). Its opening words stunned the world with a revolutionary new sociopolitical concept: "Man was born free and everywhere he is in chains."[4]

Widely misinterpreted—especially in America—Rousseau seemed to imply that, having been born in a natural state, independent of all authority other than God, man has the right to remain so. "Renouncing one's liberty," he goes on to say, "is renouncing one's dignity as a man, the rights of humanity and even its duties." To Rousseau's own consternation, however, such phrases spread across the western world without any of his qualifying words. Although Rousseau asserted that "no man has a *natural* authority over his fellow man," he insisted that man's survival depends on a "social compact, in which he surrenders many of his rights to the state."[5] In his argument against writs of assistance, Otis carefully omitted the Rousseauvian concept of the necessary alienation of some individual liberties to the state to ensure protection of other individual liberties.

"Liberty is the darling idea of an Englishman," scoffed Peter Oliver, who was on the Massachusetts Executive Council at the time of the writs of assistance case. The son of the great Boston merchant Daniel Oliver and grandson of Massachusetts Governor Jonathan Belcher, Oliver had graduated from Harvard at the head of his class in 1730, earned his M.A. three years later, and married the daughter of another prominent Boston merchant, Richard Clarke. By 1761, when Otis took up the cause of merchants opposing writs of assistance, Oliver had inherited his father's merchant-banking house with his older brother Andrew—also a Harvard graduate. In 1744 they had bought an iron works, added eight water wheels, and transformed it into North America's first rolling mill and largest iron works. After amassing a fortune supplying the Massachusetts militia with cannons during the various wars with the French, Oliver retired to the country to focus on scientific agriculture. Later, he entered public service as a justice of the peace, then, in succession, as a member of the provincial House of Representatives, a member of the Executive Council, and chief justice of the Massachusetts Bay Colony.

"There is so much magic in the sound of the word liberty," Oliver argued, "that the discord of licentiousness very seldom vibrates on the ear . . . and hence arise many evils which . . . induce anarchy and every species of confusion. . . . As to a state of natural liberty existing . . . that there is any such state of existence among the human species remains at present to be proved."[6]

The division between those who argued for or against so-called natural rights split every class of American society, from the wealthiest merchants to nomadic frontiersmen. Frontiersmen were fierce in asserting their rights to poach on anyone's land to hunt for meat, skins, and fur, and many merchants were equally fierce in asserting their right to trade with whomever they chose and to profit from their trade without sharing a penny with the government—even if they had to smuggle goods into the country to avoid doing so. For American merchants, the right to make money was as basic to life in the New World as the right to breathe the air.

Peter Oliver. The future chief justice of Britain's Massachusetts Bay Colony, he was the son of one of Boston's merchant-aristocrats and, with his brother Andrew, inherited his father's merchant-banking house. They amassed a fortune supplying the Massachusetts militia with cannon during various wars with the French. (LIBRARY OF CONGRESS)

Grenville's American Revenue Act sought to reduce the incentive to smuggle foreign molasses by reducing the duty from six to three pence a gallon. To compensate for the reductions, he placed new or slightly higher duties on non-British textiles, coffee, and indigo, and he doubled duties on all other foreign goods, including wines from Madeira, the Canary Islands, and France. The increased web of taxes provoked growing anxieties in the American merchant community, where all taxes represented tyranny and confiscation of private property. Grenville, however, responded that the American Revenue Act would extract only about £45,000 a year in annual revenues, or about two pence *a year* per capita—hardly an onerous burden.

To ensure collection of revenues, Parliament gave Grenville special powers to enforce the American Revenue Act, and he acted immediately to reform the customs service, tighten ship inspection procedures, and ban ship owners and merchants from suing the customs service for illegal seizures. He placed the burden of proof for recovering seized ships and cargoes on merchants and ship owners, and he moved the vice-admiralty court to Halifax, forcing merchants whose cargoes or ships were seized to try to recover their property in a court far from home, where they had no influence.

After passing the American Revenue Act, Parliament resolved with little fanfare that "it may be proper to charge certain Stamp Duties in the said Colonies and Plantations."[7] English lawyers, insurance firms, merchants, publishers, and stationers routinely affixed government stamps, for which they paid a nominal sum, on legal documents of all types, including liquor licenses and other permits, wills, bails, ships' papers, bills of lading, bills of sale, insurance policies, appointments to office, and articles of apprenticeship. Stamps also had to be bought and affixed to university degrees, wine containers, newspapers, almanacs, pamphlets, publicly distributed leaflets, playing cards, and dice.

After resolving to consider the stamp tax, Parliament passed Grenville's second proposal for increasing American contributions to British costs in America: the Currency Act. The measure extended the ban on local currency in New England to the rest of the colonies and forced all but the wealthiest Americans—that is, those without a hoard of gold and silver coins—to rely on barter for day-to-day transactions.[8] An inefficient method of trade, barter often left would-be buyers without enough goods or the proper goods to trade for their needs, thus slowing the pace of trade and economic activity of the region. In effect, Grenville's two acts combined to send the American economy into decline, and in April 1763, 147 Boston merchants responded by organizing a "Society for Encouraging Trade and Commerce within the Province of Massachusetts Bay" to monitor trade and try to influence Parliament to reverse Grenville's policies. As news of their activities spread to other ports, similar organizations emerged in New York, then Philadelphia. "They abhor every limitation of trade and duty on it," New York Lieutenant Governor Cadwallader Colden explained.[9]

In the months that followed, Otis sensed that British duties—and the higher costs of living they produced—represented an issue that would forge a political bond between all merchants—wealthy or not. In August 1764 he published a pamphlet entitled *The Rights of the British Colonies Asserted and Proved* and raised the first public cry against taxation without representation, citing the Magna Carta as a guarantee that "the Supreme power cannot take from any man any part of his property without his consent in person or by representation."[10]

Samuel Adams appended a declaration of his own to the Otis work, equating taxation to government confiscation of property and warning that the American Revenue Act and Currency Act were "preparatory to new taxations upon us. . . . If taxes are laid upon us in any shape without our having a legal representation where they are laid," he suggested, "are we not reduced from the character of free subjects to the miserable state of tributary slaves?"[11]

Both Adams and Otis, of course, conveniently overlooked the fact that few taxpayers in England had any representation in Parliament. Indeed, only one million of the nine million adult males in Britain were entitled to vote.[12]

"In Britain, copyholders, leaseholders, and all men possessed of personal property only, choose no representatives," explained one member of Parliament in defense of colonial taxation.

> Manchester, Birmingham, and many more of our richest and most flourishing trading towns send no members of Parliament, consequently cannot consent by their representatives, because they choose none to represent them; yet are they not Englishmen? . . . Why does not their imaginary representation extend to America as well as over the whole island of Great Britain? If it can travel three hundred miles why not three thousand? If it can jump rivers and mountains, why cannot it sail over the ocean? If the towns of Manchester and Birmingham sending no representatives to Parliament are notwithstanding there represented, why are not the cities of Albany and Boston equally represented in the assembly?[13]

What Parliament's defender failed to mention, however, was that Britain's unrepresented majority had not forfeited representation voluntarily. Generations of population shifts from rural districts into port cities had left 140, or 30 percent, of Parliament's more than 450 districts as underpopulated "rotten boroughs," with each district's vote in Parliament controlled by only one or two major landowners. Fifty districts were "pocket boroughs," where the elected member of Parliament was "in the pocket" of a single landowner who could rule his district like a tyrant and usually voted as such in Parliament, without regard to the interests of any other Englishman. Indeed, the bloc of MPs from rotten and pocket boroughs often formed a conspiracy of tyrants when voting on important issues in Parliament—especially social issues involving expanded popular rights and privileges.

Adams's fears that Grenville's laws would spawn new taxes proved prescient. In April 1765 Grenville asked Parliament to convert its resolution for a stamp tax into law. With the Molasses Act and the American Revenue Act, the Stamp Tax would be the third set of taxes on Americans that Parliament would enact without American consent. More provocative than earlier taxes, it was the first direct tax that would affect almost every American. Americans could avoid paying indirect taxes by simply not buying goods on which the cost of duties had been added. There was no way to avoid paying a direct tax.

The Stamp Act was to take effect the following November 1 and extend England's own seventy-year-old stamp tax to the colonies. The tax raised about £300,000 a year in Britain, and Grenville estimated it would yield about £60,000 a year in America, at a cost of less than a shilling a day per capita, or less than three hours' earnings a year for a skilled artisan. When added to the £45,000 to be raised from the American Revenue Act, stamp tax collections would bring total American tax revenues to about £105,000 a year, or almost one-third of the costs of maintaining Britain's army in America. Although it seemed innocuous, it would prove one of the most disastrous calculations in Grenville's storied career.

Although Grenville correctly calculated the negligible costs of the tax to the average consumer, he failed to recognize the costs to three of America's most influential groups: merchants, publishers, and lawyers. Merchants would have to buy and affix stamps to every purchase order, remittance, and receipt; publishers to every newspaper, pamphlet, and circular they printed; and lawyers to every legal document they issued. Granville's Stamp

Act would not only unite three of the most powerful, otherwise nonallied groups in America, it would teach them for the first time the power of united action against government—no matter how big or powerful.

Although America's merchants voiced few objections to Britain's maintaining defensive military garrisons, they objected to paying for British troops to man and maintain them. Indeed, Andrew Rutledge, an influential South Carolina rice planter, suggested raising £100,000 for South Carolina on its own to support four regiments of American militiamen on the frontier. Other colonist leaders agreed that the forces should be American rather than British. Even some English military leaders doubted the value of British troops in America. Colonel Sir William Johnson, the British Superintendent of the Northern Indians, told the Board of Trade in 1762 that although frontier forts might prove effective "in retarding the progress of an army, they can in no wise prevent incursions by Indians, who need not approach the forts in any of their inroads, and can destroy the inhabitants and their dwellings with very little risk."[14]

By summer 1765 some colonists suspected that Grenville's motives for expanding British military presence in America was not to fight Indians but to police and control colonists. Anger began to build when General Thomas Gage, the New York–based commander in chief of British forces in America, all but confirmed those suspicions by asking Parliament to pass a Quartering Act, requiring civil authorities in the colonies to supply barracks and provisions for British troops.

In Boston, John Hancock, whose uncle's merchant bank had become New England's largest enterprise, grew so annoyed he wrote to his agent in London, all but ordering him to lobby against passage of the Stamp Act. Breaking ranks with Boston's small circle of merchant-aristocrats, Hancock called the act "very cruel." He warned that British merchants would ultimately pay a higher price for the stamp tax than American merchants. "We were before much burdened. We shall not now be able much longer to support trade, and in the end Great Britain must feel the effects of it. I wonder the merchants and friends of America don't make a stir for us."[15] Hancock warned the royal governor: "I am determined as soon as I know that they are resolved to insist on this act to sell my stock in trade and shut up my warehouse doors."[16]

Although the friends of America were indeed ready to "make a stir," the conspiracy of tyrants in Parliament refused to budge. They believed that American merchants were profiting at their expense and they intended to snatch a share of those profits—regardless of the eventual cost in human misery and lives.

Chapter 5

Flockwork from England

$\mathcal{L}$ike Hutchinson, Oliver, Clarke, and other scions of Boston's mercantile aristocrats, Hancock had never questioned the rule of God, King, and Country. The third of his line to carry his Christian name, his forebears had arrived from England in 1634, only fourteen years after the *Mayflower*. The first John Hancock graduated from Harvard in 1685 and stepped into the pulpit of the North Precinct Congregational Church of Cambridge, Massachusetts, in 1698. After fifteen years, he led a tax revolt in which the North Precinct declared independence and adopted a new name—Lexington. Quickly dubbed "the Bishop of Lexington," he brooked no opposition to his iron-fisted rule and became the first Hancock to join the ruling class of the Massachusetts Bay Colony. His power, like that of other Congregation-alist ministers, stemmed from the determination of early Puritan settlers to found a "Bible Commonwealth" in Massachusetts. They limited free speech and political privileges and imposed in New England the same reli-gious discrimination that Anglicans had imposed on them in old England. They limited voting rights to propertied male members of their church and converted town after town into theocracies, where ministers ruled the spiri-tual world and deacons and elders the material world.

The first of the bishop's five children also bore the name John Han-cock and entered the ministry. And from the moment *his* son—John

Hancock III—was born in 1737, his family had little doubt that he would follow the first and second John Hancocks into the pulpit. In 1744, however, John Hancock III's father became ill and died, and another Hancock appeared at the manse in Lexington in an English-built, gilt-edged coach and four, attended by four liveried servants. A silver and ivory coat of arms emblazoned its doors. Beneath it, heraldic gold script proclaimed, *nul plaisir sans peine* (no pleasure without pain). Thomas Hancock, the bishop's second son, who had left as a fourteen-year-old indentured apprentice, had returned home after twenty-seven years as one of America's richest, most powerful merchants, the owner of Boston's world-renowned House of Hancock.

Like Hutchinson, Oliver, and Boston's other powerful merchants, Hancock's enterprise included retailing, wholesaling, importing, exporting, warehousing, ship and wharf ownership, commercial banking, investment banking, and real estate investments. What made his and the other merchant banks unique was that they had achieved success in what was then the richest city in the New World: Boston. Although no one had a firm idea of all the things that the House of Hancock and the other merchant-banking firms traded, everyone knew that whatever in the world one might want, one could find it at Thomas Hancock's, and if he didn't have it, he could get it for a price. Every bit as overwhelming as his father the bishop, Thomas Hancock could buy anything he wanted, and what he wanted more than anything else in the world when he strode into his dead brother's house in the summer of 1744—and what he intended to buy at any price—was a son and heir to the House of Hancock. Married but unable to have children of his own, Thomas Hancock had spent twenty-seven years building his commercial empire, and he was not about to let it fall into the hands of strangers after his death. His older brother's death provided the first opportunity to adopt an acceptable child. Thomas pledged to provide lifelong security in the most generous fashion for his brother's widow Mary and all three children—if Mary would allow him to raise the older boy, John, as his own in Boston. He promised to give the boy the finest schooling, culminating at Harvard, where he would follow in his father's and grandfather's educational footsteps. All but penniless, Mary Hancock had little choice but to yield to the forceful merchant king and watch as her little boy, the third and soon to be the greatest John Hancock, left the manse in Lexington and waved goodbye from his uncle's stately carriage.

Although Thomas Hancock lacked the Harvard credentials of Boston's other merchant-aristocrats, he more than matched them in his bearing and demeanor—from his immaculate, carefully powdered wig to his silver shoe buckles. Embroidered ruffled shirt cuffs flared from the ends of his jacket sleeves and embraced his soft, puffy hands. The rest of his costume—the magnificent knee-length velvet coat and the shirt frills that peeked discreetly from the front of his jacket—showed the care he took to compensate for his academic deficiencies with well-displayed evidence of wealth, power, and high standing. A gold chain held a magnificently fashioned watch in his waistcoat pocket.

Hancock lived on the edge of the Common at the peak of Beacon Hill in one of Boston's grandest homes—a three-story palace that differed only in its exterior architecture from the homes of Boston's other great mansions. Hancock had acquired the land for next to nothing when it was but a pasture, and he kept on buying property until he owned the entire crest of Beacon Hill and half the town below, including the massive Clarke's Wharf, Boston's second-largest wharf.

"He had raised a great estate with such rapidity," wrote Thomas Hutchinson, "that it was commonly believed that he had purchased a valuable diamond for a small sum and sold it at its full price."[1]

Built of square-cut granite blocks and trimmed at each corner with brownstone quoins, Hancock House looked out on the Common through four large windows that framed a central entrance. A large balcony above the door commanded a breathtaking, panoramic view that swept across the entire Common, the city, harbor, and sea beyond as well as the surrounding countryside. In all, the house had fifty-three windows, including those in the dormers, lighted by 480 squares of the best crown glass from London.

Outside, a two-acre landscaped green bore a variety of shade trees and elegant gardens. At the far end, a small orchard included mulberry, peach, and apricot trees from Spain. A gardening enthusiast, Hancock ordered many trees and plants from English nurseries and unwittingly enriched

Hancock House on Beacon Hill. A painting of Hancock House, the palatial Beacon Hill mansion of Thomas Hancock and his nephew John Hancock. It was torn down in 1863. (BOSTONIAN SOCIETY. PHOTO BY RICHARD MERRILL.)

the entire New England landscape with species of trees, shrubs, and flowers that were new to North America. All originated from wind-blown seeds from Thomas Hancock's gardens on Beacon Hill.

He told one horticulturist:

> to procure for me two or three dozen yew trees, some hollys and jessamine vines; and if you have any particular curious things . . . [that] will beautify a flower garden, send a sample. . . . Pray send me a catalogue of that fruit you have that are dwarf trees and espaliers. . . . My gardens all lie on the south side of a hill, with the most beautiful assent to the top; and it's allowed on all hands that the kingdom of England don't afford so fine a prospect as I have both of land and water. Neither do I intend to spare any cost or pains in making my gardens beautiful or profitable.[2]

Hancock's gardens were the most beautiful and most envied in Boston.

Inside his house, a wide, paneled, central entrance hall reached through to a set of rear doors that looked onto the formal gardens. Delicately carved, spiral balusters bounded a broad staircase that rose along the left wall of the main hall. A ten-foot-tall "chiming clock," topped with sculpted figures, "gilt with burnished gold," stood against the opposite wall. Oil portraits of important men in uniform or formal clothes stared out from large gilded frames on the walls in the rooms off the hall, casting silent judgments on all who entered. The great parlor, or drawing room, lay off the hall to the right as one entered the house, and the family sitting room sat

Hancock House interior. Engraving depicting the interior of Hancock House for an article in Harper's Weekly *in the mid-nineteenth century.* (BOSTONIAN SOCIETY)

opposite. Mahogany furniture filled the parlor, upholstered in luxurious damask that matched the drapes. Imported green-scarlet "flockwork" from England—a "very rich and beautiful fine cloth" wall covering ornamented with tufts of wool and cotton—covered the walls. Elegant brass candlesticks sparkled with reflected light from the marble hearth—one of three downstairs. Servants kept fires burning in every room during the cold Boston winters. Across the hall, English wallpaper in the family room displayed brightly colored "birds, peacocks, macaws, squirrels, fruit and flowers" that Hancock described as "better than paintings done in oil."[3]

Beyond the family room was the dining room and kitchen, which included "a jack of three guineas price, with a wheel-fly and spitt-chain to it." One of the smaller rooms behind housed Hancock's huge china collection, and the other rooms served as lodgings for servants and slaves. Hancock stocked his cellar with Madeira wines that he bought "without regard to price provided the quality answers to it." He also bought a docile slave named Cambridge for £160 to help serve his and his wife Lydia's many guests from "6 quart decanters" and "2 dozen handsome, new fashioned wine glasses" made of the finest rock crystal from London.[4]

Upstairs, above the parlor, sat the huge guest bedroom, with furnishings and matching draperies in yellow damask. Years later, its canopied four-poster bed would sleep, among others, Sir William Howe, commanding general of the British Army in America during Washington's siege of Boston in the winter of 1775–76. Opposite the guest room stretched the master bedroom, done in crimson. Two other smaller bedrooms lay on the second floor, with storage and servants' quarters scattered above, beneath the roof. "We live pretty comfortable here on Beacon Hill," Thomas Hancock purred modestly.[5]

Within hours of entering his new home on the hill, little John Hancock began a year of intensive training with a private tutor, who transformed the country boy into a city sophisticate, with impeccable manners, speech, and behavior—a model of mid-eighteenth-century Anglo-Boston society. His doting aunt Lydia, Thomas Hancock's wife, groomed and dressed him in velvet breeches with a satin shirt richly embroidered with lace ruffles at the front and cuffs. His shoes bore the same sparkling silver buckles as those of his uncle. Thomas Hancock was immensely proud of his adopted son's good looks, and as quickly as the boy's bearing and manners permitted, he made a ceremony of introducing him to the scores of military and government leaders, including the royal governor, who constantly came to pay court to the great merchant and dine at his wife's fine table.

In July 1745 John Hancock was ready to enroll in the prestigious Boston Public Latin School on School Street at the bottom of Beacon Hill behind the Anglican King's Chapel, where he joined the sons of every other merchant-banker in Boston. A two-story wooden building with a neat peaked roof and belfry, Boston Public Latin was the academic gateway to Harvard College and leadership in church, business, and government. It was no place for a rebel. Thirty years earlier, ten-year-old Benjamin Franklin had bridled under the harsh discipline and quit Boston Latin after only two years there.

Headed by Tory martinet John Lovell, the school put John through five years of torturous studies, stretching from seven in the morning to five in the afternoon, four days a week, and from seven to noon on Saturdays. There was no school on Thursdays, Sundays, and fast days, nor on Saturday afternoons. School ran the year around, with only a week's vacation at Thanksgiving and at Christmas and three weeks off in August. In the end, Hancock and other survivors of Lovell's brutal pedagogy learned to venerate the king; to read, write, and speak fluent Latin and Greek; to read and cite the Old and New Testament in both languages; and to read and cite the works of Julius Caesar, Cicero, Virgil, Xenophon, and Homer. He entered Harvard in the autumn of 1750 at the age of thirteen and a half—the second youngest in his class of twenty, but ranked fifth because of his uncle's wealth, power, and social standing and John's own heritage as the son and grandson of Harvard alumni. The prospect of a generous legacy from his wealthy uncle did not hurt his ranking. Four years later, he graduated with his degree and the right to be called "Sir Hancock" whenever he set foot on the Harvard campus. No sooner had he graduated than his uncle put him to work in the House of Hancock, learning every aspect of merchant-banking in preparation for his ascendancy to full partnership with his uncle and eventual inheritance of their vast enterprise. Young John rode to work each day with his uncle in the splendid family carriage, dined at the Merchants Club with the city's other great business magnates, joined the Freemasons, and became close friends with the heirs to other great merchant fortunes—Thomas Hutchinson, Jr., Andrew and Peter Oliver, Thomas Cushing, Jr., and James Bowdoin, Jr. All embraced wealth and its accouterments with equal passion, and they dressed and dined accordingly. All were Men of Harvard, and in unison, they sang the praises of the king and country that had blessed them with abundance.

After Hancock luxuriated in Boston's merchant banking milieu, news of Braddock's disaster in the West reached Boston and imbued the city with a sense of impending crisis. As senior military official in America, Massachusetts Governor William Shirley took immediate command of all British forces in the thirteen colonies. At Shirley's behest, Thomas Hancock assembled thirty-one ships in Boston harbor, and two regiments of New Englanders—about two thousand men—set sail for Canada. The British tacked to the northernmost shore of the Bay of Fundy in Nova Scotia and, in a surprise attack, overwhelmed Fort Beausejour, leaving the entire French garrison dead or captured. By the end of the month, the British captured all the lands along the shore of the Bay of Fundy, including settlements with about six thousand French-speaking, Roman Catholic Acadians, whom the British adjudged potential rebels. Ordered to swear allegiance to the English crown or be expelled, they chose exile, and British troops obliged, forcing three thousand men, women, and children to board eighteen Hancock ships at bayonet point and watch as other troops burned their homes and villages. The dispersal went on for months, with the House of Hancock sending bills for "digging graves" and, in one instance, for "burying of 2 French children." Thomas Hancock expressed satisfaction to his British agent that Nova Scotia was "pretty clear of those vermin. . . . For God's sake, then let us root the French blood out of America." As quartermaster general, in effect, for two enormously successful British military enterprises, Thomas Hancock had become a staunch, outspoken British imperialist, and his nephew echoed his words.[6]

In February 1757 the British government appointed Cambridge-educated Thomas Pownall, a former deputy governor of New Jersey, as governor of Massachusetts. He immediately conferred with Boston's business leaders—Thomas Hancock among them—to develop a plan for pur-

Thomas Pownall. The royal governor of Massachusetts, he pursued a policy of expelling Roman Catholic Acadians from their native lands in New Brunswick and Nova Scotia. (LIBRARY OF CONGRESS)

suing the war more vigorously. A champion of a more aggressive policy toward the French and Indians, Thomas Hancock offered Pownall his full political and logistical support. Expelling the French from America, Hancock enthused, "will be the salvation of England, for in forty years this very America will absolutely take all the manufactury of England. . . . Whoever keeps America will in the end (whether French or English) have the kingdom of England."[7] He had good reason to be enthusiastic: He was already earning more than £30,000 a year from the war, and the new governor now asked him to help raise and supply an additional militia of seven thousand men.

Hancock's zeal for punishing Acadians seemed to wane, however—especially after seeing a pitiful group that was captured in Boston trying to make their way home from the Carolinas. While they languished in prison awaiting transport back to exile in North Carolina, the Governor's Council, or upper house of the legislature, asked Hancock to provide them with food. During that time, Hancock experienced a change of heart and asked the Council to be "compassionate [about] their unhappy circumstances" and free them. The Council complied.

By 1758 Hancock had become the primary financier and procurement officer in America for the British military, and the defense ministry at Whitehall in London appointed him "His Majesty's Agent for Transports," thus putting an official cachet on the unofficial role he had played for a decade. The appointment extended Hancock's authority beyond procurement to include payment of enlistment bounties to seamen, provisioning the fleet, chartering cargo ships for the military, and handling payrolls. Generals and civilian governors were to turn to the House of Hancock for all supplies and payrolls. For his efforts, from 1754 to 1760 Thomas Hancock received 5 percent of the costs of conducting the French and Indian War as well as appointment to the Governor's Council, which handled most of the colony's finances. The huge burden of work forced him to turn over more responsibilities to his nephew John, and in 1763 he made his nephew a full partner and gave him direction of the firm, which changed its name to Thomas Hancock & Nephew.

A year later, on Wednesday, August 1, 1764, sixty-one-year-old Thomas Hancock walked down Beacon Hill for a meeting of the Governor's Executive Council at the Town House and collapsed as he entered the Council chamber. Council members carried him back to his mansion, where he died of a stroke, leaving his twenty-seven-year-old nephew John as Boston's new merchant king and one of the wealthiest men in America. John Hancock's ascension to wealth and power would change the course of America.

Chapter 6

The Flame Is Spread

*J*ohn Hancock could not have inherited his uncle's business at a worse time. After writing to all his agents, customers, and suppliers of his intention "to carry on the business . . . by myself," he pressed ahead valiantly with his uncle's expansion plans, but the postwar economic slump had deteriorated into a full-scale depression. Many merchants had overstocked because of the seemingly endless demand that the war had created. By the spring of 1763, six months after Britain had silenced her cannons, several major Boston mercantile houses collapsed while others trembled ominously on their foundations.

Part of the problem lay in slow communications. By the time the first ship arrived from London with news that the war had ended, merchants had long earlier placed their orders for merchandise that would no longer be needed. Then, toward the end of 1763, a small pox epidemic sent citizens fleeing the city, leaving merchants and shopkeepers crushed by piles of unsold Christmas inventories and no one to buy them. One after another, Boston's merchants—some of them leaders in the field—closed their doors: the gigantic house of Nathaniel Wheelwright, the equally large firm of John Scollay, chairman of Boston's Board of Selectmen, and many others.

As the end of 1764 approached, John Hancock—like Thomas Hutchinson, Thomas Cushing, the Oliver brothers, and other surviving merchants—wrote to his English agents to cancel orders for the following spring. "Trade has met with a most prodigious shock," Hancock explained. "Money is extremely scarce . . . times are very bad . . . take my word, my good friends, the times will be worse here." Hancock said that the wave of failures had left him unable to buy any more goods from England, and he warned that "if we are not relieved at home we must live upon our own produce and manufactures."[1]

Like New England's other merchants, Hancock was simply not prepared for peace when the Seven Years' War came to an end in 1763. For the better part of two centuries, New England's economy had been based on war or the threat of war. Thomas Hancock had built the House of Hancock on war profits, and his nephew John—as well as Boston's other merchants—now discovered peace to be highly unprofitable in a frontier society where consumers can provide for themselves by converting raw materials from the wilds into tools, clothes, food, and other essentials. Barter made money—and merchants—superfluous much of the time. Only the military relied on merchants on a regular basis—for arms, ammunition, clothing, food, and transport—but the end of the Seven Years' War reduced such purchases and collapsed the American economy. And it was that moment—early in 1764—that the British government picked to raise taxes. Its timing could not have been worse.

Merchants from Boston to Charleston, South Carolina, wrote to their agents in Britain protesting Grenville's American Revenue Act and Currency Act. As Parliament debated the Stamp Act, the letters grew into a torrent that goaded British merchants to protest to Parliament. In Parliament, future prime minister Charles Townshend responded angrily, calling the colonists "children planted by our care, nourished up by our indulgence . . . protected by our arms."

The colonists had their champions in Parliament, however—among them Colonel Isaac Barré, M.P. for Chipping Wycombe, who had fought in the French and Indian War and acquired many American friends. "They planted by your care?" he bellowed in response to Townshend.

*John Hancock. The young merchant is shown in his
imported wig and sartorial finery in a portrait by
John Singleton Copley.* (LIBRARY OF CONGRESS)

No! Your oppressions planted them in America. They fled from your
tyranny to a then-uncultivated and inhospitable country—where they
exposed themselves to almost all the hardships to which human nature is
liable.

They nourished by your indulgence? They grew by your neglect of
them. As soon as you began to care about them, that care was exercised in
sending persons to rule over them, in one department and another.

They protected by your arms? They have nobly taken up arms in your
defence, have exerted a valor amidst their constant and laborious industry
for the defence of a country, whose frontier, while drenched in blood, has
yielded all its little savings to your emolument. And believe me, remem-
ber I this day told you so, that same spirit of freedom which actuated that

people at first, will accompany them still. . . . The people I believe are as truly loyal as any subjects the king has, but they are a people jealous of their liberties who will vindicate them, if ever they should be violated.[2]

Although "the whole house sat a while, amazed, intently looking and without answering a word," it voted 245 to 49 in favor of proceeding with the proposed stamp tax.[3]

After word of Parliament's action arrived in America, Boston's merchants gathered to dine at the Merchants Club and, after mutters of dismay, accepted the inevitable and toasted the king and motherland. "I am heartily sorry for the great burden laid upon us," John Hancock wrote to his London agent. "We are not able to bear all things, but must submit to higher powers, these taxes will greatly affect us, our trade will be ruined, and as it is, it's very dull." Then, turning to what remained for him a more important topic, he ordered "two pipes [about 125 gallons each] of the very best Madeira for my own table. I don't stand at any price, let it be good, I like rich wine."[4] At heart, John Hancock was no rebel and, indeed, tried to mediate behind the scenes with a letter to former Massachusetts royal governor Thomas Pownall, who had retired in England but had been a close friend of Thomas Hancock and the rest of Boston's mercantile aristocrats.

"I seldom meddle with politics," Hancock opened.

> I know the goodness of your disposition towards us, and I wish we could be helped out of our present burden and difficulties. Our trade is prodigiously embarrassed and must shortly be ruined under the present circumstances, but we must submit. . . . I, however, hope we shall in some measure be relieved, and doubt not your good influences to forward it.[5]

As merchant protests against the Stamp Act grew in intensity, Otis and Adams stepped into the picture, citing the Magna Carta again to argue against taxation without representation. Grenville tried to strike back, reiterating that the vast majority of British taxpayers went unrepresented in Parliament and that representation could actually work to the disadvantage of American taxpayers. For one thing, members of Parliament were unpaid and any parliamentarians from America would incur inordinately high costs of transportation and living expenses that would add to the burden of American taxpayers. In addition, the number of colonial representatives in Parliament would be too small to exert any legislative influence or quash demands of the majority of British taxpayers that colonists pay their fair share of taxes.

American printers and publishers refused to publish his or any other arguments in favor of the Stamp Act, however, because of its particularly harsh effects on their industry. "The Stamp Act . . . will affect the printers more than anybody," grumbled Benjamin Franklin, Philadelphia's printer and copublisher of the *Pennsylvania Gazette*. With a stamp required for every newspaper they printed and sold, Franklin and the editors of almost all twenty-six newspapers in America rallied behind merchant protests and gladly featured Otis's diatribes.

The Stamp Act infuriated many lawyers as well, enticing the otherwise retiring thirty-year-old country lawyer John Adams into politics for the first time in his young career. He went before the Braintree Board of Selectmen to demand that they instruct the Massachusetts agent in Parliament to seek repeal of the act. "We can no longer forbear complaining," Adams barked, "that many of the measures of the late acts of Parliament have a tendency . . . to divest us of our most essential rights and liberties." Calling the Stamp Act too burdensome, he predicted that it would "drain the country of its cash, strip multitudes of all their property, and reduce them to absolute beggary.

> We further apprehend this tax to be unconstitutional.* We have always understood it to be a grand and fundamental principle of the constitution that no freeman should be subject to any tax to which he has not

---

* Britain did not have (nor does it now have) a constitution in the form of a single, American-style document—only a "customary" or conceptual constitution made up of documents (letters, opinions, declarations, decisions from the bench, etc.), written statutes, and common law, often based on old, established, and widely practiced customs. Under the British "constitution," Parliament, as primary law giver and center of power in eighteenth-century England, could do anything it wanted, thus refuting arguments that the Stamp Act was unconstitutional and leaving opponents of such acts to choose between either obeying or declaring independence.

given his own consent, in person or by proxy . . . that no freeman can be separated from his property but by his own act or fault.

Adams went on to demand "explicit assertion and vindication of our rights and liberties . . . that the world may know . . . that we can never be slaves."[6]

With all-but-universal opposition to the Stamp Act among merchants, newspapers, and lawyers, the outrage spread across the nation. In Virginia, Assemblyman Patrick Henry, a lawyer himself, resolved that

> the General Assembly of this colony have the only and sole exclusive right and power to lay taxes . . . upon the inhabitants of this colony, and that every attempt to vest such power in any person or persons . . . other than the General Assembly . . . has a manifest tendency to destroy British and American freedom.[7]

Although the Speaker of the House interrupted Henry with an angry cry of "Treason, sir!," Henry responded by warning, "Caesar had his Brutus, Charles the First his Cromwell, and George the Third may profit by their example! If *this* be treason, make the most of it!"[8]

The House erupted in a cacophony of angry shouts and jubilant cheers. "Violent debates ensued," Henry recalled. "Many threats were uttered, and much abuse cast on me. After a long and warm contest, the resolutions passed by a very small majority, perhaps of one or two only."[9] After hearing Henry's condemnation of the Stamp Act, both Richard Henry Lee and George Washington, the owners of two of Virginia's largest plantations, abandoned the ranks of pro-British planters in the Assembly and voted with Henry. Henry, in fact, had prepared seven resolutions, but presented only five before deciding he had gone far enough. His last two called for outright disobedience of the Stamp Act and rebellion against the motherland.

Outraged by what he considered nothing less than a coup d'état, Virginia's conservative Speaker of the House acted swiftly to reassert his authority, engineering a reassessment and rejection of Henry's resolutions—but his action came too late. Henry had already given the editor of the *Virginia*

Patrick Henry speaks against the Stamp Act. An idealized painting of Patrick Henry delivering his oration denouncing the Stamp Act in 1765, with a warning to King George III that "Caesar had his Brutus, Charles the First his Cromwell. . . ." (FROM A NINETEENTH-CENTURY PHOTOGRAPH IN THE AUTHOR'S COLLECTION)

Gazette all seven resolutions to copy, and under a news-sharing agreement among newspaper printers in most of the colonies, the *Gazette* editor had already sent them across America. "The alarm spread . . . with astonishing quickness," Henry chuckled. "The great point of resistance to British taxation was universally established in the colonies."[10]

A week later, Henry's resolutions appeared in the Annapolis, Maryland, newspaper; by mid-June they were in the Philadelphia, New York, and Boston papers, and by early August in the Scottish and British press. Newspaper publishers in Britain were at one with American publishers in despising the Stamp Act, which required them to put a stamp on every copy they sold in Britain. With each publication of Henry's resolutions, collective exaggerations, misinterpretations, and copying errors transformed them into nothing less than a call to revolution. His sixth resolution, according to the *Maryland Gazette*, declared that Virginians were "not bound to yield obedience to any law or ordinance whatsoever, designed to impose taxation upon them, other than the laws or ordinances of the General Assembly," and his seventh resolution called anyone who supported Parliament's efforts to tax Virginians "AN ENEMY TO THIS HIS MAJESTY'S COLONY."[11]

The *Boston Gazette*, which was published by two vitriolic antiroyalists, Benjamin Edes and John Gill, also printed all seven of what they called Henry's original resolutions and claimed falsely that Virginia had adopted them all intact. Described as "foul-mouthed trumpeters of sedition" by the rival, pro-British *Boston Chronicle*, Edes and Gill had met as apprentice printers and formed a partnership printing books, broadsides, and pamphlets that featured only sermons at first but gradually included betterselling polemics by gifted provocateurs such as Samuel Adams.

Publication of Henry's resolutions fired up colonist antipathy toward British government intrusion in their affairs and Parliament's efforts to tax them. Stamp Act opponents rallied in every city, forming secret societies called Sons of Liberty, which would soon evolve into the Tea Party movement.

"The flame is spread through all the continent," Virginia's royal governor Francis Fauquier warned his foreign minister in London, "and one colony supports another in their disobedience to superior powers."[12] Governor Sir Francis Bernard of Massachusetts agreed, warning the ministry that Henry's resolutions had sounded "an alarm bell to the disaffected."[13]

After reading Henry's resolutions in the *Boston Gazette*, the Massachusetts assembly called on all colonies to send delegates to an intercolonial congress to be held in New York City in October, one month before the Stamp Act was to take effect.

On August 8, the British government published the names of colonial distributors who would sell stamps. The distributor for Massachusetts was Andrew Oliver, the wealthy Boston merchant who was also Chief Justice Hutchinson's brother-in-law. The appointment seemed proof positive of James Otis's charges two years earlier that wealthy merchants and the royal government were conspiring to forge "chains and shackles for the country" and "grind the faces of the poor without remorse, eat the bread of oppression without fear, and wax fat upon the spoils of the people."[14] Andrew Oliver ignored Otis's charges, pointing out that no less a man than Benjamin Franklin had applied to be a stamp distributor. Far from grinding the faces of the poor, Oliver had been one of Boston's most generous philanthropists, using his own money to help pave Boston's streets and to feed and house the poor. A leader in the effort to send Congregationalist missionaries among the Indians, he was a major supporter of Eleazar Wheelock's missionary school for Indians (later Dartmouth College).

Publication of Henry's resolutions, however, aroused too many pent-up emotions. As one, Bostonians seemed to snap. Debts had piled high, there was no work, shops had closed—with nothing left for rent or food, many tramped off into the wilderness, hoping that something would turn up. Early in the morning on August 14, an effigy of Andrew Oliver dangled from the limb of a huge oak tree on High Street near Hanover Square, drawing the attention of the curious at first. Planted three years before the beheading of King Charles I in 1649, the oak had quickly acquired an appropriate title—the Liberty Tree.

As angry faces began crowding around it, Governor Bernard ordered deputies to disperse them, but the deputies refused, saying any effort would put them in "imminent danger of their lives." Sam Adams appeared with a group of followers that included printer Edes of the radical *Boston Gazette*, and distillers John Avery and Thomas Chase, who wielded an inordinate amount of power in local government by offering political leaders a room in the distillery as a clubhouse and assuring them a steady flow of free "punch, wine, pipes, and tobacco, biscuit and cheese."[15]

After Adams and the others had spoken, the mob dispersed and the men returned to work, but at Adams's invitation, they pledged to return later in the day. The second, bigger rally drew a rougher crowd of water-front workers and laborers, who set to drinking free rum offered by the Chase and Speakman distillery. They soon raged out of control, tore down Oliver's effigy, and carried it to the windows of the governor's office at the Town House, or state capitol, where they chanted defiantly, "Liberty, Property, and No Stamps."

Growing in number, they moved toward a half-finished brick building near the waterfront where Oliver planned to let out shops. Believing it would house the stamp office, the mob tore it down, brick by brick, ripping off and burning the wooden sign that bore Oliver's name. With nothing left to destroy, they rushed off to Oliver's beautiful estate—the mangled effigy still in tow. Once in front of the Oliver mansion, they beheaded and burned the straw dummy with great ceremony, then set to stoning the windows and uprooting fruit trees and flowers in the beautiful garden. Unsatisfied, they cried for a hangman's rope, smashed the windows and broke down the mansion's doors. When they realized Oliver had fled with his family, they destroyed the magnificent furniture, art, mirrors, china, crystal, and everything else they could lay hands on.[16]

Chief Justice Hutchinson and the county sheriff raced to the scene and tried to reason with the mob, but its leaders responded with volleys of epithets and stones—driving the two away. Governor Bernard ordered the colonel of the militia to summon his regiment, but the drummers who normally sounded the alarm were part of the mob, as were many of the employees of the Hutchinson, Hancock, and Oliver merchant-banking houses.

"Everyone agrees," the governor wrote to the Board of Trade in London, "that this riot had exceeded all others known here, both in the vehemence of action and mischievousness of intention."[17] The teapots of Boston had come to a boil and threatened to explode into a tempest.

Chapter 7

A Diabolical Scene

After the destruction of Andrew Oliver's beautiful home, Lieutenant Governor Thomas Hutchinson tried to make sense of what seemed an unimaginable spasm in an edenic land that had harbored and nurtured generations of their families for 150 years.

> Americans were convinced in their own minds that they were very miserable—and those who think so are so. There is nothing so easy as to persuade people that they are badly governed. Take happy and comfortable people and talk to them with the art of the Evil One, and they can soon be made discontented with their government, their rulers, with everything around them, and even with themselves. This is one of the weaknesses of human nature of which factious orators make use of to serve their purposes.[1]

Although Samuel Adams was a familiar figure in Boston's taverns and had certainly harangued the mob at the Liberty Tree, there is no evidence he personally took part in the Oliver attack. He took full advantage of the excitement it generated, however, to organize a Boston branch of the Sons of Liberty. Its membership, which would remain known only to him and the group's other leaders, would later gain national and international fame as Boston's Tea Party Patriots.

The next morning, an unidentified "group of gentlemen" approached Andrew Oliver, threatening to destroy what was left of his property and menacing him and his family unless he resigned as stamp distributor.

"He was carried to the Tree of Liberty by the mob," his younger brother Peter Oliver recalled, "and there he was obliged on pain of death to take an oath and resign his office."[2]

Although Sam Adams said the night's events and those of the following day "ought to be forever remembered . . . [as] the happy day, on which liberty rose from a long slumber,"[3] merchant John Hancock was appalled at the mob attack on one of his friends. Thirty years older than Hancock, Oliver was also a Harvard graduate, son of a great merchant, grandson of a prominent surgeon and ruling elder of the Boston church—the third generation in a distinguished Massachusetts family whose roots reached back to 1632, twelve years after the landing at Plymouth. John Hancock knew that a large number of near-bankrupt smaller merchants and shopkeepers had been in the mob that attacked Oliver. Hancock suddenly felt isolated in an increasingly polarized city. As a wholesaler, he had strong ties to the small merchants and shopkeepers whom he supplied, but his wealth, his international merchant-banking enterprise, and his fleet of ships made him an intimate member of the plutocracy of large merchants like Hutchinson, Oliver, and others with deep loyalties to Mother England.

Thinking he could influence events in England and douse the embers of rebellion in America, Hancock again wrote to his London agent of the "general dissatisfaction here on account of the Stamp Act, which I pray may never be carried into execution. . . . It is a cruel hardship upon us and unless we are redressed we must be ruined. . . . Do exert yourselves for us and promote our interest. We are worth saving but unless speedily relieved we shall be past remedy."[4]

Hancock's warnings proved all too accurate. The epidemic of mob violence spread to Newport, where a mob plundered the homes of a wealthy lawyer and an eminent physician for defending the Stamp Act. Similar assaults ravaged homes in towns along the Hudson River Valley, in New York City, Philadelphia, Charleston . . . rioting erupted again in Boston on August 26, when rumors swept through the city that the "whole body of Boston merchants had been represented as smugglers" in depositions by the royal governor seeking their arrest. Although Governor Bernard denied making any such charges, merchants "descended from the top to the bottom of the town" to Town House. A mob gathered, lit a bonfire, and began drinking and shouting "Liberty and Property"—which Governor Bernard described as "the usual notice of their intention to plunder and pull down a house."[5] The mob eventually marched to the home of the marshal of the vice-admiralty court, who saved his home by leading them to a tavern and buying a barrel of punch. Now drunker than before, they staggered to the home of another court official, broke down the doors, and burned all court records before wrecking the house and its contents. A second mob smashed into the elegant new home of the comptroller of the customs, who had just arrived from England. After the mob had sacked the house—and finished drinking all the wines in its cellar—Ebenezer Mackintosh, a leatherworker/shoemaker and fire brigade commander, led both mobs to Lieutenant Governor Thomas Hutchinson's home.

Peter Oliver later charged Samuel Adams, James Otis, and other anti–Stamp Act activists with hiring Mackintosh to do "their dirty jobs for them." Oliver said Mackintosh

> dressed genteely . . . to convince the public of that power with which he was invested. . . . He paraded the town with a mob of 2,000 men in two files, and past by the Stadthouse when the General Assembly was sitting, to display his power. If a whisper was heard among his followers, holding up his finger hushed it in a moment, and when he had fully displayed his authority, he marched his men to the first rendezvous and ordered them to retire peaceably . . . and was punctually obeyed.[6]

Lieutenant Governor Hutchinson's home had stood as one of North America's architectural jewels: a palatial Inigo Jones–style residence with Ionic pilasters framing its facades, crowned by a delicate cupola on its roof. Warned of the mob's approach, Hutchinson ordered his family to leave while he and Governor Bernard confronted the mob. His daughter refused to leave without him, however, and they fled with Bernard to the protection of British troops on Castle William, the island fortress in Boston Harbor (see map 2, page 82). The mob broke down the massive doors and,

Castle William. The island fortress in Boston Harbor was built to defend the town of Boston and to house British troops. (LIBRARY OF CONGRESS)

room by room, destroyed everything they could lay their hands on, including Hutchinson's legendary collection of manuscripts—many of them significant public papers documenting the history of Massachusetts. "One of the rioters declared that the first places which they looked into were the beds, in order to murder the children," according to Peter Oliver. "All this was joy to Mr. Otis, as also to some of the considerable merchants who were smugglers and personally active in the diabolical scene."[7]

It took the mob three hours to dislodge the cupola from the roof, and only fatigue and the rising sun put an end to the systematic destruction they wreaked on the Hutchinson home. "If the Devil had been here last night," one Bostonian commented the next day, "he would have gone back to his own regions ashamed of being outdone and never more have set foot upon the earth."[8]

In the course of the following day, rumors swirled through Boston that the mob had a list of fifteen "prominent gentlemen" and contemplated "a war of plunder, of general leveling and taking away the distinction of rich and poor."[9] Fearful that his name might be on the list, Hancock joined other Boston selectmen in refusing to bring the looters to justice. The Governor convened the Council, the upper house of the state legislature, in the safety of outlying Cambridge. They agreed that the previous night's rioting "had given such a turn to the town that all gentlemen in the place were ready to support the government in detecting and publishing the actors in the last horrid scene."[10] Although the Council issued a warrant to arrest Mackintosh, Sam Adams led a group that demanded and won his release. After others were jailed, a mob broke into the jailer's house, seized his keys, and released the prisoners before they could be tried. They never were.

By the end of September, events continued isolating John Hancock. Only the wealthiest merchants and men of great property—a tiny elite—remained united behind the royal governor. The base of those in opposition had broadened to include a sizable—and most respectable—majority that included almost all of Boston's small merchants and shopkeepers; its printers, tavern owners, land speculators, and smugglers; a few of its ship owners; and many ordinary citizens who worked for the merchants, shopkeepers, printers, and so forth. All would have to pay stamp taxes on everything from playing cards to wills. For most, it would have been the first direct tax they had ever had to pay, although all paid indirect, hidden taxes such as customs duties, which merchants tacked onto wholesale and retail prices.

Publicly, Hancock sided with no one, and when a vacancy occurred in the House of Representatives, voters rejected him brusquely. He finished last on the list of candidates with a mere forty votes. Instead, they elected the outspoken James Otis and his friend Sam Adams—despite the prison term hanging over Adams's head for embezzling public monies. As titular leaders of the radical majority, Otis and Adams used veiled threats of mob retaliation to gain control of every important committee in the House of Representatives. As Governor Bernard noted with dismay, the "faction in perpetual opposition to Government" took complete control. "What with inflammatory speeches within doors and the parades of the mob without," the Otis-Adams radicals "entirely triumphed over the little remains of government."[11]

Hancock thus remained in a precarious position on the fence around his hilltop mansion. Rather than put his property and personal safety at risk, he spent more time within sight of his home at the nearby Merchants Club and at the Green Dragon Tavern, where his fellow Freemasons assembled. Although most of the Green Dragon Freemasons were wealthy Harvard alumni, they did not exclude less-schooled applicants or skilled craftsmen such as Paul Revere. The son of a silversmith of Huguenot descent, the younger Revere had eschewed higher education in favor of an apprenticeship in his father's shop and eventual ownership of their prosperous enterprise. Sam Adams was not a Freemason, but he stopped at the Green Dragon Tavern on the daily rounds he made of Boston taverns, coaxing and cajoling imbibers to support his quest for political power. Step by step, tavern by tavern, he assumed leadership over the disparate elements of Boston's malcontents—the small merchants facing bankruptcy, the skilled artisans struggling to keep their shops open, and those out-of-work laborers who were too poor to feed their children or heat their hovels. Nor did he overlook any Green Dragon Utopians—the rich sons of Harvard who had studied and believed in the principles set forth in the works of John Locke, Voltaire, Rousseau, and others.

According to his cousin John Adams, Sam Adams had the most thorough understanding of "the temper and character of the people" along with a gift for intellectual seduction.

> Although erudite, he spoke the common tongue and dressed in the common cloth—not miserable, but as a working artisan, say, after a day's work. Everywhere he went, in every tavern, on the streets, he recruited ceaselessly for his rebellion against royal rule and those who had destroyed his father. He made it his constant rule to watch the rise of every brilliant genius, to seek his acquaintance, to court his friendship, to cultivate his natural feelings in favor of his native country, to warn him against the hostile designs of Great Britain.[12]

His tactics varied with each recruit—flattery for one, cajolery for another, pledges and promises for another. From the moment he stepped into the General Court, he began organizing a group of powerful allies from rural districts to expand his political power beyond Boston to the rest of the province.

Although he could count on a broad-based throng of rebels and wealthy young malcontents, Sam Adams had failed to recruit anyone from the merchant elite, and he knew he would never overturn the royal governor without the political and financial support of at least a few merchant-

The Green Dragon Tavern. This was a public tavern that served as the meeting house for Boston's Freemasons. (LIBRARY OF CONGRESS)

aristocrats to buy arms, ammunition, and rum for the mobs. His cousin John Adams called Sam a "designing person" who, in public, "affects to despise riches, and not to dread poverty, but no man is more ambitious."[13]

Sensing Hancock's fear and indecision, Sam Adams pounced on the young merchant. His technique of ingratiating himself was "the same manner that the devil is represented seducing Eve, by a constant whispering at the ear," according to Peter Oliver. The seductive whispers left unsuspecting listeners "closely attached to the hindermost part of Mr. Adams as the rattles are affixed to the tail of a rattlesnake." Whenever anyone tries to disengage himself from Adams's thrall, Oliver went on, Adams "like the cuttlefish would discharge his muddy liquid, and darken the waters to such a hue that the other was lost."[14]

Hancock listened closely to what Sam Adams had to say. Knowing that Adams was perhaps the only man in Boston who could guarantee the safety of his property, Hancock decided to pay for that guarantee—at least for a while—with financial support for Adams and what would soon evolve into the Tea Party movement. Adams soon dug so deeply into Hancock's pockets that the merchant won the reputation of being Adams's "milch cow."[15]

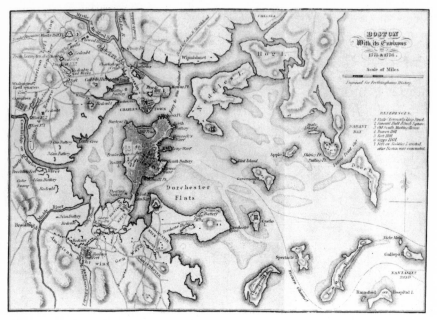

Boston, its harbor and environs, 1775–1776. Charlestown lies across the water to the north, with Breed's Hill on the right extremity and Bunker's Hill to the northwest, near the neck. (BOSTONIAN SOCIETY)

On September 23, fourteen boxes of stamps arrived in Boston, but with no stamp distributor to accept them, they went to the British garrison on Castle William. Boxes destined for Rhode Island and New Hampshire remained on board ship, guarded by two men-of-war. A few days later, stamps for other states arrived in Philadelphia and New York in anticipation of November 1, when the act would take effect. Calling the stamps "the most disagreeable commodity that was ever imported," Hancock continued appealing to influential friends in London, predicting that if the stamps were "carried into execution they will entirely stagnate trade here, for it is universally determined here never to submit to it . . . and nothing but the repeal of the act will right the consequence of its taking place. . . . For God's sake use your interest to relieve us. I dread the event."[16]

Five colonies—Connecticut, Rhode Island, Pennsylvania, Maryland, and South Carolina—responded to the call of the Massachusetts General Court to meet in New York, and delegates from three other states that failed to respond—New York, New Jersey, and Delaware—showed up anyway. The Stamp Act Congress, as the gathering was called, brought together for the first time leaders from all sections of the American colonies.

From the opening session on October 7, however, it was clear that delegates harbored a wide range of opinions on dealing with Parliament. Erudite moderates who favored conciliatory negotiations with Parliament outnumbered the radicals, and dismissing all suggestions for public protests and boycotts, the moderates took control of the proceedings. Although James Otis headed the Massachusetts delegation, Congress rejected, by one vote, his nomination as chairman in favor of a more moderate delegate.

After eleven days the congress approved a "Declarations of Rights and Grievances of the Colonists in America," written largely by the brilliant moderate John Dickinson, a prominent Philadelphia lawyer and member of the Pennsylvania legislature. Dickinson adopted the position of John Hancock—that the only way to force repeal of the Stamp Act was by recruiting the help of English merchants. Dickinson's declaration maintained that the Stamp Act deprived colonists of "two privileges essential to freedom"—taxation by consent and trial by jury. Devoid of inflammatory language, the document reiterated the argument against taxation by Parliament without colonist representation but, in effect, agreed to colonist taxation by their own legislatures if the Stamp Act were repealed.

"The invaluable rights of taxing ourselves," Dickinson declared, "are not . . . unconstitutional but confirmed by the Great Charter of English liberties." He called it unjust to try American ship owners and merchants in a far-off Halifax admiralty court, adding that such trials would deprive the accused of the constitutional right to trial by a jury of his peers. His document dissociated itself from antiroyalist radicals, however, by asserting that American colonists "glory in being subjects of the best of kings having been born under the most perfect form of government . . . and esteem our connection with Great Britain as one of the great blessings." Dickinson said he believed that Parliament would almost certainly redress American grievances when it receives assurances "that the inhabitants in the colonies have the most unbounded affection for his majesty's person, family and government, as well as for the mother country, and that their subordination to the parliament is universally acknowledged."[17]

John Dickinson. A prominent Philadelphia lawyer and member of the Pennsylvania legislature, he wrote a series of stirring essays— Letters from a Farmer in Pennsylvania—*that united American opposition to Britain's Townshend Acts.* (LIBRARY OF CONGRESS)

Even the obsequious whimper at the end of Dickinson's declaration, however, left delegates too fearful of British government retaliation to affix their names to the document. Only one signature appeared—that of the clerk of the congress—and only six colonies agreed to sponsor the petitions to the king and Parliament. Otis was furious. He arrived in Boston railing irrationally against the Stamp Act, the British in general, and Thomas Hutchinson in particular. In what Otis's friends called "incoherent ravings," Otis urged citizens at a town meeting to march to the ruins of Hutchinson's home and destroy its remaining fragments. He challenged British Prime Minister George Grenville to a one-on-one duel on the floor of the House of Commons to determine whether the colonies were to be free or enslaved by British tyranny. Thomas Hutchinson responded by call-ing Otis "more fit for a madhouse than the House of Representatives."[18]

On October 31, 1765, 250 merchants in Boston, 200 in New York, and 400 in Philadelphia agreed to stop importing all but a select list of goods from England and Europe on the following day, when the Stamp Act was to take effect. The merchants hoped the boycott would so dam-age English trade that their agents and suppliers in England would force Parliament to repeal the Stamp Act. John Hancock recognized he would have little choice but to join the boycott. Not doing so would have been tantamount to pledging allegiance to the royal governor, after which he surely would have had to flee to Castle William and abandon his beloved Beacon Hill property to Sam Adams's mob. In a letter designed for Sam Adams as much as for his London agent, he wrote of his fears and of his intention to join the boycott. If his ships left England before November 1, he pledged to unload them when they arrived, refill them with whale oil, and send them back to England. If the ships left after November 1, however, he said he would remove their cargoes, haul the vessels ashore, and cancel his orders for all spring goods.

"I now tell you, and you will find it come to pass, that the people of this country will never suffer themselves to be made slaves of by a submis-sion to the D——d act," Hancock wrote.

> But I shall now open to you my own determinations. A thousand guineas—nay, a much larger sum—would be no temptation to me to be able to be the first that should apply for a stamp, for such is the aversion of the people to the stamps that I should be sure to lose my property, if not my life. . . . Any further taxes must ruin us. . . . It is the united resolution and determination of the people here not to carry on business under a stamp. . . . I would sooner subject myself to the hardest labor . . . than carry on this business as I now do. . . . I am determined as soon as I know that they are resolved to insist on this act to sell my stock in trade and shut up my warehouse.[19]

As it turned out, Hancock had nothing to lose and everything to gain by supporting the merchant boycott. Financially, the boycott could not have come at a better time. Sales were slow, and his warehouse was filled with unsold goods. He could not have bought another shilling's worth of goods even if he had wanted to. Along with that of many other American merchants, his credit had run out in London, and as he wrote, a letter from his London agent demanding payment of old bills stared up at him. The merchant boycott, therefore, gave him time to sell off inventories and accumulate some cash. Moreover, his inability to buy stamps left him unable to pay any London bills. All remittances as well as other financial and legal documents required stamps, and there were none to be had.

Hancock assailed the Stamp Act with passion:

> I believe that not a man in England, in proportion to estate, pays the tax that I do. I now pay yearly . . . £300 sterling, besides all duties, imposts, ministers and many other additional taxes. . . . I will not be a slave. I have a right to the liberties and privileges of the English Constitution, and I as an Englishman will enjoy them.[20]

By the time the Stamp Act was due to take effect, all stamp officers in the colonies had resigned, and with no stamps available, the Act was irrelevant except as a symbolic affront. Americans nevertheless greeted November 1 as a day of mourning, with bells tolling throughout the day. The Sons of Liberty—Adams, Edes, and the others—gathered at the Liberty Tree to hang effigies of Grenville and another member of parliament. That evening, they put the effigies in a cart, and as thousands marched behind, they wheeled it past the Town House and on to the gallows on Boston Neck. The courts and customs houses had no choice but to close. Business came to a standstill.

After a few unanticipated days of festivity, however, Boston resumed its normal activities, ignoring the Stamp Act completely. Newspapers published, the courts heard cases, and stores reopened—all without stamps. The customs house also reopened and allowed goods to flow in and out normally. Ships from London arrived with autumn merchandise after the stamp tax deadline, and merchants like Hancock simply refilled them with whale oil and sent them back to London as they had always done. Although they sent completed documents with purchase orders for spring merchandise, they told their London agents not to fill them until Parliament repealed the Stamp Act. Excusing his inability to repay his outstanding debts, Hancock chuckled to himself that English law alone was preventing him from issuing remittances without stamps. Although he distanced himself from the violence that the Stamp Act had engendered, he warned that he would remain unflagging in his support of the merchant boycott.

"The injury that has been done to Hutchinson," Hancock wrote, "is what I abhor and detest as much as any man breathing and would go to great lengths in repairing his loss. But any opposition to the Stamp Act is commendable."[21]

The Stamp Act took effect a week before Pope's Day, which was Boston's version of Guy Fawkes Day, when England celebrated the execution of the leader of a Catholic conspiracy to blow up Parliament in 1604. Instead of a single, traditional parade, with dancing and other festivities, however, Boston's Pope's Day had turned ugly a year earlier in 1764, when two rival gangs—each a neighborhood crime family of sorts—staged parades that inevitably met head on. After the bloodshed subsided, a little girl lay dead.

Sam Adams subsequently befriended the leaders of both gangs and, by the following summer, he had united them into a single, powerful armed force under the shoemaker Mackintosh and added what was now a street army of toughs—mostly part-time waterfront workers—to his political protests. In August 1765 the Mackintosh force had formed the core of the mob that sacked the homes of Andrew Oliver and Thomas Hutchinson—and frightened John Hancock off his political fence on Beacon Hill. On the evening before Pope's Day, in November 1765, Adams displayed the street power he now wielded at a "Union Feast" he sponsored for the two gangs to mingle with merchants and politicians— "with heart and hand in flowing bowls and bumping glasses."[22] John Hancock was there—indeed, had not dared stay away—and in the end, to Adams's delight and everyone else's cheers, he picked up the $1,000 tab for the entire dinner.

Although Adams and Otis had whipped up crowd hatred against Boston's merchant kings, that hatred had never touched Hancock. Always ready to offer credit to customers, Hancock was not only an outspoken opponent of the Stamp Act, he was a generous employer and well liked by the hundreds of colonists who depended on him to sell the products of their fields or workshops and relied on him for their own supplies. One of the rare Boston plutocrats who seemed to understand the plight of ordinary men, he had a loyal following of his own, whom Sam Adams recognized as a constituency he would have to court.

The following morning, on Pope's Day, Adams's "trained mob" marched in disciplined military formation before a startled governor and general court at the Town House. To the governor's astonishment, the volatile Ebenezer Mackintosh led the force, marching in uniformed splendor, stride for stride, arm in arm, with—of all people—the colonel of the governor's own militia. A few days later, the governor wrote to England that he had "ordered some companies of militia to be mustered" to thwart the marchers, "but the militia refused to obey my orders."[23]

Pope's Day in 1765 marked a sharp turning point in John Hancock's relationship with Boston radicals, and in the months that followed he drew ever closer to them—always motivated by self-preservation. It proved a wise move. Six weeks later Adams's mob hauled poor Andrew Oliver down to the Liberty Tree again, and as all of Boston watched this time, the mob forced him to make a public apology: He cried out that he detested the Stamp Act and swore never to attempt to enforce it. After the crowd released Oliver amid hoots of derision, Hancock left the scene of his friend's humiliation to sign another boycott agreement with other Boston merchants. "In case the Stamp Act is not repealed," they all wrote to their London agents, "my orders are that you will not . . . ship me one article." Their common letter, dictated by Sam Adams, said that their boycott reflected the "united resolves of not only the principal merchants . . . of this town, but of those of the other trading towns of this province."[24]

By mid-winter 1766 the American merchants' boycott had taken a dreadful toll on English merchants. The Americans owed them about £4 million before the boycott began, and as the flow of orders and cash from America dried up, British exports dropped 14 percent by the beginning of 1766 and continued plunging, with no end in sight. As goods piled up inside and outside warehouses in Bristol, Liverpool, Manchester, Leeds, Glasgow, and every other trading town in Britain, British merchants inundated Parliament with petitions demanding repeal of the Stamp Act. London merchants asked Parliament to grant "every ease and advantage the North Americans can with propriety desire."[25]

For whatever reasons, Hancock's London agents had ignored his previous entreaties, but when he made good on his threat not to repay them or order any spring goods, they quickly joined the protest. In Virginia, George Washington could not resist mocking the miscalculations of Parliament and the British merchants: "I fancy the merchants of Great Britain trading to the colonies," Washington laughed, "will not be among the last to wish for a repeal of it."[26]

The storm clouds in New England were spreading down the Atlantic coast.

Chapter 8

A Blackguard Town

*E*arly in 1766 Governor Bernard warned London that he would need massive military support to restore order in Boston: "I am more and more assured that the people of this town, who have now got all the power in their hands, will know no bounds, until the authority of Great Britain shall interpose with effect."[1] Although Grenville expressed his "resentment and indignation at the outrageous tumults and insurrections . . . in North America," he faced a growing multitude of English merchants on the verge of financial ruin unless trade with the colonies resumed.[2] They warned Parliament that the use of troops to enforce the Stamp Act would provoke rebellion. If Parliament wanted to tax the colonies, they counseled, it should continue the traditional practice of external taxation with hidden, indirect taxes such as import duties.

"I have been charged with giving birth to sedition in America," William Pitt assailed Grenville in Parliament:

> I rejoice that America has resisted. . . . If the gentleman does not understand the difference between internal and external taxation, I cannot help it. . . . The gentleman asks when were the colonies emancipated? But I desire to know when they were made slaves? . . . I will beg leave to tell the

*William Pitt, Earl of Chatham. As British prime minister,
Pitt tried to crack down on smuggling in America but
fought Parliament's efforts to impose a stamp tax on the
colonists.* (FROM A NINETEENTH-CENTURY ENGRAVING
IN THE AUTHOR'S COLLECTION)

House what is really my opinion: It is that the Stamp Act be repealed absolutely, totally, immediately.[3]

By the end of February the pressure to repeal the Stamp Act grew overwhelming, and when a group of thirty-nine leading English merchants
joined in the protests, Parliament promised that repeal was indeed imminent. The merchants sent a circular letter to their American correspondents
predicting repeal, but they warned against further rebellion and "intemper-
ate proceedings of various ranks of people on your side of the water. . . .

> If therefore . . . you have a mind to do credit to your friends and strengthen
> the hands of your advocates, hasten, we beseech you, to express filial duty
> and gratitude to your parent country. Then will those who have been . . .

your friends, plume themselves on the restoration of peace to the colonies. . . . But if . . . [repeal of the stamp tax] is talked of as a victory, if it is said the Parliament have yielded up the right [to tax the colonies], then indeed your enemies here will have a complete triumph. Your friends must certainly lose all power to serve you. Your tax masters probably will be restored and such a train of ill consequences follow as are easier for you to imagine than for us to describe.[4]

Only four and a half months after the Stamp Act had taken effect, a chastened Parliament voted to repeal it, without a single stamp ever having been affixed to a colonial document. It was a humiliating defeat—particularly because it had been inflicted by a constituency without a single direct vote in either the House of Commons or House of Lords. In the end, the British government collected no new taxes and left its own treasury—and many British merchants—far poorer than they would have been had they never passed the act. Moreover, passage of the act created the first organized opposition to royal rule and government taxation in the colonies—an opposition that radical rabble-rousers such as Sam Adams would convert from a modest espousal of free enterprise into an unyielding movement for independence.

Tragically for England, Parliament's petty tyrants who ruled the nation's rotten boroughs and pocket boroughs refused to recognize defeat or seek reconciliation with the colonies. Intent on governing the empire as they governed their captive constituents, they lit the fuse for the next colonial explosion by passing what they called a Declaratory Act—on the very day they had repealed the Stamp Act. The act asserted that "the Parliament of Great Britain had, hath and of right ought to have, full power and authority to make laws and statutes of sufficient force and validity to bind the colonies and people of America subjects of the Crown of Great Britain in all cases whatsoever."[5] Although a lower court in Britain held the law "contrary to fundamental laws of nature and . . . this constitution," England's Chief Justice ruled,

1st, that the British legislature, as to the power of making laws, represents the whole British Empire, and has authority to bind every part and every subject without the least distinction, whether such subjects have a right to vote or not, or whether the law binds places within the realm or without.

2nd, that the colonies, by the conditions on which they migrated, settled, and now exist, are more emphatically subjects of Great Britain than those within the realm; and that the British legislature have in every instance exercised their right of legislation over them without any dispute or question till the 14th of January last. . . . I know no difference between laying internal and external taxes.[6]

Even before the news of repeal reached Boston, Samuel Adams and his followers were satisfied that Hancock had proved his loyalty by supporting the merchant boycott, and Adams recognized that Hancock, as an important New England merchant and member of the mercantile elite, could add a crucial element to the all-but-bankrupt radical movement: money. On May 6, Adams and his supporters assured Hancock's election to the General Court, or legislature, with 437 votes. By allying himself with the radical wing in the Court, Hancock believed he was espousing the cause of commercial freedom, but in fact, London believed his election had made him "one of the leaders of the disaffected"—especially after he foolishly declared that he "would not suffer any of our [English customs] officers to go even on board any of his London ships."[7]

On the afternoon of Hancock's election, Sam Adams walked with John Adams, who was still building his law practice, and is said to have told his younger cousin, "This town has done a wise thing today."

"What?" John Adams inquired.

"They have made that young man's fortune their own."[8]

Ten days later, in one of the most fortuitous events of his budding political career, one of Hancock's ships brought him the official notice of repeal. London's merchants had selected him, as one of America's most important merchants, to announce the news to Boston at a selectmen's meeting. The selectmen cheered him and set aside the following day—Repeal Day—for celebration. At 1:00 in the afternoon, church bells—and every other bell in town—began pealing. Bostonians poured from their houses, firing guns in the air and shouting Hancock's name. As the shouts proliferated, they grew convinced—as he apparently did—that he had been the instigator of repeal rather than a simple messenger. Flags flew from every building in town, and bands marched through the city. Sam Adams and the Sons of Liberty gathered at the Liberty Tree before parading to debtor's prison with John Hancock's cash to buy the release of all the inmates.

Edes published a special Repeal Day issue of the *Gazette*:

> At one o'clock the castle and batteries and train of artillery fired a royal salute and the afternoon was spent in mirth and jollity. In the evening the whole town was beautifully illuminated. On the Common the Sons of Liberty erected a magnificent pyramid, illuminated with 280 lamps. The four upper stories of which were ornamented with the figures of their majesties and fourteen worthy patriots who have distinguished themselves by their love of liberty.[9]

Not to be outdone, Hancock set off his own, even larger display of fireworks on a huge stage in front of his mansion. All eyes turned toward the merchant king and his beautiful home, which he swathed in illuminations. Gradually, the crowd worked its way up the Common to Hancock's gate, where he set up a pipe—a cask holding 125 gallons—of Madeira wine. When they emptied it, he sent out another. He came out on his balcony and waved to the cheering crowd, calling out greetings and looking every bit the hero of repeal. He not only convinced the crowd of his new role, he believed it himself. While the mob stood cheering and drinking outside, "John Hancock Esq . . . gave a grand and elegant entertainment to the genteel part of the town" inside the mansion.[10]

The celebration continued the next day. Hancock entertained twenty-nine merchants at the Bunch of Grapes, another popular merchants' tavern, near the end of Long Wharf. At Province House, the governor's mansion on Marlborough Street, Governor Bernard celebrated Repeal Day with his council by drinking to his majesty's health before stepping out courageously to mingle with the rest of Boston. Bernard clearly thought Repeal Day marked the beginning of peace in the colonies.

Unfortunately, Hancock's fellow merchants had unleashed forces they could no longer control. Having called their workers and the rest of Boston's underclass to rebellion against British "taxes and tyranny," they aroused ambitions for liberties that most could not distinguish from license, and the result was madness. New York's Lieutenant Governor Cadwallader Colden warned that the merchants "who excited this seditious spirit in the people" no longer "have it in their power to suppress it."[11]

In addition to stirring discontent among Boston's lowest social echelons, the city's merchants alienated some of the most brilliant and influential members of their own social and economic class—and weakened the ability of merchants as a group to control future political events. Indeed, the peaceful reconciliation with Britain that the merchants thought they had wrought marked but the beginning of all-out war for Otis and Adams. Seeking neither peace nor reconciliation, they saw repeal as the first victory in a war for American independence from Britain—and political power for themselves.

They fired their next shot in the House of Representatives on May 28, when Sam Adams's political coterie took firm control. It named Otis speaker, Adams clerk, and antiroyalists, including Otis's father, to the Governor's Council, or upper house. Governor Bernard picked up the gauntlet and, under his charter powers, rejected Otis as speaker and vetoed the Council elections. Sam Adams responded sarcastically, "Had your Excellency been pleased . . . to have favored us with a list and positive orders whom to choose, we should in your principles have been without excuse. But even the most abject slaves are not to be blamed for disobeying their master's will and pleasure, when it is wholly unknown to them."[12]

Adams replaced Otis as speaker with the pleasant, unassuming Thomas Cushing, Jr., who, like Hancock, had graduated from Harvard, inherited a huge mercantile empire, and been lured into the radical camp leadership by the siren songs of the cunning Sam Adams. Also like Hancock, he envisioned the Stamp Act's repeal as a harbinger of calm over the seas that linked the colonies to their motherland.

Bernard, however, muddied the waters by presenting the General Court with a Parliamentary demand to bring Stamp Act rioters to justice and force them to compensate those who had suffered losses in the riots. Caught unprepared, assembly radicals recognized that refusal might cost them the support of moderates who supported Stamp Act repeal but condemned violence. Otis and Adams finally pushed through a compromise bill that com-

*Thomas Cushing, Jr. Speaker of the Massachusetts House of
Representatives, he was an unassuming Harvard College
graduate who had entered his father's prosperous merchant-
banking firm before joining Samuel Adams's radicals and
entering Boston politics.* (LIBRARY OF CONGRESS)

pensated riot victims but granted full amnesty to rioters. In defying Parliament and the governor, Otis and Adams called the amnesty a victory, but as
British merchants had warned in their circular letter to their Massachusetts
counterparts, it proved a costly victory that turned moderates in England
and the colonies against Boston for condoning criminal acts and failing to
respect basic English law.

What little warmth England retained for New England colonists disappeared after Parliament had to raise English duties and taxes at home to
compensate for American refusal to pay the stamp tax and cover British defense costs in America. The increased property taxes forced farmers to raise
the price of wheat, which raised the costs of flour and bread. Increased duties
lifted prices of imported produce, wines, and other European essentials.

"Grievous are the complaints of the poor in every part of the Kingdom," one newspaper reported, "on account of the extravagant price of provisions of all sorts. Every post brings fresh accounts of tumults, occasioned by the high price of bread. . . . There is nothing but riots and insurrections over the whole country, on account of the high price of provisions."[13]

John Hancock tried to stay out of the line of fire between Governor Bernard and the Sam Adams–James Otis forces. For him, Repeal Day had marked the beginning of new opportunities to expand his business and make money—and he set to work doing just that. He outbid the market for whale oil, expanded exports to England, expanded the number of his retail stores, and ordered about £8,000 worth of new inventories to stock them. "He changed the course of his uncle's business, and built, and employed in trade, a great number of ships," wrote Thomas Hutchinson, "and in this way, and by building at the same time several houses, he found work for a great number of tradesmen, made himself popular, was chosen selectman, representative, and moderator of town meetings, etc."[14]

The expansion of his business expanded his spirit, and as his uncle had done, he became a major benefactor of his community. On May 22, he went to Cambridge, where he received enthusiastic applause at a pomp-filled public ceremony installing the first Hancock Professor of Oriental Languages at Harvard College. As business slowed for summer, he paid more attention to his new position as a member of the General Court. Its activities suddenly enthralled him, and he accepted posts on thirty different committees, whose functions ranged from regulating potash production to auditing the provincial treasurer's government accounts. Other court members deferred to his knowledge and experience as one of the colony's most successful merchants and head of what had become its largest enterprise. He discovered a gift for mediating differences, and delegates turned to him in increasing numbers for help in resolving disputes. His popularity grew daily—and nightly at the lavish dinners he offered at various taverns and on Beacon Hill. To Sam Adams's consternation, Hancock was also accumulating power as a spokesman for Boston's shopkeepers and merchants and eroding Adams's own political base. In response, Adams stepped up his personal propaganda in the *Boston Gazette* and in public speeches. He staged demonstrations, parades, and fireworks to commemorate even the slightest triumph over royal governance.

"Otis and Adams," wrote John Adams, "are politic in promoting these festivals, for they tinge the minds of people; they impregnate them with the sentiments of liberty; they render the people fond of their leaders in the cause, and averse and bitter against all opposers. To the honor of the Sons of Liberty, I did not see one person intoxicated, or near it."[15] In contrast, Loyalists scorned those who marched in the Adams demonstrations as "the rabble," ignoring their potential political strength because few, if any, owned enough property to make them eligible to vote.

In early 1767 John Hancock celebrated his thirtieth birthday at one of his never-ending entertainments that sealed his political position as leader of an important merchant faction. Otis and Adams had little choice but to offer him a seat at their inner political circle, which met regularly above Edes's print shop. Sam Adams's political star, meanwhile, began to lose a bit of its luster as loyal royalists worked behind the scenes to produce some propaganda of their own, demeaning Adams as an embezzler of public funds. With Adams on the defensive, Hancock moved into the leadership breach, with coincidences continually working in his favor.

On the night of February 3, fire broke out in the bakehouse of one of his tenants. By morning, it had razed more than twenty buildings, including many of his own, and left fifty families homeless. After the General Court appropriated £400 for their relief, Hancock added £400 of his own money and saw to the distribution of huge stacks of free firewood to the poor throughout the city for the rest of what was one of the coldest winters in memory. Hancock constantly rode through town in his golden coach on the lookout for opportunities to relieve the most hard-pressed of Boston's underprivileged, both directly and indirectly. Boston had never seen any man of such evident wealth show such deep concern for the unfortunate. In addition to outright gifts of firewood, food, or free rent, he made substantial contributions to almost every church in the city, with seats and Bibles for the needy, window glass, communion tables, and pulpits. He paid for a three-hundred-pound bell at one church and gave cash gifts to churches to minister to the needy. The ministers did not forget him in their sermons, and he gained a justifiable reputation as a great humanitarian with a deep devotion to his community and its citizens.

As the city's affection for Hancock increased, its disaffection with Sam Adams increased proportionately. In March the selectmen appointed a committee to examine the tax collector's books and found Sam Adams's collections for the provincial treasury short £2,300, whereas collections for the town were short £1,700. Bostonians were outraged and asked James Otis, of all people, as attorney for the town treasury, to charge his friend Adams with embezzlement. Otis called Boston's electors "a pack of damned stupid fools," to which his enemies replied by calling him a "mad dictator."[16] Although Otis had no choice but to prosecute Adams, Sam Adams's political friends handpicked a lower court jury, which acquitted him. Forced by the governor to appeal the Adams verdict, Otis filed a less-than-enthusiastic appeal and—to his own surprise—won a surprising appellate court reversal of the lower court decision. The higher court issued a judgment against Adams for £1,463 based on the total amount missing, less the salary due him as tax collector. The court gave him nine months—until March 1767—to repay the city.

Although Sam Adams's political machine managed to reelect him and Otis to the House of Representatives in the May elections, John Hancock out-polled them both with 618 votes—44 votes more than the tarnished Adams. Hancock easily won reelection as selectman as well, and both Adams and Otis reluctantly recognized Hancock, the merchant king, as a new and unexpected full partner in Boston politics. Had a vengeful Parliament not acted just then, Otis and Adams might have disappeared from the political scene and left the moderate conciliator John Hancock to maneuver Boston's political machine between the conflicting interests of England and her colonists.

England, however, faced economic collapse and social upheaval. To quell the ongoing bread riots, Parliament reduced English farm and other property taxes 25 percent, cutting government revenues by £500,000 and leaving Chancellor of the Exchequer Charles Townshend desperate for new sources of money. Without the political strength to reduce the size of the military or the king's £800,000-a-year allowance—and without even considering tax increases for England's financially bloated nobility—

Townshend had no choice but to try to make colonists pay the full costs of the British military in North America.

Townshend's opponents—those who had fought for Stamp Act repeal—urged the House of Commons not to fan the flames of discontent in America, but those seeking to avenge the humiliation of repeal insisted that Massachusetts had usurped powers of the king by granting amnesty to Stamp Act rioters. Although Townshend scoffed openly at the distinction between external and internal taxes, in the interest of reconciling with the colonies, he agreed to impose only new external taxes.

On June 29, 1767, Parliament passed the Townshend Acts—the fourth and what would prove to be the decisive set of taxes that would incite Americans to rebel and declare independence. The Townshend Acts imposed import duties on five types of glass, red and white lead, paints, a full range of paper—and tea. Tea had become the rage among wealthy ladies in America after London magazines described it as the favorite beverage of the royal family and British aristocrats of note. Tea now entered the collective American mind as a symbol of British wealth and power.

Together the new duties would yield an estimated £40,000 a year for defending the colonies and "defraying the charge of the administration of justice and the support of the civil government." Nor did the new acts leave any escape from paying duties. All the taxed items except tea were made only in England, thus preventing smugglers from bringing in cheaper goods from elsewhere. As for tea, the government effectively halved the sixpenny duty on East India Company tea, leaving the net cost to American merchants below the price of smuggled Dutch tea.

In addition to new taxes, the Townshend Acts created new vice-admiralty courts to try smugglers and their accomplices without juries and provided for direct payment of judges and governors by Parliament rather than by colonial legislatures, thus making them independent of colonial influence. Townshend himself died before the acts took effect on November 20, and he never saw the havoc his vengeful scheme would wreak on the British Empire.

News of the Townshend Acts arrived in America in September 1767 and spread consternation across the colonies. The new taxes were particularly galling in colonies that had repaid their debts from the French and Indian

War. Indeed, Massachusetts had liquidated most of its war debt by 1767 and halved the rest of its provincial debt to a mere £40,000—a figure that the provincial government could erase by selling lands in the wilderness. With its debt all but eliminated, Massachusetts rescinded all the extra taxes it had exacted during the war, thus adding impetus to the colony's economic expansion. Adding still more impetus to the colony's economic growth was a dramatic shift in the Massachusetts balance of trade with the mother country, creating a huge inflow of specie—silver and gold coins and ingots—into the vaults of Boston's merchant bankers. The Townshend Acts threatened to reverse that flow, and rather than stand by idly, John Hancock called together the town's merchants to urge reimposition of the partial boycott of English imports that had proved so effective two years earlier in forcing Stamp Act repeal. As he had in '65, Hancock urged targeting only nonessential luxury goods—gloves, shoes, gold and silver thread, silks, and the like, which provided the most profits to English merchants.

"It is surprising to me," he wrote to a London associate, "that so many attempts are made on your side to cramp our trade. New duties every day increasing. In short, we are in a fair way of being ruined. We have nothing to do but unite and come under a solemn agreement to stop importing any goods from England."[17]

On October 28, a Boston town meeting approved Hancock's proposal for a partial boycott of British luxury goods. The limited scope of the boycott reflected Hancock's views that a moderate approach would be more likely to bring Parliament to its senses and, more likely, to win support from merchants elsewhere in the colonies. At the same time, Hancock pushed through a resolution urging colonists to reduce their dependence on other British goods by making their own clothing, jewelry, cheeses, malt liquors, cordage, and anchors. Until then, England had forbidden colonists' production of such goods to prevent competition with similar manufactures in Britain.

New Englanders responded enthusiastically, with churches organizing women's circles to spin textiles while forming close-knit social ties. "The female spinners kept on spinning six days of the week," Peter Oliver noted acidly, "and on the seventh the parsons took their turns and spun out their prayers and sermons to a long thread of politics."[18]

At least twenty-eight towns in Massachusetts set up spinning bees, according to local newspapers, with one town—Middletown—weaving more than 20,500 yards of cloth in 1769, or almost a yard and a half for every man, woman, and child in Boston. According to the *Boston Gazette*, a group of lesser entrepreneurs—among them William Molyneux—"erected a building 50 feet in length and two stories high for a manufactury house" in which they installed looms and hired workers to weave woolens.[19] Like Paul Revere, Molyneux was of Huguenot descent and bore an all-but-instinctive passion for individual liberties, including freedom of worship and freedom from taxation. Born to a family of modest means, he lacked the Harvard education of Boston's more prominent merchants but nonetheless succeeded in establishing a successful, albeit small, merchant house amidst the giants of Boston's competitive trade world.

By adding a nonconsumption agreement to the nonimportation agreement and expanding home manufacturing, Boston now threatened to effect a virtual end to trade with Britain. Even proroyalist merchants such as the Hutchinsons, Olivers, and Clarkes could not continue importing if American customers refused to buy their goods. The nonconsumption agreement amounted to a declaration of commercial independence and cleared the first barrier to political independence.

A few days later, on November 5, 1767, the *Pennsylvania Chronicle* published the first of twelve stirring essays by Philadelphia's John Dickinson, who had drafted the declaration at the Stamp Act Congress. His essays—*Letters from a Farmer in Pennsylvania*—appeared in twenty of the twenty-six newspapers in all thirteen colonies and in pamphlet form. They united American opposition to the Townshend Acts by supporting Boston's declaration of commercial independence and calling the debate over external and internal taxes meaningless. He charged that Britain could bleed the colonies as effectively with external as with internal taxes and that there was no difference between the Townshend Acts and the Stamp Act. Both, he said, burdened the colonies with unconstitutional taxes.

Dickinson argued that "if Britain can order us to come to her for necessities, we want and can order us to pay what taxes she pleases before we take them away or when we land them here, we are . . . slaves." There was no need for Americans to pay taxes for military protection, he said, because the colonies had already more than compensated Britain with commercial benefits from trade. The colonists were "pouring the fruits of all their labors into their mother's laps. . . . How many British authors have demonstrated that the present wealth, power and glory of their country are founded on these colonies?"

Dickinson spared no vitriol in attacking the Townshend Acts for stripping colonial assemblies of financial control over judges and governors:

> Is it possible to form an idea of slavery more complete, more miserable, more disgraceful, than that of a people where justice is administered, government exercised . . . AT THE EXPENSE OF THE PEOPLE, and yet WITHOUT THE LEAST DEPENDENCE AMONG THEM. . . . If we can find no relief from this infamous situation . . . we may bow down our necks, and with all the stupid serenity of servitude, to any drudgery which our lords and masters shall please to command.

Dickinson warned that the Townshend Acts would make America another Ireland, where British taxes had been of benefit to only British sinecures and pensioners. "Besides the burdens of pensions in Ireland," he added, "all the offices in that poor kingdom have been . . . bestowed upon strangers. . . . In the same manner shall we unquestionably be treated."[20]

The *Letters* provoked deep anger among colonists and equally deep anxiety among Loyalists. Newport and Providence joined the Massachusetts boycott, and New York did the same near the end of the year. Massachusetts Governor Bernard conceded that the *Letters* were "artfully wrote" and sent "a compleat set" to a friend in Parliament with the warning that they had been "universally circulated" and that if they "should receive no refutation . . . they will become a kind of colonial Bill of Rights." On December 5, four weeks after his first *Letter* appeared in Philadelphia, Dickinson sent copies of all twelve to James Otis in Boston and urged that Massachusetts, as the center of colonial trade with England, take the lead in organizing colonial opposition.

"The liberties of our common country appear to me to be at this moment exposed to the most imminent danger," he wrote to Otis, "and this apprehension has engaged me to lay my sentiments before the public in

Letters, of which I send you a copy. . . . Only one has yet been published and what their effect may be, cannot yet be known, but whenever the cause of American freedom is to be vindicated, I look towards the Province of Massachusetts Bay. She must, as she has hitherto done, first kindle the sacred flame, that on such occasions must warm and illuminate the continent."[21]

The first Dickinson *Letter* appeared in all three Boston newspapers on December 21, 1767, and the following day, Otis, Sam Adams, John Hancock, and Thomas Cushing petitioned the king to repeal the Townshend Acts as violations of their "sacred rights" as Englishmen "of being taxed only by representatives of their own free election." Adams and Otis sent a circular letter to the other North American colonial assemblies urging them to send similar petitions. Governor Bernard called the letter seditious and dissolved the General Court, but it was too late. In England, the Secretary of State for Colonial Affairs, Lord Hillsborough, shot off two letters—one to Governor Bernard with the king's order that the Massachusetts House condemn the circular letter and the second to all other provincial governors to prevent their assemblies from acting on the Massachusetts resolution—by dissolving them if necessary.

Like Bernard, Hillsborough acted too late to thwart the inexorable march of the colonies toward independence. Indeed, far from slowing the march, Hillsborough's letters spurred it forward. In Boston, Hancock called for expanding the partial boycott of British goods to a total boycott. Virginia, New Jersey, and Connecticut issued their own petitions to the king, with Virginia sending a circular letter to other colonies, urging support for the Massachusetts boycott. By the end of 1767 Maryland, Pennsylvania, Delaware, New Hampshire, South Carolina, North Carolina, and New York had ignored the admonitions of their royal governors and sent their own petitions to the king.

On March 14, 1768, the Boston Town Meeting overwhelmingly reelected Hancock as selectman and appointed him to several key committees—one of them to enforce the judgment against Sam Adams for the missing funds in his accounts at the tax collector's office. With his payments already a year overdue, Adams asked for another six-month stay to put his financial affairs in order. After a long debate that tarred Adams with epithets ranging from patriot to pilferer, the town decided to ask the treasurer to stay all action against Adams until Hancock's committee could reexamine town accounts. The tide of events, however, quickly washed away memories of Adams's embezzlement. Although Hancock loaned Adams some of the money and Adams collected additional funds here and there, he would never repay his entire debt.

Indeed, Adams managed to refocus Boston's attention after the Town Meeting by announcing plans for another of his constant demonstrations and parades—this one to celebrate Repeal Day again, a "Day of Triumph over Great Britain," on March 18. Anticipating tar and feathers, the customs commissioners went into hiding, but to their own and the governor's surprise, Sam Adams astonished his followers by announcing, "NO MOBS—NO CONFUSIONS—NO TUMULTS." To ease the mob's disappointment, he added, "We know WHO have abused us . . . but let not a hair of their scalps be touched: The time is coming when they shall lick the dust and melt away."22

On April 8, 1768, three weeks after his reelection as selectman, Hancock's brig *Lydia* tied up at Hancock Wharf with spring orders from London that the commissioners suspected included tea, paper, and other dutiable goods. Two customs agents boarded her the following morning. Hancock charged from his office to the wharf and, with a small mob, including the ship's captain, rushed on board and blocked the men's access to the hold. That night, one of the customs agents sneaked below deck under cover of darkness, but Hancock was waiting with about eight or ten men, one of whom shone a lantern in the frightened agent's face. Hancock demanded to see the agent's orders and writ of assistance, or search warrant. His orders were undated and he had no writ. Hancock told his men to seize the agent and carry him topside. With the mate and boatswain suspending the terrified young man by his arms and thighs, Hancock asked him, "Do you want to search the vessel?" He insisted he did not, and they let him go ashore unharmed.

Hancock's assault on the British agent was the first physical attack on British authority in the colonies, and overnight, it raised him to hero's status in Boston. Although the commissioners appealed to the attorney general of Massachusetts to prosecute Hancock, the attorney general decided that the men who had carried the agent ashore had borne no arms. More-over, the agent had boarded the vessel illegally, without a writ or the per-mission of the captain. Several days later, a mob stoned two commissioners while they rowed away from Long Wharf. The commissioners blamed Hancock for the incident, calling him "an idol of the mob" and adding that, "this infatuated man now gives out in public, that if we, the commis-sioners, are not recalled he will get rid of us before Christmas."[23]

On May 4, Boston jubilantly reelected Hancock to the provincial House of Representatives, which, in turn, elected him to the Governor's Council. The governor, however, rejected Hancock, as well as Adams, Otis, and other Patriot leaders. Five days later, at sunset on May 9, another Han-cock ship, the sloop *Liberty*, sailed into port. It had come from Madeira, and customs inspectors expected to find a shipload of wine. Because of the darkness, they postponed their inspection until morning, by which time they found the ship bobbing high in the water, with only twenty-five pipes in its hold—less than one-quarter of the ship's capacity. When questioned by the commissioners, the inspectors could not explain the curious void and insisted they had seen no wine taken ashore during the night.

A month later, after Hancock had unloaded the *Liberty* and reloaded her with cargo bound for England, the *Romney*, a fifty-gun, British man-of-war, sailed into Boston Harbor, commanded by a ruthless captain who thundered to all within earshot, "The town is a blackguard town and ruled by mobs . . . and, by the eternal God, I will make their hearts ache before I leave."[24] As he aimed his cannons at the town, Bostonians prepared for far worse pain than heartache.

Chapter 9

Farewell the Tea-board

*T*rue to his word, the captain of the *Romney* sent monstrous press gangs swarming ashore to terrorize the waterfront and impress whatever unlucky young men happened to cross their paths. With the menacing silhouette of the *Romney* and her big guns to protect them, the commissioners leaped at the chance to avenge Hancock's insults and insolence. One of the customs inspectors who had inspected the *Liberty* reversed his earlier testimony: He told of Hancock's men forcibly holding him aboard the *Liberty* on the night of May 9, that he heard the squeal of tackles hoisting goods, but his captors threatened to kill him and burn his home if he told what he knew.

A senior customs official responded by painting a broad arrow on the *Liberty*'s mast—a signal she was now government property—and on June 10, the captain of the *Romney* sent a detachment of marines to haul the *Liberty* to a mooring beneath the *Romney*'s massive guns. While marines made fast their lines, a mob of about five hundred "sturdy boys and Negroes" gathered on the wharf and pelted the marines with paving stones ripped from the streets.

As the sailors towed the *Liberty* out of range, the mob focused its attack on the customs official and his aide, beating them as they ran to their homes, catching one and dragging him through the streets while pelting him with rocks and filth until friends could rescue him. The mob then gathered about the officials' homes, beating drums, blowing horns, and smashing windows with rocks while letting forth "the most hideous howlings—as the Indians do when they attack an enemy."[1] Another group at the harbor pulled the customs boat from the water and set it afire. The commissioners, meanwhile, fled with their families to the customs house to retrieve government cash and then rowed away under cover of darkness to the safety of the *Romney* and Castle William. Signs went up on the Liberty Tree urging citizens to attack the commissioners if they should reappear and attempt to collect duties. Sensing an imminent popular uprising, Governor Bernard prepared to flee and sent an urgent message to the New York headquarters of General Thomas Gage, the commander in chief of British forces in America, to send troops "to rescue the government out of the hands of a trained mob."[2] Gage ordered two regiments to sail to Boston.

For Samuel Adams, the seizure of the *Liberty* and its cargo and the threat of British troops were the sparks he had awaited to light the flames of outright rebellion against British rule. He called his mob to the Liberty Tree.

"If you are men," he cried out, "behave like men. Let us take up arms immediately and be free and seize all the king's officers. We shall have thirty thousand men to join us from the country . . . with their knapsacks and bayonets fixed. . . . We will take up arms and spend our last drop of blood."[3] Adams pledged that the English masses would join in the uprising, citing "the great tumults and risings of the people all over England and Ireland . . . the weavers' mob, the seamen's mob, the tailors' mob, the coal miners' mob, and some say the clergymen's mob . . . will unite in one general scene of tumult . . . at the very gates of the palace, and even in the royal presence."[4]

In contrast to Adams, Hancock saw the seizure of the *Liberty* as a serious business loss. Months might pass while his loaded cargo ship lay idle awaiting a resolution of the court case. On Saturday morning, June 11, he sent his lawyers and his friend and fellow Freemason Dr. Joseph Warren to try to negotiate its release. Five years younger than Hancock, Warren—like everyone else of consequence in Boston—was a Harvard graduate. Although he started his adult years as a schoolmaster in 1759, he switched course in 1761 to study medicine and gained fame by developing an unusual method of inoculating small pox patients—one of whom was the increasingly renowned John Adams. Warren's marriage to the daughter of a wealthy merchant bought him the luxury of dabbling in politics. He joined the Freemasons and became Grand Master of the Masonic Grand Lodge, where he formed close ties to John Hancock and other young Freemasons. Like them, he soon fell under the spell of Samuel Adams at the Green Dragon, and passage of the Stamp Act saw him plunge irretrievably into the maelstrom of Patriot politics. Opposed to and eager to prevent violence, he frequently offered to mediate local disputes between radical American merchants and British authorities. In the dispute over Hancock's *Liberty*, he offered to post a bond to guarantee the ship's availability when the case went to court. Meanwhile, Hancock would be able to send his ship and its cargo to London and carry on his trade. Fearful that the mobs might riot following Sunday Sabbath, the customs commissioners agreed. In the interests of restoring calm, the commissioners promised to return the ship to Hancock on Monday morning and forego pressing charges against him. Other merchants—as fearful of the possible effects of riots as the commissioners—poured into Hancock's house urging him to accept the settlement, and he did—happily and triumphantly.

Otis and Adams, however, stormed into Hancock's mansion, angrily accusing him of capitulating to the Customs Commission, the royal governor, and the Townshend Acts—in effect, committing treason against the Patriot cause. Although Hancock favored a moderate approach of accommodation and reconciliation with Britain, Otis and Adams shocked him into acting in the interests of self-preservation—to protect himself and his property against mob violence. He recognized that sheer numbers in the Boston streets favored the radical Otis-Adams camp. Even if British troops eventually crushed the mob, it would have ample time to destroy properties of all perceived enemies before the troops arrived, and Hancock had no intention of being one of those enemies. Rather than risk a fallout with the radicals, he decided to swallow his financial losses and assume the role of martyr and symbol of Patriot resistance. On Sunday evening, Hancock canceled his deal to recover the *Liberty* and threw his lot in with the radical Sons of Liberty street mobs.

On June 30, Governor Bernard asked the General Court to rescind its petition to the king to repeal the Townshend Acts. The Court refused, resolving defiantly "that this House do concur in and adhere to . . . that essential principle, that no man can be taxed, or bound in conscience to obey any law, to which he has not given his consent in person, or by his representative."[5] With Gage's troops on their way, however, the House suddenly moderated the tone of the resolution to read, "That the sole right of imposing taxes on the inhabitants of this his majesty's colony of the Massachusetts Bay, is now and ever has been vested in the House of Representatives . . . with the consent of the council, and of his majesty the king of Great Britain, or his governor for the time being."[6] Much as with Patrick Henry's inflammatory resolves, however, only the most offensive resolve went out to newspapers across the colony, and an infuriated governor dissolved the House of Representatives.

On August 1, sixty "Merchants and Traders of the Town of Boston" adopted a sweeping two-part nonimportation agreement. The first part banned imports of paper, glass, painters' colors, and tea beginning January 1, 1769, "until the acts imposing duties on these articles are repealed." The second part of the agreement was a one-year ban on all other products imported from Britain except ten essentials, including salt, coals, fish-hooks and lines, hemp, duck, and shot. In the months that followed, merchant groups in New York, Philadelphia, Connecticut, Delaware, and Rhode Island adopted similar agreements, although the products and degree of enforcement varied. Because Townshend duties applied largely to products that were made only in England, Americans could no longer turn to smuggling to evade them; the only way around the duties was to produce comparable products in America. Smuggling Dutch Tea and Portuguese Madeira wines, however, continued apace.

The boycott of dutiable goods was hardly universal. New Hampshire and New Jersey merchants refused to boycott British goods, and Loyalist merchants such as Boston's Hutchinson, Oliver, and Clarke added to their orders of British merchandise, knowing that large numbers of less vocal but nonetheless loyal subjects of the crown were ready and eager to pay the price for British tea and other products—duties and all.

In Virginia, the wealthy planter George Washington led the effort for agreement on nonimportation. In the South, the owners of great plantations such as Washington bought large enough quantities to buy directly from British merchants, without using American intermediaries like Boston's merchant houses. Having determined to cut back on his imports, Washington wrote to his friend and neighbor George Mason at Gunston Hall, another large plantation comparable to Washington's Mount Vernon:

> At a time when our lordly masters in Great Britain will be satisfied with nothing less than the deprivation of American freedom, it seems highly necessary that something should be done to avert the stroke and maintain the freedom that we have derived from our Ancestors. . . . How far then their attention to our rights and privileges is to be awakened or alarmed by starving their trade and manufactures remains to be tried.[7]

Throughout the summer, Hancock's captive *Liberty* bobbed in the water beneath the guns of the British man-of-war. Merchants and artisans—and even the poor—made the pilgrimage up the hill to Hancock House to pay homage to Hancock for his martyrdom. At the Liberty Tree, Otis and Adams kept the mob's war fever burning with furious calls to arms. If British troops marched into Boston, Otis raged at a Town Meeting on July 14, there was "nothing more to do but to gird the sword to the thigh and shoulder the musket. . . . We should one and all resist even unto blood. There are your arms," he shouted, and gestured at an armory containing four hundred muskets. "When an attempt is made against your liberties, they will be delivered to you."[8] The meeting ended with Hancock, Adams, and other leaders going off in a convoy of carriages to petition the governor to recall the General Court. Bernard rejected the appeal, and Adams responded with a call to all the towns in Massachusetts to send delegates to a convention in Boston on September 22 to discuss "the peace and safety of his majesty's subjects in this province."[9]

Early in August, the trial of John Hancock and the *Liberty* got under way. John Adams agreed to represent Hancock. After two weeks, the court ordered forfeiture of the *Liberty*. Although the customs commissioners put her up for sale, there were no buyers, so they decided to arm her and send her roaming the coast in search of smugglers. A year later, the *Liberty's* searches and seizures so infuriated Newport merchants and ship owners that they sent a mob to pierside to set fire to the ship and cheered as they watched the *Liberty* burn to her waterline.

On September 19, Governor Bernard announced he had sent for a thousand troops from Halifax, and Sam Adams saw his support begin to erode as anxiety over the approaching British troops undermined the bravado of many farmers and the less robust members of the mob. On September 22, only about seventy delegates from the colony's more than one hundred counties answered Adams's call to convention in Boston's Faneuil Hall. Few were eager to take up arms against professional British soldiers; indeed, they were terrified. The *New Hampshire Gazette* fed their fears, proclaiming,

> We are not to act like rebels. Scorn the thought—we have a good king and his royal ear is not wilfully shut against us. . . . We are represented as rebels against the crown and dignity—but let us convince him by a dutiful submission to his government, and the British constitution, that we are oppressed, and that we have a right to petition him thereon.[10]

Hatfield, Massachusetts, in the western part of the state, not only refused to send delegates to the Adams convention, it urged rural Massachusetts to let the Boston mob, which had started the rebellion on its own, fight British troops on its own. After it became evident that most delegates opposed violence, merchant Thomas Cushing, who, like Hancock, was helping to finance the Patriot cause, abandoned Sam Adams and joined the moderates.

Aware of the changing mood, Otis did not even show up for the first three days of the convention, and Hancock darted in and out, pretending that the press of business did not allow him to attend for any length of time. Although Governor Bernard called the convention illegal and warned delegates to return home, he reveled in the political schism between radicals and moderates and considered inviting Hancock to resume his place in the ruling oligarchy by offering him a seat in the Council, or upper house. When British men-of-war pulled within sight of the Massachusetts coast on the fourth day of the convention, the delegates dashed off an innocuous petition for relief from taxation and military coercion and "rushed out of town like a herd of scalded dogs."[11] That afternoon, the governor rejected the petition, and five days later, on October 1, an armada of British naval vessels rode into Boston Harbor with twelve hundred regular, red-coated troops aboard. The ships pulled close enough to shore for Boston to see the fierce faces of the force they opposed. For the first time in American and British history, the government had deployed the vaunted British Army not to protect the empire, but to police it and enforce hated laws on British subjects.

Boston greeted the ships with silence as the commander of the troops, Lieutenant Colonel William Dalrymple, stepped ashore to meet selectmen and arrange quarters for the troops. All agreed to try to avoid violence. The selectmen suggested quartering the troops at Castle William, but the colonel rejected it as too small. The colonel agreed not to quarter troops in private homes, but fearing an outbreak of disease and violence if his men remained in tight quarters aboard ship, he insisted that his troops disembark and spend the weekend in Faneuil Hall. The selectmen had no choice but to agree.

One by one, longboats rowed to Long Wharf, discharging Redcoats in full battle regalia, each bearing sixteen rounds of ammunition, until two regiments—twelve hundred soldiers for a city with barely fifteen thousand people—stood smartly at attention at the pier. Suddenly, a staccato of commands pierced the stillness of the harbor, and "with drums beating, fifes playing and colors flying," they marched in precision up King Street onto the Common, "as if taking possession of a conquered town."[12] After a drill on the Common to intimidate the Boston mob, they went off to Faneuil Hall for the weekend. Silversmith Paul Revere, whose anger had been building as he watched the troops land, walked back to his shop at the end of Hancock Wharf to engrave the "insolent parade" on copper.[13] When General Gage arrived from New York, some troops moved to the Common to establish a permanent encampment. Rumors swept across town that Gage would declare martial law and send troops into every home to disarm the citizenry and arrest "a number of gentlemen, who have exerted

British troops drill on Boston Common. In 1768, they drilled after landing in Boston to quell the beginning of the American Revolution. Hancock House, the palatial mansion of Tea Party Patriot John Hancock, sits on the upper right. (ENGRAVED BY SIDNEY L. SMITH FROM A WATERCOLOR BY CHRISTIAN REMICK IN 1768. PUBLISHED BY CHARLES E. GOODSPEED, BOSTON, IN 1902. PHOTO COURTESY OF THE CONCORD MUSEUM, CONCORD, MA)

themselves in the cause of their country."[14] Gage's only goal, however, was to restore order in the streets and the smooth functioning of the royal provincial government. By the end of the month, he felt confident enough to report "the appearance of peace and quiet in this place."[15]

To Hancock and the rest of Boston, however, the troops seemed a disease, infecting every nook and cranny of the city. They had turned the green of the Common into a sea of muck, sprouting tents and reeking of campfires, rotting garbage, human and animal wastes, and all other imaginable filth. Despite their promise to leave, troops continued living in Faneuil Hall—and in Town House, the Massachusetts state capitol. In the harbor, the fleet commander had anchored his ships along shore, one behind the other, broadsides facing the town with the maws of their big guns agape, ready to belch cannon balls. Backed by armed sailors, customs commissioners boarded every vessel that entered or left the harbor.

On October 13, less than two weeks after the fleet arrived, a New York newspaper published an anonymously written article called "Journal of Transactions in Boston," purportedly chronicling events in Boston. It proved to be the first of a yearlong series that would appear in newspapers across the colonies and in England under the eventual title "Journal of Occurrences." Insisting its report was "strictly fact," the "Journal of Occurrences" described daily, blood-curdling atrocities of British troops in Boston—of their beating small boys, raping young girls . . . of their violations of the Sabbath with gunfire, drinking, and gambling. It described the inconsolable grief of an elderly Patriot who "the other morning discovered a soldier in bed with a favorite grand daughter."[16] The anonymous author was the consummate propagandist Sam Adams, who used the Journal to promote the cause of independence and venerate its heroes. Governor Bernard called the articles a "collection of impudent, virulent, and seditious lies; perversions of truth and misrepresentations."[17] Suspecting Adams as author, he accused him of publishing the articles in far-off New York to prevent Bostonians from disputing their accuracy.

Misrepresentations notwithstanding, the Journal would not have succeeded without the arrogance and miscalculations of British political and military leaders. Most refused to believe that anyone fortunate enough to be a British subject would dare or even want to rebel. As Thomas Hutchinson put it, "I cannot think that, in any colony, people of any consideration have ever been so mad as to think of revolt. Many of the common people have been in a frenzy and talked of dying in defense of their liberties and have spoke and printed what is highly criminal; and too many of rank above the vulgar, and some in public posts have countenanced and encouraged them."[18]

Ignoring all appeals from saner minds—at home and abroad—for restraint, the British political and military high commands remained intent on asserting their authority in the most provocative ways. In doing so, they fed Sam Adams more fuel than he needed to keep the flames of discontent raging in Boston and everywhere else his "Journal of Occurrences" appeared. On October 29, British troops in Boston abandoned the Common for winter quarters in various public buildings. Hancock and other Bostonians were just beginning to relax in their absence when the troops returned two days later in full force, at slow march, with drums rolling ominously. In their midst was a young soldier, draped in white, accompanied by a chaplain reading from an open Bible. The procession halted. A firing squad snapped to the ready, aimed, fired, and marched away, leaving the body and its pale shroud in a pool of blood and mud. As echoes of the fatal round resounded through the silent grove, the drums resumed their eerie roll while commanders led their regiments on an endless, slow march around and around the corpse, to demonstrate the inevitable fate of deserters.

Adams had no sooner written his description of the grizzly scene when, on the evening of November 2, the British once again went out of their way to provoke colonists with an order to the troops to stand ready for possible rioting the next day. The next morning, the marshal of the vice-admiralty court marched up Beacon Hill and arrested John Hancock. Not satisfied with having confiscated the *Liberty*, Governor Bernard decided to crush Hancock and the Sons of Liberty by filing criminal charges against the merchant for smuggling goods aboard the *Liberty*. Bernard believed he could destroy the Patriot movement by cutting off its source of funds at the House of Hancock. To avoid imprisonment, Hancock posted a £3,000 bond—an amount equal to the value of the goods the crown said he had smuggled on the *Liberty*. John Adams agreed to defend him.

From the outset, the trial was illegal. Although offloading a vessel without a true and perfect inventory was grounds for seizure and forfeiture, there was no eye witness or evidence of such offloading. Nevertheless, the attorney general of the province charged Hancock with landing one hundred pipes of wine, worth £3,000. The law subjected smugglers to fines equal to triple the value of the goods they smuggled—in this case, £9,000, with one-third to go to the crown, one-third to the governor, and one-third to the informer. To ensure Hancock's subsequent bankruptcy, the attorney asked for penalties adding up to another £100,000 for failing to obey lawful orders of a crown agent, and encouraging assault on and illegal imprisonment of the agent. The attorney general made the case as costly as possible for Hancock and everyone he knew, demanding that all Hancock's friends, relatives, business associates, and employees appear in court for hours of endless questioning. He even considered calling Hancock's aging aunt, the widow of Thomas Hancock. One after the other, the witnesses answered the attorney general's questions with expressions of ignorance or lapses of memory. The case dragged on day after day, week after week, exhausting the entire town.

"I was thoroughly weary and disgusted with the court, the officers of the crown, the cause, and even with the tyrannical bell that dongled (sic) me out of my house every morning," John Adams grumbled.[19] As the trial enervated the rest of Boston, it energized Samuel Adams, whose accounts of the trial in the "Journal of Occurrences" lifted John Hancock to national prominence as a martyred hero for what Patriots now called "the Glorious Cause."

John Adams argued that the law under which the court had tried his client was illegal because it denied his client the right of a jury trial and, in effect, repealed the Magna Carta "as far as America is concerned" and "degraded John Hancock below the rank of an Englishman." The court agreed, and after three months, when government prosecutors were unable to present any evidence or eye-witness testimony to substantiate the charges against Hancock, the government backed down. "The Advocate General prays leave to retract this information and says Our Sovereign Lord the King will prosecute no further hereon."[20]

Boston greeted the decision with a mixture of joy and anger—joy at Hancock's acquittal; anger at the mean-spirited governor and attorney general who had put Hancock and the rest of the town through the unnecessarily long and painful ordeal of a trial. Hancock himself sat at ease in his home, luxuriating in the adulation that enveloped Beacon Hill. Letters of praise, encouragement, and congratulations arrived from across the colonies, from Britain, from Europe. Sam Adams had created a new champion of resistance who, to Adams's eventual regret, would ultimately displace him in the front ranks of the revolutionary leadership.

In February 1769 the events associated with the *Liberty* had so aroused Parliament that it decided to apply Henry VIII's ancient "Treason Act" to punish those responsible. Long unused, the act ordered those suspected of treason brought to trial in England, regardless of whether the crimes were committed in or out of the realm.

The Treason Resolution produced angry counter resolutions in Massachusetts and nine other colonies. In addition to protesting the Treason Resolution and Townshend Acts, the Massachusetts Assembly complained about "the establishment of a standing army in the colony in time of peace without the consent of the General Assembly."

At the Town Meeting in March 1769, Hancock garnered the most votes for selectman, and in May he won 500 of the possible 508 votes for the House of Representatives, which immediately elected him Speaker *pro tem* and a member of the Governor's Council. Governor Bernard was out of town and had named Chief Justice Hutchinson as lieutenant governor, who promptly vetoed the election of his old friend Hancock for both posts. The House replaced Hancock with Dr. Joseph Warren. Less outspoken than Otis, Adams, or Hancock, Warren may have seemed more ineffectual to Hutchinson, when, in reality, he was at least as dangerous to royal governance as the others.

By mid-July Royal Governor Bernard had had enough of the Boston mobs and decided to return to the peace and dignity of his stately home in Mother England. On August 1, Boston steeple bells rang out defiantly, flags all but enveloped the huge Liberty Tree, and guns fired continuously from Hancock Wharf as Bernard sailed off, leaving Lieutenant Governor Thomas Hutchinson, the former merchant and still chief justice, as new governor *ex officio*. Two weeks later the Sons of Liberty marched under the noses of British troops to the Liberty Tree to toast the anniversary of their founding four years earlier, when they hung Andrew Oliver's effigy and attacked his home. That evening, Hancock's coach led a procession of 119 carriages—with Otis taking up the rear—across the neck to a tavern in Dorchester on the mainland to toast victory at another of Hancock's elegant dinners.

By the time Bernard left Boston, it was clear to Massachusetts merchants that their partial boycott of British imports had been ineffective, and they now imposed a near-total boycott that shut down the flow of all but a handful of British products into the province. Every colony except New Hampshire followed suit, and by the end of the year British imports into the colonies had plunged 38 percent to about £1.34 million, from £2.2 million the previous year. In Boston, Hancock promoted the boycott tirelessly, even supplying substitute merchandise on credit to small merchants faced with closing for lack of English merchandise. Once mocked as the milch cow for Sam Adams, Hancock was buying so much personal political power that if the Patriot conflict with England had ended then, he would have had a near-monopoly on Massachusetts banking, retailing, and wholesaling.

Some English goods continued to flow to a handful of Loyalist importers who refused to join the boycott, but Hancock, Adams, and other Patriot leaders rallied consumers to support it. Ordinary citizens curtailed purchases of British-made hats, gloves, lace, clocks, glue, furniture, mustards and cheeses—and tea. Although men seldom drank it, tea had acquired widespread popularity among women after winning the royal family's imprimatur. "They all drink tea in America—as they drink wine in the south of France," one French observer concluded. Indeed, every home of substance had a silver, silver plate, or china tea service, complete with a tea pot, sugar and creamer, tongs, and tea "dishes," which were, in fact, small bowls with no handles. Americans drank only chocolate and coffee from cups with handles.[21] Although the requisite china tea service graced his parlor, John Hancock preferred Madeira wine, and Sam Adams, who abstained from alcoholic beverages for religious reasons, didn't like it. Ebenezer Mackintosh and his waterfront thugs swilled only ale and rum and refused even to taste tea. But the drinking of tea had become a quasi-religious ritual for Britain's aristocrats along with those Americans—especially the ladies—who aped the mother country's nobility. So it was inevitable that tea acquired a symbolic value that far exceeded its economic importance. Not every cargo ship carried English lace or glue, but most ships sailing into Boston harbor carried some East India Company tea—until the boycott.

Even some of Boston's grandest dames, however, joined the boycott and abandoned English tea. Encouraged by such lyrical appeals as *A Lady's Adieu to her Tea-Table*, many tea boycotters turned—quite courageously at times—to substitutes such as raspberry bush leaves ("a detestable drink, which the Americans had the heroism to find good") and labradore, or hyperion tea, an insipid concoction the American Indians had derived from the red root bush that grew in New England swamps.

A Lady's Adieu to her Tea-Table

FAREWELL the Tea-board with your gaudy attire,
Ye cups and ye saucers that I did admire;
To my cream pot and tongs I now bid adieu;
That pleasure's all fled that I once found in you.
Farewell pretty chest that so lately did shine,
With hyson and congo and best double fine;
Many a sweet moment by you I have sat,
Hearing girls and old maids to tattle and chat;
And the spruce coxcomb laugh at nothing at all,
Only some silly work that might happen to fall.
No more shall my teapot so generous be
In filling the cups with this pernicious tea,
For I'll fill it with water and drink out the same,
Before I'll lose LIBERTY that dearest name.
Because I am taught (and believe it is fact)
That our ruin is aimed at in the late act,
Of imposing a duty on all foreign Teas,
Which detestable stuff we can quit when we please.
LIBERTY'S the Goddess that I do adore,
And I'll maintain her right until my last hour,
Before she shall part I will die in the cause,
For I'll never be govern'd by tyranny's laws.[22]

To support the anti-tea-drinking movement, almost every shopkeeper and craftsman began carrying tea substitutes in an effort to encourage their use. Even the printers Edes and Gill began selling labradore tea, and some Bostonians began cultivating Chinese tea bushes (without much success) in their kitchen gardens.

In addition to poetic appeals to the average citizen's love of liberty, Adams and his propagandists spread rumors that tea had baneful effects on the health of its imbibers. Consumption of tea, insisted "A Countryman" in the *Boston Gazette*, "had produced such strange disorders as . . . tremblings, apoplexies, consumptions, and I don't know what all."[23]

Although all Americans made a pretense of avoiding tea, too many ladies loved the leaf too much to give it up, and East India Company tea sales held relatively steady in the face of anti-tea pronouncements in the press. For the moment, at least, the tea-drinking habit had become too ingrained in American culture to break easily. Apart from its social value, tea offered many health benefits. Unlike fresh water or milk, tea was safe, tasty, and settled the stomach. Although some merchants refused to stock East India Company tea, at least nine Loyalist merchants in Boston alone ignored the boycott and continued business as usual with their British suppliers, who simply labeled tea chests as containing textiles to conceal their contents. After two years, from 1768 to 1770, the nonconsumption charade had reduced East India Company tea exports by only 30,000 pounds, from 870,000 to 840,000 pounds, or about 3.5 percent.

The major houses of Richard Clarke & Sons and Thomas & Elisha Hutchinson (the sons of Lieutenant Governor Thomas Hutchinson) were quite bold in offering East India Company tea for sale to Boston's tea drinkers. Using the same argument as merchants who defied the authority of Parliament, they declared the Boston Town Meeting to be without authority to interfere in the conduct of their business. Like all American merchants—and, indeed, most Americans generally—they did not like others telling them how to run their lives.

"It always seemed strange to me," wrote Theophilus Lillie, one of the Loyalist merchants resisting the boycott, to the Boston *News-Letter*,

> that people who contend so much for civil and religious liberty should be so ready to deprive others of their natural liberty. . . . I own I had rather be a slave under one master, for if I know who he is, I may perhaps be able to please him, than a slave to an hundred or more whom I don't know where to find nor what they will expect from me.[24]

Knowing they had become the last sources of English tea, Clarke, the Hutchinsons, and other Loyalist merchants ignored mob threats and filled their warehouses to capacity with English tea and other English goods. Determined to obey the law of the land, they paid whatever duties were required and simply raised prices to compensate, knowing that consumers would have no choice but to pay the higher prices if they wanted English merchandise. The Hutchinsons alone imported fifty thousand pounds of English tea in 1769—much of it carried by John Hancock's ships.

"My sons tell me they have sold their tea to advantage," Lieutenant Governor Hutchinson confided, "though with the utmost difficulty. . . . Beside the danger to their persons there was a design to destroy the tea. . . . It was one of the sellers of the Dutch tea who made the greatest clamor."[25]

An American correspondent wrote to a Liverpool, England, newspaper calling the tea boycott "really a joke. . . . As to our people's quitting the use of tea . . . it would be full as reasonable to imagine they will cease to drink New England rum or cider. . . . I don't believe there are ten chests of tea less consumed in this province in a year than there were before the act took place."[26]

Peter Oliver—by then a superior court judge—agreed, saying it was

the art of the great traders to ruin the lesser ones and engross the whole of the business to themselves. . . . Notwithstanding their solemn promises, they imported goods enough for the demand for them. The ladies too were so zealous for the good of their country that they agreed to drink no tea except . . . in case of sickness . . . and they could be sick just as suited their convenience or inclination. Chocolate and coffee were substituted for tea, and it was really diverting to see a circle of ladies about a tea table and a chocolate or coffee pot in the midst of it filled with tea, one choosing a dish of chocolate and another a cup of coffee. Such a finesse would not only be a laughable scene to a spectator, but it must have been a fund of mirth to themselves.[27]

The irony of Hutchinson's English tea arriving on Hancock's ships was not lost on John Mein, a Scottish printer who founded the *Boston Chronicle* with a partner and produced what had been a nonpartisan weekly, then semiweekly. In early summer 1769, he discovered that in the first five months after January 1, when the nonimportation agreement was in effect, twenty-one ships had arrived in Boston from Britain, bearing 162 trunks, 270 bales, 182 cases, 233 boxes, 1,116 casks, 139 chests, 72 hampers, and other containers of goods bound for 190 signers of the nonimportation agreement. The list did not include containers from at least four other vessels lost at sea. On August 21, 1769, the *Chronicle* began printing Customs House lists—fifty-five in all—with the names of every merchant importing British goods in violation of the nonimportation agreement they had endorsed. John Hancock owned four of the ships and their contents. Mein then printed four thousand copies of the lists and sent them to newspapers and influential people across the colonies and in England.

"John Hancock, one of the foremost of the Patriots of Boston," wrote the *Newport Mercury* on September 4, 1769, "would perhaps shine more conspicuously . . . if he did not keep a number of vessels running to London and back, full freighted, getting rich by receiving freight on goods made contraband by the colonies."[28]

Focusing on Hancock as the boycott organizer, the newspaper published a manifest from one of Hancock's ships, which showed he had imported a handsome new carriage for himself and expensive table linen—fraudulently listed as canvas—for his aunt. The newspaper pointed out that the boycott did not prevent merchants from importing goods duty-free if they stated that they had no intention of reselling them. They could thus continue importing unlimited quantities of goods listed for their personal use or belonging to others. Newspapers throughout the colonies reprinted the *Chronicle* stories, with Boston merchants, including Hancock, portrayed as liars and charlatans. For the first time, Loyalist newspapers went on the offensive, assailing Hancock in New Hampshire, Newport, and New York.

Although Hancock denied having violated the nonimportation agreement, the *Chronicle* articles undermined merchant support for nonimportation, and Hancock had to call Boston merchants together to sign an amended nonimportation agreement not to bring in any dutied goods on their vessels, regardless of who owned the goods. He then packed his things and set off for New York and Philadelphia to shore up support in those towns. In Philadelphia, he convinced John Dickinson, the author of the *Farmer's Letters*, to stand by him, and together they managed to restore some merchant support for nonimportation, but the articles substantially weakened the agreement.

The royalist *Chronicle* persisted in its attacks, calling Hancock

Johnny Dupe, Esq., alias the Milch-Cow . . . a good natured young man with long ears—a silly conceited grin on his countenance—a fool's cap on his head—a bandage tied over his eyes—richly dressed and surrounded with a crowd of people, some of whom are stroking his ears, others tickling his nose with straws while the rest are employed in rifling his pockets; all of them with labels out of their mouths bearing these words: OUR COMMON FRIEND.[29]

Two days later, a mob marched to the *Chronicle* office to lynch its two editors. Each editor carried guns and warded off his attackers before fleeing to the main Redcoat guardhouse, opposite Town House. As the crowd swelled to almost two thousand, the commanding officer sent word to his commander, Colonel Dalrymple, who in turn notified Lieutenant Governor Hutchinson. As Dalrymple awaited word from Hutchinson, a part of the mob went off toward Mein's house and, by coincidence, crossed paths with George Gailer, a crewman from Hancock's *Liberty* whom mob leaders accused of being an informer for the Customs House and for Mein's subsequent articles. The mob pounced, threw him into the ever-present tumbrel, stripped him naked, and slathered a thick coat of hot tar over his entire body, "then feathered and in this condition carried through the principal streets of the town in the cart followed by a great concourse of people."[30] Peter Oliver reported,

Thus tarring and feathering . . . and riots reigned uncontrolled. The liberty of the press was restrained by the very men who, for years past, had been halloowing for liberty herself. Those printers who were inclined to support government were threatened and greatly discouraged, so that people were deprived of the means and information.[31]

With the fateful tumbrel following behind, the mob found its way to Mein's house, where it leveled a volley of stones at the windows. When one of Mein's apprentices fired a musket shot in retaliation, the mob broke down the door, and as the boy fled through the rear of the house, they searched the house for Mein, destroying most of his papers and books before leaving with some weapons they found and retracing their steps toward the guard house where Mein had taken shelter. On the way, they passed the Customs House, where the young Private Thomas Burgess stood guard and loaded his musket. The mob swarmed over him before he could fire.

"They closed me up and struck at and abused me most grossly." After stripping the boy naked, they "threatened to hoist me in the cart and use me as they did the man they had tarred and feathered." Wiser voices cautioned against harming one of the King's Own, however, and they returned the soldier's clothes and released him.

Lieutenant Governor Hutchinson, meanwhile, recognized that neither he nor Dalrymple's troops could control Boston mobs. Samuel Adams seemed to be winning the war.

Mein remained in the safety of Redcoat barracks for about a month until the captain of a British frigate offered him safe haven and the means of escape to England. Sometime thereafter, John Hancock received a letter from Thomas Longman, a prominent London bookseller and stationer, who asked Hancock to assume power of attorney and collect some £2,000 in long overdue debts from, of all people, the editors of the *Boston Chronicle*. After sending a disingenuous "anything for a friend" reply, Hancock set out to destroy the publication. With John Adams as attorney, he won a judgment against the newspaper. The sheriff seized the printing shop, book store, and its assets; Hancock closed the newspaper, sold the press and everything else in the shop, and sent the proceeds to Longman, thus crushing the opposition press in Boston.

In September 1769 James Otis swaggered into the British Coffee House, all but daring the British army and navy officers who peopled it to challenge him. Brushing past one after another, he spotted Customs Commissioner John Robinson and rushed up to him. "A number of sticks at once were over Mr. Otis's head," according to Sam Adams, who took full advantage of the brawl to provoke the Boston mob. "A drawn sword," Adams's depiction continued, "the cry in the room 'G-d d—n him,' meaning Mr. Otis, 'knock him down—kill him—kill him. . . .' Can anyone . . . entertain the least doubt but that some persons in the company had a design to assassinate Mr. Otis?"[32]

In the brawl that ensued, Otis emerged bloodied, badly beaten, and incoherent after repeated clubbing about the head and at least one severe cutlass blow. Otis sued one of the officers and won £2,000 in damages and an apology, but he never recovered from the effects of his head injuries. "He loses himself," John Adams commented, "rambles and wanders like a ship without a helm. . . . I fear he is not in his perfect mind."[33] He had always exhibited some eccentricities, but now he wavered between fits of verbosity and melancholy, and he lamented—to Governor Hutchinson, of all people—his responsibility for the violence then plaguing Boston. "I meant well," he mewled to the governor, "but am now convinced I was mistaken. Cursed be the day I was born."[34]

Otis sank deeper and deeper into insanity, giving up his law practice and turning to drink. "He talks so much," reported John Adams, for whom Otis had been a friend and sometime mentor in the law, "and fills it with trash, obsceneness, profaneness, nonsense and distraction. . . . I never saw such an object of admiration, reverence, contempt, and compassion, all at once. I fear, I tremble, I mourn for the man and for his country; many others mourn over him, with tears in their eyes."[35] In February, the following year, Otis snapped and began smashing the windows at Town House before he was "finally bound hand and foot, loaded into a chaise, and carted out of Boston, an apparently hopeless maniac."[36] The Patriots named John Adams to fill his seat in the General Court. As one of the luminaries of the Boston Patriots went into eclipse, a bright new star was ascending.

By the end of 1769 mob threats against dissenting merchants forced all but a few staunch Loyalists to agree to abide by the nonimportation agreement. The Hutchinson brothers and Clarke & Sons remained obstinate in their refusal to abandon their commercial ties to Britain or cede authority over the conduct of their business to a mob.

By then, however, the Townshend duties had proved a dismal failure. They had produced less than £5,000 in added revenues for the govern-

John Adams. The Boston lawyer who defended John Hancock in the
Liberty *smuggling case and the British soldiers accused of murder in*
the Boston Massacre, he would later become the first vice president
and second president of the United States. (LIBRARY OF CONGRESS)

ment and cost British merchants a colossal £7,250,000 in lost annual
revenues—about two years' worth of trade. Although tea consumption
had actually increased, Americans had simply substituted cheap smuggled
Dutch Tea for costly East India Company tea, cutting purchases of dutiable English tea from 850,000 pounds in 1770 to 550,000 in 1773 and
buying 900,000 tons of smuggled duty-free Dutch tea instead. The
Townshend Acts, therefore, had failed to increase British government revenues from duties and succeeded only in provoking colonist fury and
uniting Americans in defiance of mother-country rule. The boycott that
began in Boston had spread across the colonies—to Connecticut, Rhode
Island, New York, New Jersey, Delaware, Philadelphia, Baltimore, Virginia, North and South Carolina, and Georgia. Only New Hampshire refused to join the continent-wide boycott. With the three great ports of
Boston, New York, and Philadelphia united in nonimportation measures,

*Frederick Lord North. Educated at Eton and Oxford
University, he became British chancellor of the exchequer and
coaxed Parliament into repealing the notorious Townshend Acts
but urged retention of a tax on tea as a symbol of Parliament's
right to legislate for the colonies.* (LIBRARY OF CONGRESS)

the author of an anonymous letter to London's *Public Advocate*—probably
Benjamin Franklin—warned that Parliament's continued efforts to tax
the colonies would inevitably lead to a revolution that would require an
army of 25,000 men to suppress and cost Britain at least £100 million
over ten years.

In January 1770 a new chancellor of the exchequer took office. God-
son of the Prince of Wales, Frederick Lord North had been educated at
Eton and Trinity College, Oxford, and was known for his wit, easy-going
good humor, and mediation skills. Assuming, in addition to his chancel-
lorship, a second post as first lord of the British treasury, he urged Parliament to repeal the Townshend Acts and almost all their duties, and in
March 1770 Parliament complied. With merchants able to renew prof-

itable, duty-free trade with the mother country, Sam Adams's nonimportation agreement in Boston fell apart.

At North's urging, however, Parliament had, without fanfare, retained the duty on one export to America—an all-but-minuscule, symbolic, three-penny-per-pound duty on tea that he urged Parliament to retain "as a mark of the supremacy of Parliament and an efficient declaration of their right to govern the colonies."[37] Although some members of Parliament argued that retaining the tea duty would prolong smuggling of less-costly Dutch tea, the majority voted in favor of what they saw as an important face-saving measure and symbol of their authority over the colonies. As William Pitt, Lord Chatham, put it, the Tea Act would keep colonists from carrying "their notions of freedom too far—especially if they would disengage themselves from the laws of trade and navigation."[38] In repealing the Townshend Acts, Parliament succeeded in dousing the flames of rebellion in America, but it foolishly left one ember burning in the form of the Tea Act.

Chapter 10

"Damn You! Fire!"

$\mathscr{S}$am Adams used the Otis brawl as kindling to reignite the fury of Boston's radicals, provoking their literate supporters with inflammatory propaganda in the press and rousing the illiterate with fiery orations in Boston's taverns and at the Liberty Tree. Adams also reorganized the radicals into three groups. He put about 150 waterfront toughs under the leadership of Ebenezer Mackintosh to train as a hard-hitting strike force—"as regular as a military corps," according to Governor Hutchinson. Adams assigned craftsmen and some shopkeepers—the less vicious but nonetheless well-armed second mob—to William Molyneux, the merchant who had helped found Manufactury House to develop locally made cloth. Adams himself took charge of the Sons of Liberty, whose membership included many small merchants along with some craftsmen and shopkeepers. Often wrapping themselves in Indian blankets to symbolize the Rousseauvian "natural" man, living and hunting in freedom, in unblemished fields and virgin forests, they soon became known as "Adams's Mohawks."[1]

Adams and Otis had secretly organized a fourth "mob" of sorts, however. Peter Oliver called it a "black regiment"—made up of Congregational ministers who inherited from their ancestors [the Puritans] an aversion to episcopacy and . . . the Church of England. . . . The town of Boston being . . . the metropolis of sedition . . . those who were the most distinguished of the Boston clergy distinguished themselves in encouraging seditions and riots. . . . One of those preachers, with the reputation of learning, preaching upon the Sixth Commandment to his large parish, declared to them that it was no sin to kill the Tories.[2]

With the black regiment echoing his every word on Sundays, Adams pounced on Lord North's retention of the tea tax as a symbol of tyranny, provoking many Bostonians to near anarchy—especially after he demanded full compliance with the old nonimportation agreement. Personal feuds and rivalries deteriorated into accusations of royalist collaboration—and, inevitably, broken windows, vandalism, and vicious graffiti.

In January and February 1770 reports poured into Boston of serious clashes in New York between bayonet-wielding British soldiers and mobs armed with clubs. In Boston, fights erupted nightly in the city's many taverns and spilled into the streets. In every alley, small gangs lay in wait to assault any lone Redcoat who chanced by. Sam Adams roamed the taverns spreading the seeds of anarchy among small merchants, shopkeepers, and craftsmen who frequented them. Boston's children contributed to tension in the streets by pelting Redcoats or suspected Redcoat sympathizers with snowballs, oysters, or worse. In London, Pitt, who had sided with the colonists, now warned the House of Lords that colonists had carried "their notions of freedom too far . . . [and] will not be subject to the laws of this country."[3]

Early in February, a mob of radicals marched to the door of Governor Hutchinson's house with a petition that his sons, who now managed their father's merchant house, turn over a shipment of tea they had received from the British East India Company. The lieutenant governor shouted in defiance, "I am the representative of the king of Great Britain, the greatest monarch on earth, and in his name require you to disperse."

Recognizing that mob leaders usually spoke only for themselves or a tiny minority, he demanded to see the petition with its signatures, which the mob spokesman refused even to display. "Gentlemen," Hutchinson now shrieked, "when I was attacked before, I was a private person. I am now the representative of the greatest monarch on earth, which majesty you affront in thus treating my person."[4] Hutchinson went on to denounce Adams's Town Meeting as an illegal usurpation of powers relegated to the state legislature and the royal governor.

As the mob retreated and dissolved, other Loyalist merchants took heart from Hutchinson's stand, and Adams and his radicals responded in kind, deeming four such merchants "obstinate and inveterate enemies to their country and subverters of the rights and liberties of this continent." A second vote condemned six other recalcitrant merchants "to be driven to that obscurity from which they originated and to the hole of the pit from whence they were digged [sic]." And a third vote demanded an end to tea consumption "under any pretense whatever."[5]

But an end to tea consumption rubbed many ladies the wrong way.

"The people take a great deal of tea in the morning," French Baron Cromot du Bourg reported in his diary, *Journal de mon séjour en Amérique.* "They drink tea with dinner at two in the afternoon," he said, and "about five o'clock they take more tea, some wine, Madeira, and punch."[6] Indeed, tea had addicted most American women in the upper social and economic classes, along with those with aspirations of attaining or pretensions to that status. Foreign visitors to America at the time found that tea had become a standard breakfast drink of the wealthy in both New York and Philadelphia. Naturalist Peter Kalm noted that for upper social classes in Albany, New York, "their breakfast is tea, commonly without milk. . . . With the tea was eaten bread and butter or buttered bread toasted over the coals so that the butter penetrated the whole slice of bread. In the afternoon about three o'clock tea was drunk again in the same fashion, except this time the bread and butter was not served with it."[7] And in Boston, "The ladies here visit, drink tea, and indulge in every little piece of gentility to the height of the mode and neglect the affairs of their families with as good grace as the finest ladies in London."[8] An end to tea consumption, therefore, represented a considerable sacrifice for many an American lady—especially for those who tried substituting the vile "labradore" tea derived from swamp bushes. As one Virginian wrote plaintively to her friend in England, "I have given up the article of tea, but some are not quite so tractable. However, if we can convince the good souls on your side of the water of their error, we may hope to see happier times."[9]

Patriot newspapers supported the end of tea consumption with lyrical appeals: "Throw aside your Bohea and your Green Hyson Tea," urged a self-styled poet in the *Boston Post-Boy*,

> and all things with a new fashion duty;
> Procure a good store of the choice Labradore,
> For there'll soon be enough here to suit ye;
> These do without fear, and to all you'll appear
> Fair, charming, true, lovely, and clever;
> Though the times remain darkish, young men may be sparkish,
> And love you much stronger than ever.[10]

With Hutchinson and Clarke standing tall against the radicals, Molyneux led a mob to the homes of the smaller, less-resilient recalcitrants, shattering the windows of one after another and forcing them to turn over their shipments of tea to the mob. On February 22, 1770, they marched to the shop of Ebenezer Richardson, and as he took refuge inside, a barrage of stones shattered the building's windows. An out-of-work seaman came to his aid, and as the mob broke down the door, Richardson appeared at the window above, a musket barrel poised and protruding. As the rain of rock persisted, he fired a blast of swanshot—small pellets that spread as they approached their target. The pellets wounded a nineteen-year-old and killed an eleven-year-old German boy, Christopher Seider. Seider's death inflamed Boston's street mobs. In effect, it proved to be the first death of what evolved into the American Revolution.

Sam Adams turned the Seider funeral into the largest ever held in America—an enormous mass mourning of a martyr that began at 5 P.M. at the Liberty Tree, where Adams had affixed a board bearing the inscriptions

> *Thou shalt take no satisfaction for the life of a MURDERER—he shall surely be put to death.*
>   and
> *Though hand join in hand, the wicked shall not pass unpunish'd.*

The procession stretched more than a half-mile, with more than four hundred carefully groomed, angelic schoolboys marching two by two, cloaked in white, leading the coffin. Six youths carried the coffin; two thousand mourners led by the boy's family and friends followed, with thirty chariots and chaises behind them.

"Mine eyes have never beheld such a funeral," said John Adams. "This shows there are many more lives to spend if wanted in the service of their country. It shows too that the faction is not yet expiring—that the ardor of people is not to be quelled by the slaughter of one child and the wounding of another."[11] The radical *Boston Gazette* said Seider's death "crieth for vengeance. . . . Young as he was, he died in his country's cause."[12]

Relations between colonists and British troops—already vicious—reached a new low. The air filled with a constant staccato of catcalls and cries of "Lobster; hey lobster!" at red-coated British officers. Fights erupted on the waterfront between "lobsters" and "mohawks"—with Sam Adams never far away, goading his street toughs to harass, insult, and provoke violence. General Gage recognized his error in ordering troops to Boston:

> The people were as lawless and licentious after the troops arrived as they were before. The troops . . . were there contrary to the wishes of the Council, Assembly, magistrates, and people, and seemed only offered to abuse and ruin. And the soldiers were either to suffer ill usage and even assaults upon their persons till their lives were in danger, or by resisting and defending themselves, to run almost a certainty of suffering by the law.[13]

More than soldiers, customs commissioners remained the targets of the mob, with more than one of them overtaken, stripped, and doused with scalding tar, then feathered and carried about the town and subjected to unconscionable humiliations.

At the beginning of March, the king appointed Hutchinson governor, who, in turn, ceded his post as chief justice to his brother-in-law Peter Oliver. As two of Boston's great merchant-bankers, they had the support of Loyalist merchants and moderates in Boston's business community who had tired of the violence that political radicals generated. Most now longed for stability and peace in a tax-free climate that would allow them

Bostonians paying the excise man. A newspaper cartoon portrays a Boston mob tormenting a customs commissioner, whom they tarred and feathered and now force boiling tea down his throat. (LIBRARY OF CONGRESS)

to prosper. In elevating Americans to the chief posts in the executive and judiciary, the king hoped also to placate Boston's malcontents by giving them a sense that two of their own now controlled provincial affairs. The king went a step farther by appointing Hutchinson's brother-in-law, Peter Oliver's brother Andrew, lieutenant governor. In effect, three Americans, whose roots stretched to the first settlements in the New World, now held the three most powerful posts in Massachusetts, and Britons were nowhere to be seen in government.

Hutchinson and Oliver could not have assumed their new posts at a worse time, however. "I thought I could support myself well enough at first," Hutchinson wrote in dismay to former Governor Pownall in London, "but the spirit of anarchy which prevails in Boston is more than I am able to cope with."[14]

From the moment the Seider boy went to his rest, townsmen seldom let a moment pass without provoking fights with soldiers. On March 2, ropemaker Samuel Gray, one of Mackintosh's most brawl-hardened street toughs, approached a soldier who was seeking part-time work and offered the Redcoat a job cleaning the ropemaker's privy. As onlookers cawed with laughter, the soldier called to his comrades; together, they plunged into a brawl that flashed intermittently for the next three days and nights. Gangs of boys continually provoked conflict by pelting the Redcoats with snowballs, pieces of ice, whole oysters in their shells, stones, glass bottles, and other missiles.

On the evening of March 5, belligerent bands of laborers and boys roamed the streets, provoking fights with British soldiers wherever the opportunity presented itself. A wigmaker's apprentice, of all people, set off a ruckus on King Street, accusing a British officer of not paying his bill. As a small mob surrounded them, another ruckus erupted near the British barracks on Brattle Street, where a mob leader confronted a British officer, demanding, "Why don't you keep your soldiers in their barracks?" As the mob drew closer, a small boy—perhaps seven or eight—emerged screaming, his hands cupping his head, and asserting that the British officer had killed him. And at one end of Boylston's Alley, another mob had surrounded a contingent of junior officers, pelting them with snowballs while screaming accusations: "Cowards! Afraid to fight!" Meanwhile, a fourth mob of about two hundred surged into the market on Dock Square, brandishing wood bats, breaking into market stalls and crying, "Fire! Fire!"

"It is very odd to come to put out a fire," Scotsman Archibald Wilson remarked, "with sticks and bludgeons."[15]

At 9 P.M., as if on signal, the town's bells began pealing, and a young barber's apprentice taunted a sentry at the Customs House on King Street. The sentry slapped the boy, sending him sprawling onto the street. He bounded up and went off screaming for help as the bells continued their mournful peals. A crowd of boys materialized and pelted the sentry with snowballs, all the while shouting, "Kill him, Kill him. Knock him down."[16] And the bells continued pealing.

A crowd of men joined the boys in taunting the Redcoats while men everywhere rushed out of their homes thinking a fire had broken out. Mobs surged through the streets in every direction. At Faneuil Hall a man variously described as tall and wearing a red cloak and white wig was haranguing a crowd of men into a frenzy, while another crowd gathered at the Redcoat barracks.

By this time, Captain Thomas Preston, the officer of the day, had heard of the sentry's predicament at the Customs House. He marched six privates and a corporal to the scene, bayonets fixed, intent on escorting the sentry into the Customs House, away from the mob's missiles and taunts. By the time he reached the sentry's post, small gangs swept in from all directions. The mob swelled and made it impossible for Preston to march away. Volleys of ice, oyster shells, and sticks rained on the troops. Ropemaker Samuel Gray, Crispus Attucks (a massive "mulatto fellow," according to later testimony), ship's mate James Caldwell, and Patrick Carr, "a seasoned Irish rioter," pushed their way to the front of the crowd with a group of sailors.[17]

"The multitude was shouting and huzzaing, and threatening life; the bells were ringing, the mob whistling, screaming and rending Indian yells; the people from all quarters were throwing every species of rubbish they could pick up in the streets"—all the while, daring the soldiers to fire. As the missiles rained on the soldiers, some townsmen lunged at them with sticks held as swords, crying "bloody backs," "lobsters," and other epithets.[18] Attucks then hurled his club at one of the soldiers. It found its mark, the soldier fell, then staggered to his feet. The cry of "Damn you! Fire!" resounded across the scene, and he fired into the crowd. A second soldier fired a hole into Gray's skull, and before his body hit the ground, a volley of shots left four others dead. Attucks and Caldwell fell at the feet of the beleaguered soldiers. Eight others lay wounded, including Carr and a seventeen-year-old, both of whom later died of their wounds. The other six recovered.[19] Samuel Adams now had the massacre he had sought to incite a revolution against British rule. He sent messengers into the country to alert farmers to arm themselves but to await ignition of a bonfire on Beacon Hill as a signal to march on Boston.

In the terrifying moments after the shootings, Preston and his men returned to the main guard house and prepared for an assault by the mob, now rumored to have reached five thousand. The British regiment quartered at Town House, already seething from months of insults and assaults, moved toward King Street prepared to crush a rebellion. Governor Hutchinson knew that unless he took control immediately, "the whole town would be up in arms and the most bloody scene would follow that had ever been known in America."[20] Hutchinson raced to Town House, and as the crowd gathered beneath the second-floor balcony, he called on them to return to their homes. "The law shall have its course," he promised. "I will live and die by the law."[21]

Enough of the mob went home to restore a semblance of peace, and Hutchinson decided to implement his pledge immediately. The sheriff brought in Captain Preston at 2 A.M. Although he insisted he had never given the order to fire, witnesses claimed he did, and a justice sent Preston to prison at 3 A.M. The next morning, more than three thousand people gathered at Town House as the eight soldiers under Preston's command surrendered, were indicted for murder and imprisoned to await trial.

For a while, Boston awaited an even greater massacre. Merchants tried as best they could to protect their shops from looters. Appalled by the violence, Hancock remained cloistered in his mansion on Beacon Hill. Messengers from town—his clerks, various followers, and others—bounded up and down Beacon Street with breathless reports of the goings-on below. He was trapped in a war of madmen—each set on destroying the other. He realized his own survival might depend on his taking personal control of the Patriots, unseating Sam Adams and the fanatics who controlled the mobs, and restoring calm to the streets of Boston. Regardless of the outcome of the conflict with Britain, reason would have to prevail. Hancock, like other moderate Boston merchants—Loyalist and Patriot alike—now sought peace in the streets and a return to normal life. Unfortunately, the radical merchants had encouraged their waterfront workers to march with the mob and allowed a hitherto docile, obedient underclass to experience independence, individual liberties, and the orgiastic satisfaction of successfully defying authority. In effect, the merchants had set loose beasts unable to distinguish between liberty and license—and would never be able to encage them again.

"Endeavors had been systematically pursued for months by certain busy characters," John Adams noted, "to excite quarrels, encounters, and combats . . . in the night between the inhabitants of the lower class and the soldiers . . . to enkindle a mortal hatred between them. I suspected this was the explosion which had been intentionally wrought up by designing men who knew what they were aiming at better than the instruments employed."[22]

The court postponed the trial of Captain Preston and his troops until autumn to allow a return to calm and improve the chances of finding an impartial jury. Adams, Cushing, Hancock, and another assemblyman met with Hutchinson, Oliver, and British military commander Colonel Dalrymple at Town House to try to end the violence. With House Speaker Cushing acting as moderator, Hancock warned Oliver that "there were upwards of 4,000 men ready to take arms . . . and many of them of the first property, character and distinction in the province."[23] Ten thousand more, he said, stood poised, muskets in hand, on the outskirts of Boston, their eyes fixed on Beacon Hill for the signal to march into Boston if British troops did not withdraw from the city.

Hancock was bluffing, of course, and both Dalrymple and Hutchinson knew he was bluffing, but all agreed that the violence had gone on too long and reached unnecessarily tragic proportions. Dalrymple agreed to withdraw his troops, and a few days later the Redcoats retreated to Castle William. A few weeks later Dalrymple eased tensions further, sending one of the two regiments at Castle William to New Jersey, thus cutting his troop strength in half.

Sam Adams, of course, could not reveal his role in provoking the Boston Massacre without incurring merchant outrage—not to mention charges of treason from the governor. Fearful of losing control, he rallied the Sons of Liberty, elevated the dead hooligans to near sainthood, and staged a grandiose procession with more than ten thousand mourners to carry them to their graves. Adams encouraged James Bowdoin, a friend from Harvard days, to write (anonymously) an inflammatory pamphlet. Entitled *A Short Narrative of the Horrid Massacre of Boston*, it called the shootings part of a conspiracy between the British army and customs commissioners to silence their critics. Although born to mercantile wealth,

The Boston Massacre. Paul Revere's engraving of the event, copied without permission from a drawing by Henry Pelham, the half-brother of portrait artist John Singleton Copley. Pelham threatened legal action against Revere for the theft. (BOSTONIAN SOCIETY)

Bowdoin was a radical who seldom let facts stand in the way of his conclusions. He sent his pamphlet to newspapers across the colonies and in Britain, where it received widespread circulation. The *Boston Gazette* of March 12 displayed Bowdoin's words edged in black mourning, charging that British soldiers had provoked the massacre by "parading the streets with drawn cutlasses and bayonets, abusing and wounding numbers of the inhabitants."[24] The issue included a provocative and grossly inaccurate drawing by Henry Pelham, the half-brother of portrait artist John Single-ton Copley. Entitled "Fruits of Arbitrary Power, or The Bloody Massacre in King Street," Pelham's drawing showed soldiers slaughtering helpless townsmen. Paul Revere made an engraving and sold prints of it, without permission or attribution.[25]

In the days after the massacre, Sam Adams, Cushing, and Josiah Quincy, a lawyer who was the youngest son of Colonel Josiah Quincy of Braintree, wrote influential friends in London, including former Massa-chusetts Governor Pownall, "acquainting them with the circumstances and facts relative to the late horrid massacre and asking the continuance of their good services in behalf of this town and province." The letter was designed "to prevent any ill impressions from being made upon the minds of his Majesty's ministers and others of the Town of Boston."[26]

Although Governor Hutchinson tried to restore calm by appealing to the General Court for help, Sam Adams and his followers would have none of it. They packed meetings with three and four thousand people to shout, hoot, cheer, sing, and do whatever else they could to disrupt proceedings. On March 15, Hutchinson followed the example of his predecessor Governor Bernard and ordered the General Court to meet in mob-free Cambridge across the water from Boston. The Court met there intermittently over the next six months, in an increasingly frustrating de-bate over whether the governor had the constitutional right to tell the House where to meet. In a surprise split with Samuel Adams, Hancock supported the governor. He sensed a growing alienation of rural represen-tatives toward Adams and the Boston radicals for forcing delegates from across the state to travel into the dirty streets of Boston every time the Assembly convened. They welcomed the opportunity to meet in Cam-bridge, and Hancock joined them. After weeks of inaction, however, the governor finally ordered the Court adjourned until the following year.

Despite Sam Adams's efforts to rekindle the embers of violence, calmer voices began to prevail. Members of the Suffolk County Bar Association took the lead by organizing a force of three hundred lawyers, merchants, and other moderate townsmen to stand armed watch and patrol the town to prevent further mob violence. Equipped with a musket, bayonet, broadsword, and cartridge box, the short, round, thirty-five-year-old attorney John Adams volunteered for and took his regular turn on sentry duty outside Town House. Recalling the Boston Massacre, he later concluded, "On that night the foundation of American independence was laid."[27]

Chapter 11

"Let Every Man
Do What Is Right!"

 ews of the repeal of the Townshend Acts cheered Boston's rational citizens and calmed the irrational—except for the redoubtable James Otis, who continued acting so irrationally his family confined him to his home. At the end of May, he erupted in uncontrollable rage and began firing guns from his window over the heads of a large, frightened crowd. Friends subdued him and moved him to a safe haven in the country.

As with Stamp Act repeal, the official announcement of Townshend Acts repeal arrived on one of Hancock's ships—again confusing the Town Meeting as to whether Hancock had been a facilitator or simply a messenger. He did nothing to discourage their cheers, however, and, indeed, displayed numerous letters he had sent to men of influence in England that may or may not have affected repeal. Boston's eligible voters cast a resounding 511 of the possible 513 votes for Hancock in the May elections for the Massachusetts House of Representatives.

With the end of the Townshend Acts, trade between England and the colonies returned to normal. Renewed prosperity created jobs for the unemployed and weakened popular support for Sam Adams and the Sons of Liberty. The city also lost its appetite for vengeance against the

British soldiers who had languished in prison since the Boston Massacre. Moreover, two outstanding Patriot lawyers—John Adams and Josiah Quincy—had agreed to represent the soldiers. Sam Adams tried to renew public hysteria, but to his dismay, the court allowed his cousin John to select a jury of men from outside Boston. None had ever lived under Redcoat occupation or harbored any animosities toward British troops. Several even had business ties to the British army, and five jurors later became Loyalist exiles. Using their challenges expertly, Adams and Quincy prevented the seating of even a single Son of Liberty or Bostonian on the jury. The first trial, *Rex v. Preston,* began on October 24, with Robert Treat Paine appointed prosecutor, with no option to refuse. Although a brilliant lawyer who, like all his colleagues and Boston friends, had graduated from Boston Latin and Harvard, he inherited a case that was laughably weak.

The first prosecution "witness" admitted he had not been on King Street the night of the tragedy. Other prosecution witnesses agreed that the crowd, not Preston, had shouted, "Fire!" John Adams and young Quincy quickly dismantled the prosecution's case, presenting thirty-eight witnesses to testify that civilians had plotted to attack the soldiers. In addition, they had the deathbed confession of Patrick Carr that the townspeople had been the aggressors and that the soldiers had not fired until attacked by "a motley rabble of saucy boys, Negroes and mulattoes, Irish teagues and outlandish jack tars."[1]

At the end of the six-day trial, Chief Justice Peter Oliver presented the case to the jury and all but assured victory for the defense: "I feel myself deeply affected that this affair turns out so much to the disgrace of every person concerned against him [Preston], and so much to the town in general."[2] The jury immediately acquitted Preston, but with Sam Adams's ruffians still calling for Preston's neck, the officer sought refuge at Castle William and returned to England, where the crown awarded him a handsome life pension of £200 a year—twice the average annual income of a skilled craftsman. Dr. Charles Chauncy, the longtime head of Boston's First Congregational Church and a leading member of Adams's "Black Regiment," declared that if he had been a member of the jury, "I would bring him in guilty, evidence or no evidence."[3]

The trial of the eight soldiers began a month later on November 17, and on December 5, the jury acquitted six of them and found two guilty of manslaughter, with mitigating circumstances. They were punished in the court-room by being branded on their thumbs and released. On December 12, the jury, without leaving their seats to deliberate privately, dismissed charges that four customs officials had fired on the mob from the Customs House windows. Adams and Quincy proved that the boy who had been the star Patriot witness was a perjurer, coached and bribed by "divers high Whigs."[4]

With his power to control events in Boston slipping away, Sam Adams tried to incite resentment against the court and its verdicts in a series of anonymous articles in the *Boston Gazette* signed "Vindix."[5] Although he portrayed the massacre as a slaughter of innocents by evil tyrants and their bloodthirsty mercenaries, his articles had little effect. The testimony at the soldiers' trials had unmasked Sam Adams as a sinister, power-hungry plotter willing to sacrifice innocent lives and destroy the city, if necessary, to further his designs. As the trial progressed, Adams's carefully constructed coalition of street toughs, laborers, artisans, merchants, lawyers, and Harvard intellectuals fell apart. The mob violence that Adams had generated the night of the massacre had turned even those merchants who opposed British rule against Adams and the radicals. Given a choice of tyranny by street toughs or tyranny by tariffs, all preferred the latter. The British not only maintained peace, their merchants paid in sterling. With all its faults, royal government, at least, represented stability. Governor Hutchinson reported to Lord Hillsborough that Massachusetts was displaying more "general appearance of contentment" than at any time since passage of the Stamp Act and that he hoped to build a Loyalist party as a political sanctuary for merchants and farmers.[6]

New York's Lieutenant Governor Colden was leading that colony in the same direction. "All men of property are so sensible of their danger from riots and tumults," he boasted, "that they will not rashly be induced to enter into combinations which may promote disorder for the future."[7]

Thomas Cushing, the quiet, thoughtful merchant who was Speaker of the Massachusetts House of Representatives, agreed, urging moderates to prevent "a rupture fatal to both countries."[8]

And John Adams confessed in his diary, "I shall certainly become more retired and cautious. I shall certainly mind my own farm and my own office."[9]

THE
Boſton-
AND
COUNTRY

Gazette,
JOURNAL.

No 831.

Containing the freſheſt Advices,   *Foreign and Domeſtic.*

MONDAY, March 11, 1771.

From the ESSEX GAZETTE.   SALEM, MARCH 5, 1771.

As a ſolemn and perpetual MEMORIAL

Of the Tyranny of the Britiſh Adminiſtration of Government in the Years 1768, 1769, & 1770:

Of the fatal and deſtructive Conſequences of quartering Armies, in Time of Peace, in populous Cities:

Of the ridiculous Policy, and infamous Abſurdity, of ſupporting *Civil Government* by a *Military Force:*

Of the great Duty and Neceſſity of firmly oppoſing Deſpotiſm in its firſt Approaches:

Of the deteſtable Principles and arbitrary Conduct of thoſe *Miniſters* in Britain who adviſed, and of their *Tools* in America who deſired, the Introduction of a Standing Army into this Province in the Year 1768:

Of the irrefragable Proof which thoſe Miniſters themſelves thereby produced, that the Civil Government, as by them adminiſtered, was weak, wicked, and tyrannical:

Of the vile Ingratitude and abominable Wickedneſs of every *American*, who abetted and encouraged, either in Thought, Word or Deed, the Eſtabliſhment of a Standing Army among his Countrymen:

Of the unaccountable Conduct of thoſe *Civil Governors*, the immediate Repreſentatives of his Majeſty, who, while the *Military* were triumphantly inſulting the whole LEGISLATIVE AUTHORITY OF THE STATE, and while the Blood of the maſſacred Inhabitants was flowing in the Streets, perſiſted in repeatedly diſclaiming all Authority of relieving the People, by any the leaſt Removal of the Troops:

And of the ſavage Cruelty of the IMMEDIATE PERPETRATORS;

B E it forever Remembered,

That this Day, THE FIFTH OF MARCH, is the Anniverſary of

Preſton's Maſſacre--in King-Street--Boſton, N. England--

1770.

In which Five of his Majeſty's Subjects were ſlain, and Six wounded,

By the Diſcharge of a Number of Muſkets from a Party of Soldiers under the Command of Capt. *Thomas Preſton.*

GOD ſave the PEOPLE!

BOSTON,   March 11.

TUESDAY laſt was the Anniverſary of the never-to-be-forgotten Fifth of March, 1770, when Meſſieurs *Gray, Maverick, Caldwell, Carr,* and *Attucks,* were inhumanly murdered by a Party of Soldiers of the XXIXth Regiment in King-Street :—The Bells of the ſeveral Congregational Meeting-Houſes, were tolled from XII o' Clock at Noon till 1 :—In the Evening there was a very ſtriking Exhibition at the Dwelling-Houſe of Mr. PAUL REVERE, fronting the Old-North Square.—At one of the Chamber-Windows was the Appearance of the Ghoſt of the unfortunate young Seider, with one of his Fingers in the Wound, endeavouring to ſtop the Blood iſſuing therefrom : Near him his Friends weeping : And at a ſmall diſtance a monumental Obeliſk, with his Buſt in Front :—On the Front of the Pedeſtal, were the Names of thoſe killed on the 5th of March : Underneath the following Lines,

Seider's pale Ghoſt freſh-bleeding ſtands,
And Vengeance for his Death demands.

In the next Window were repreſented the Soldiers drawn up, firing at the People aſſembled before them—the Dead on the Ground—and the Wounded falling, with the Blood running in Streams from their Wounds : Over which was wrote FOUL PLAY. In the third Window was the Figure of a Woman, repreſenting AMERICA, ſitting on the Stump of a Tree, with a Staff in her Hand, and the Cap of Liberty on the Top thereof,—one Foot on the head of a Grenadier lying proſtrate graſping a Serpent.—Her Finger pointing to the Tragedy.

The whole was ſo well executed, that the Spectators, which amounted to many Thouſands, were ſtruck with ſolemn Silence, and their Countenances covered with a melancholy Gloom. At Nine o'Clock the Bells tolled a doleful Peal, until Ten ; when the Exhibition was withdrawn, and the People retired to their reſpective Habitations.

An Oration containing a brief Account of the Maſſacre ; of the Imputations of Treaſon and Rebellion, with which the Tools of Power endeavoured to brand the Inhabitants, and a Diſcant upon the Nature of Treaſons, with ſome Conſiderations on the Threats of the Britiſh Miniſtry to take away the Maſſachuſetts Charter, was delivered on the Evening by Dr. Young at the Factory-Hall, being the Place where the firſt Effort of Military Tyranny was made within a few Days after the Troops arrived.

The Boston Gazette's *front page. This commemorated Massacre Day, the first anniversary of the Boston Massacre.* (LIBRARY OF CONGRESS)

Like many merchants in Boston, farmers outside Boston and across New England turned against Boston's radicals for misrepresenting the events leading up to the massacre, and in England the testimony from the Preston trial turned public opinion squarely against the people of Boston. As Parliament debated appropriate punishment for Boston's duplicity, even the staunchest colonist defenders spoke of Boston as a lawless city of ruffians and a hotbed of anarchy.

As distaste increased for the rowdyism of Sam Adams and the Sons of Liberty, Governor Hutchinson sensed an opportunity to reconcile with John Hancock. The entire merchant community was abandoning Adams and the street toughs, who had sullied Boston's reputation, hurt trade, and given Philadelphia and New York opportunities to surpass Boston as primary trade centers in America. Hancock's own tolerance for street mobs had also worn thin—along with his inclination to cover the personal and public debts of the profligate Sam Adams.

In the spring, a Loyalist resoundingly defeated Sam Adams—by a two-to-one margin—in the election for Suffolk County Registrar of Deeds. After Hancock easily won reelection to the General Court, Hutchinson confided, "I was much pressed by many persons well affected in general to consent to the election of Mr. Hancock. They assured me he wished to be separated from Mr. Adams. . . . I have now reason to believe that, before another election, he will alter his conduct so as to justify my acceptance of him."[10] Although the House of Representatives had consistently elected Hancock to serve on the Governor's Council, Hutchinson had exercised his veto just as consistently. In June 1771, however, he assured Hancock he did not bear "any degree of ill-will towards him" and that "it would be a pleasure to consent to his election to the Council." Hancock surprised the governor by refusing the offer, saying he intended to abandon public affairs to attend to his private business, which, he said, he had neglected for too long. And at the governor's festive official Christmas banquet, Hancock confided to the governor that he would "never again connect himself with the Adamses."[11]

As the new year began, Sam Adams's radical movement faced collapse. In a letter to former Governor Bernard in London, Hutchinson all but proclaimed victory: "Hancock has not been with their club for two months past and seems to have a new set of acquaintances. . . . He will be a great loss to them, as they support themselves with his money."[12] He omitted the news that a court had declared James Otis *non compus mentis* and appointed his younger brother as guardian.

Hancock's relations with the governor warmed considerably, as did those of Thomas Cushing. Together, the two moderates approached Hutchinson about moving the General Court back to Boston from Cambridge. They agreed to base their resolution solely on convenience rather than the constitutional grounds that Sam Adams had cited. Even radicals had wearied of Adams's all-but-mindless obstructionism in the General Court. In fact, one of his closest allies, Dr. Benjamin Church, switched to the Loyalists and wrote newspaper articles that all but ridiculed Adams. The proroyalist movement spread elsewhere, with conservatives winning elections in New York, Philadelphia, and even in Patrick Henry's Virginia. Samuel Adams raged in the *Boston Gazette* against "the silence of the other assemblies of late upon every subject that concerns the joint interest of the colonies." He asked John Dickinson to write more "Letters" to rouse the people from "dozing upon the brink of ruin," but Dickinson declined.

As spring elections approached, Hutchinson and the resurgent Loyalists hoped to oust Sam Adams from government and silence his voice. Knowing that he was too incompetent to support himself in normal trade, they believed his removal from political power would extinguish the last embers of rebellion. Although one-third of Boston's eligible voters cast their ballots against him, Adams nevertheless won reelection. Both Hancock and Cushing received nearly 40 percent more votes than Adams, and they teamed up to defeat his radicals in the House of Representatives by passing a modest request for the General Court to return to Boston. In June the governor replied, "It is his Excellency's pleasure that the great and General Court or Assembly be adjourned till Tuesday next at ten the clock in the forenoon, then to meet at the Court House in Boston."[13] Sam Adams continued trying to disrupt the General Court, as Hancock and other moderates yawned—and finally adjourned.

In the autumn King George ordered the royalist leadership to court Hancock's allegiance, and Governor Hutchinson bestowed one of the province's highest honors on the thirty-five-year-old merchant: "His Excellency the Captain-General has been pleased to commission John Hancock, Esq., to be Captain [commander] of the Company of Cadets, with the rank of Colonel." Sam Adams lashed out angrily, scoffing that "it is not in the power of the Governor to give a commission for that company. Their officers are chosen by themselves. Mr. Hancock was elected by a unanimous vote."[14] In fact, Adams was correct. The governor had no authority to "commission" Hancock. Called the Independent Corps of Cadets, Hancock's new command was a fraternal, "gentlemen's militia" of eighty men who served as the governor's honor guard, marched at official ceremonies, and spent as much time as possible at the Bunch of Grapes tavern. Hancock had joined the guard, as he had the Freemasons and the Merchants Club, for informal fellowship with men of similar backgrounds and interests. As Adams stated, the corps did, indeed, elect Hancock, but his election was a recognition of Hancock's leadership among Boston's wealthiest, most responsible citizens, and the governor's meaningless commissioning was a gesture of reconciliation.

The election/appointment sent Hancock into spasms of ecstasy—a military command to complement his civic and political leadership. For someone who adored the trappings of leadership—and recognized their importance in commanding awe and respect—command of the corps could not have been a more perfect acquisition for John Hancock. He envisioned himself in regimentals with sparkling gold epaulets, atop a white horse, sword at his side. He set to work immediately, passionately, converting his vision into reality. He ordered magnificent new uniforms for the entire corps: scarlet coats with buff lapels, white gaiters with black buttons, and three-cornered beaver hats with brims turned up smartly—one of them bearing a rosette secured by a gilded button. He drew up a small manual of arms and asked his former adversary, the British commander Colonel Dalrymple, to assign a sergeant to drill the cadets in precision marching. A few days later, Boston newspapers carried this advertisement:

> Wanted. Immediately—For his Excellency's Company of Cadets.
> Two Fifers that understand playing. Those that are
> masters of musick and are inclined to engage with the
> Company are desired to apply to Col. John Hancock.[15]

The Corps of Cadets began drilling twice a month in Faneuil Hall and moved onto the Common for compulsory weekly drills on Wednesdays when the weather turned warm in spring. Hancock fined those who missed drills—usually a round of ale at the Bunch of Grapes. It was not long before Colonel Hancock and his Corps of Cadets looked every inch a precision marching team, and rumors circulated that the crown was preparing to confer a title on him. Hutchinson knew that John Hancock's adoration of pomp and life at the highest levels of British society as Lord Hancock would end his association with Sam Adams and the radicals.

Neither King George nor his minions, however, were as farsighted as Hutchinson (or democratic enough) to consider elevating American commoners to the nobility as a tool to command colonist loyalties. Hutchinson did the next best thing, however, by again inviting Hancock to join the Governor's Council, and again Hancock refused. Hutchinson wrote that Hancock's refusal was simply an effort "to prevent a total breach" from the radicals and "show the people that he had not been seeking after it."[16]

Hancock's refusal, however, probably had nothing to do with either. He had simply grown frustrated with politics and the inability of the General Court to produce practical benefits for Boston. Through the entire winter of 1771–72, the only accomplishment of Boston's selectmen was to name a Massacre Day orator to commemorate the March 2 confrontation. His boredom with selectman meetings reduced his attendance dramatically. He decided he could accomplish more on his own—as his uncle had done in restoring and maintaining the Common. With Thomas Cushing, who preferred to keep his contributions all but anonymous, he financed the building of a bandstand on the Common and organized and paid a band to give free concerts. He planted a row of trees along the edge of the Common fronting Beacon Street and installed walkways that criss-crossed the park and allowed strollers to enjoy the green without destroying it. He contributed £7,500 to rebuild the crumbling Brattle Square Church. In March 1772 the town appointed him chairman of a committee "to consider the expediency of fixing lamps in this town," and a year later, with Hancock and Cushing pledging to cover costs, they ordered three hundred white globes, which used whale oil for illumination and would be the most advanced type of street lamps in America. Having lost some of his own properties to the perennial fires that raged through Boston's narrow streets and alleys, Hancock ordered the latest model fire engine from England as a gift for the town. To thank their benefactor, the town meeting named the engine "Hancock" and ordered it housed "at or near Hancock's Wharf and in case of fire, the estate of the donor shall have the preference of its service."

More and more, Hancock relished the power he could exert with his wealth and the immediate, visible improvements he could effect in Boston—without having to coax ignorant, timid, or imperious government officials and political opponents. With Cushing always offering support but preferring to remain in the background, Hancock's lavish contributions quickly made him Boston's most popular political leader, eclipsing Sam Adams. The radical majority at the town meeting voted him, rather than Sam Adams, moderator, or presiding officer. Adams was furious. He had invented Hancock and the radical movement, and both now ignored him.

Adams could do nothing, however, but await Parliament's first misstep to reignite mob passions with inflammatory propaganda and seize control of Boston politics again. Parliament did not disappoint him. It enacted a bill restoring the element of the Townshend Acts that made the crown, rather than colonial legislatures, responsible for paying the salaries of judges, thus making the courts dependent on the king instead of the colonial legislatures.

"The judges," Chief Justice Peter Oliver recalled, "had agreed to accept it, but . . . four of them who lived at and near the focus of tarring and feathering . . . were so pelted . . . with cursings and threatenings" that they resigned. Oliver himself accepted the king's order that he be paid by the crown—only to have Adams order his mob "to attack the chief justice when he came to court."[17]

Adams converted the new law into a cause célèbre, writing in the *Boston Gazette*, "Let every town assemble. Let associations and combinations be everywhere set up to consult and recover our just rights." His article caused a furor. Overruling Hancock's and Cushing's objections, Adams organized a "Committee of Correspondence" at the town meeting "to state the rights of the colonists and of this province in particular, as men, as Christians, and as subjects: to communicate and publish the same to the several towns in this province and to the world."[18]

His committee would prove the first link in a chain of committees he encouraged the colonies to establish. The Intercolonial Committee of Correspondence that resulted was the first permanent system of communication between the American colonies and their first union of sorts. Adams demanded that the committee encourage other towns and colonial assemblies to establish similar groups to work in unison to overthrow royal rule. Recognizing that Adams would use the Committee of Correspondence as a springboard to revolution and power, Hancock, Cushing, and other moderates objected. Adams had enough votes, however, to form a twenty-one-man committee that Governor Hutchinson called the "foulest, subtlest, and most venomous serpent ever issued from the egg of sedition."[19] Hancock, Cushing, and other moderates refused to serve on the Adams committee, with Hancock using the press of business as an excuse. Adams, however, did not intend to allow Hancock's money to slip from his grasp, and cunningly set about repairing the political machine he had earlier assembled so carefully.

Incredibly, he brought in the demented hero James Otis to chair the committee. Otis was experiencing one of his occasional moments of lucidity, and Adams convinced his keepers to release him from his straitjacket to return to Boston. Then, with Adams barking orders, the committee agreed to produce documents of "Rights, Liberties and Privileges" for the people of Massachusetts. Three weeks later, the committee presented a seven-thousand-word declaration of the "State of the Rights of Colonists," written by Sam Adams; a "List of Infringements and Violations of those Rights," written by Dr. Joseph Warren; and "A Letter of Correspondence," written by Dr. Benjamin Church, who had, apparently, abandoned his brief flirtation with Loyalists and re-espoused the "Glorious Cause."

"Gentlemen," Church's letter began, "We the freeholders and other inhabitants of Boston . . . can no longer conceal our impatience under a constant, unremmitted, uniform aim to enslave us, or confide in an administration which threatens us with certain and inevitable destruction."[20]

Governor Hutchinson condemned the documents for inciting rebellion, saying their principles "would be sufficient to justify the colonies in revolting, and forming an independent state."[21] Although Hancock and Cushing also disapproved, the cunning of Sam Adams trapped both into playing roles neither had sought. After the Town Meeting had approved the Adams declaration and the Church resolution, the moderator would have to sign them or resign. Hancock had little choice but to pen his legendary signature across each near-treasonous document or flee to London as quickly as possible with as many of his assets as he could salvage. So much of his wealth was real property, however, he knew he would not be able to leave with enough money to live in his accustomed style in London. With the words *JOHN HANCOCK, moderator,* scrawled across the front page of Adams's incitement to rebellion, John Hancock suddenly reemerged as the reluctant leader of Boston's radicals.

After the Town Meeting, Edes and Gill at the *Gazette* printed six hundred copies of Adams's declaration for distribution to selectmen in nearly every town in Massachusetts. All saw John Hancock's signature and believed he was leading the rebellion against royal rule in Massachusetts. As the malevolent Samuel Adams had planned, Hancock was left with little choice but to resume his role as Adams's milch cow or try to seize control of the radicals and sweep Adams aside. He could no longer remain neutral and befriend both Loyalists and radicals.

The Adams statement of colonist rights and the circular letter produced a network of Committees of Correspondence throughout Massachusetts, and when the General Court met in January, it declared that Parliament had no authority to tax colonists without their consent. "I know no line that can be drawn between the supreme authority of Parliament and the total independence of the colonies," Governor Hutchinson thundered in reply. "It is impossible that there should be two independent legislatures in one and the same state, for although there may be but one head, the king, yet two legislative bodies will make two governments as distinct as the kingdoms of England and Scotland before union."[22]

Ironically, John Adams agreed with the royal governor, adding that

it is difficult, if possible, to draw a line of distinction between the universal authority of Parliament over the colonies . . . and no authority at all. . . . If there be no such line, the consequence is either that the colonies are vassals of the Parliament, or, that they are totally independent. As it cannot be supposed to have been the intentions of the parties in the compact that we should be reduced to a state of vassalage, the conclusion is, that it was their sense, that we are thus independent.[23]

In effect, John Adams wrote what was America's first "Declaration of Independence," and Parliament received it as further proof that the time had come to crush the treasonous activities in Massachusetts.

Instead of trying to rally merchant support in the colonies, however, the English government persisted in driving them into the rebel camp. Earlier in 1773, East India Company shares had plunged from 280 to 160 pence on the London Stock Exchange. Tea Act duties had cut American consumption and left the company near bankruptcy, with seventeen million pounds of unsold tea spilling out of its British warehouses. Although the company asked the government to eliminate the tea duty in North America, Lord North refused, saying colonists would interpret repeal as a sign of weakness. Instead, Parliament, many of whose members owned East India shares, passed a new law: the Tea Act of 1773, which gave the company a tea monopoly in America by letting it appoint its own licensees to sell tea directly to consumers and bypass wholesalers and retailers. By eliminating "middle men," a handful of East India Company licensees would be able to sell tea at prices below even the cheapest smuggled tea, although they would drive untold numbers of small colonial merchants and shopkeepers out of business.

Despite the occasional nonimportation and nonconsumption agreements—or perhaps because of them—tea had remained a popular beverage among American women—a staple that meant survival for some storekeepers and small merchants—many loyal to the crown and opposed to the violent upheavals in the streets of Boston. To compound the government's blunder, the East India Company named as agents in the politically volatile province of Massachusetts the two merchant-banking houses run by the sons of Royal Governor Hutchinson and the sons of Loyalist Richard Clarke, whose daughter had married one of the Hutchinson boys. Both the Hutchinsons and Clarkes had ignored colonist nonimportation agreements, and their appointment as East India Company agents would now give them a monopoly on the tea trade in Massachusetts.

With no way of reconciling the Hutchinson-Clarke interests with those of Boston's many wholesalers and small merchants, Hancock had no choice but to ally himself with the larger group. To solidify his leadership, he sought to restore political ties with Sam Adams. The opportunity came almost immediately when Benjamin Franklin—then in London—received a packet of letters that Governor Hutchinson and his brother-in-law Lieutenant Governor Andrew Oliver had sent to a friend in Parliament several years earlier. The letters urged "an abridgment of English liberties" in the American colonies and stripping self-government from "the hands of the populace . . . by degrees."[24]

Franklin, who served as agent for Massachusetts and Pennsylvania in Britain, sent the letters to Thomas Cushing, who passed them on to Sam Adams, who read them to the House of Representatives. A committee headed by Hancock concluded that the letters were "designed to overthrow the [provincial] government and introduce arbitrary rule into the Province."[25] Adams published them and sent copies to the king with a petition asking that Hutchinson and Oliver be removed from office.

The scandal over the Hutchinson-Oliver letters allowed Hancock and Adams to close ranks, but Hancock made it clear he would no longer tolerate the violence, vandalism, and disruptions of democratic town meetings by Adams's gangs of ruffians. As long as he continued to finance the Sons of Liberty, Hancock declared, he, not Adams, would now dictate broad strategy. Although Hancock's new, aggressive stance took Adams aback, Adams recognized that without the political and financial support of the stable elements of Boston society, his independence movement would die, so he agreed to Hancock's terms. Energized by his new leadership role, Hancock set out to woo an entirely new class of colonist to "the Glorious Cause." On June 29, the House adjourned, and a month later John Hancock attended the first service in the all-but-new Brattle Square Church that he had paid to restore. The cornerstone bore the name "Hon. John Hancock." Harvard's trustees also honored their Patriot son—and benefactor—by naming him treasurer of the college, a position they hoped would serve to remind him of the college's constant need for financial gifts and bequests.

In September 1773 the *Boston Gazette* reprinted a series of inflammatory articles against the Tea Act that had appeared in Philadelphia and New York newspapers. The articles argued that the government-backed East India Company monopoly on tea sales would drive small merchants out of business, encourage establishment of other government monopolies, and eventually destroy free enterprise. Sam Adams dusted off the plans he had used to prevent implementation of the Stamp Act: He would send his mob to frighten East India Company agents into resigning, then prevent ships from landing and offloading their tea—much as it had done with stamps in 1765.

On October 21, the Massachusetts Bay Committee of Correspondence wrote to similar committees in other colonies calling on them to prevent East India Company tea from landing in America. Five days later the *Boston Gazette* printed a handbill from Philadelphia that threatened the lives of "the Commissioners appointed by the East India Company for the sale of tea in America" unless they resigned.[26]

On Tuesday, November 2, 1772, a staccato of knocks on their respective front doors roused Thomas and Elisha Hutchinson from their beds. Each found a note nailed to their doors demanding their appearance at the Liberty Tree the following day "to resign your commission" as East India Company consignees. "Fail not upon your peril," the notes warned. They bore the cryptic signature: "O.C." [officer in charge].[27]

On November 3, Sam Adams, John Hancock, Dr. Joseph Warren, and other selectmen and Patriot leaders led more than five hundred Sons of Liberty to the Liberty Tree and demanded the resignation of the Hutchinson boys and Clarke's sons as tea agents. The Hutchinsons and Clarkes refused, and two days later, Hancock chaired a Town Meeting that declared them "daringly affrontive to the town."[28]

By morning the following day, John Boyle wrote in his "Journal of Occurrences in Boston" that Bostonians "found a note stuck up in all parts of the town . . . at almost every corner . . . and a large flag was also hung out on the pole at Liberty-Tree, and at 11 O'Clock all the bells in town were set a ringing."[29]

"Gentlemen," the note began.

> You are desired to meet at the Liberty Tree this day at Twelve o Clock at noon. Then and there to hear the persons to whom the tea shipped by the East India Company is consigned make a public resignation of their office as consignees upon oath—And also to swear that they will re-ship

any teas that may be consigned to them by said company by the first vessel sailing for London.

Boston, Nov. 3, 1773. O.C. Scy

"Shew us the Man that Dare take down this."[30]

By noon, Hancock, Sam Adams, Molyneux, and Warren had arrived
at the Liberty Tree, where more than five hundred were waiting in vain
for the Hutchinsons and the other merchants. Incensed by the demands
on the unsigned notice, the merchants sent word to the gathering refusing to bend to the will of a self-appointed group with no legal standing
either as a body elected by the people or appointed by the government.
Adams pronounced the response "daring [and] affrontive" and led the
mob to the Hutchinson building, where it battered down the front doors
and surged into the ground floor, smashing fixtures, but the mob was unable to breach the upper floors, where the merchants had barricaded
themselves in.

A week later, Governor Hutchinson responded with a letter to Hancock, ordering him as commander of the Governor's Company of Cadets
to "summon each person belonging to the company to be ready to appear
in arms at such place . . . whensoever there may be a tumultuous assem-
bling of people in violation of the laws."[31] In effect, the governor's note
forced Hancock to choose sides once and for all. Hancock chose to ignore
the governor's order. There would now be no turning back.

"Now, brethren," Sam Adams wrote in a circular letter for the Boston
Committee of Correspondence to committees in other eastern Massachusetts towns, "we are reduced to this dilemma, either to sit down quietly
under this and every other burden that our enemies shall see fit to lay
upon us as good natured slaves or rise and resist this and every plan laid for
our destruction as becomes freemen." Adams declared that "this tea now
coming to us [is] more to be dreaded than plague or pestilence."[32]

In London, meanwhile, a few ships' captains, including James Scott,
who commanded John Hancock's ship *Hayley*, refused to load their vessels
with tea bound for America, but the East India Company quickly bribed
its way onto other vessels, and by the end of October, 1,700 chests, with
one hundred pounds of tea in each chest, sailed off to America.

On November 18, the Sons of Liberty gathered at the Liberty Tree and again demanded that the tea agents resign. Again, the agents refused. On Saturday, November 27, the *Dartmouth*, the first of four ships bound for Boston, anchored outside the harbor, and the next day, as it glided to the wharf, Sam Adams and a group of his "Mohawks" prevented it from tying up. On Monday morning, posters appeared throughout the town:

> Friends, Brethren, Countrymen! That worst of plagues, the detestable tea shipped for this port by the East India Company is now arrived in this harbor. The hour of destruction or manly opposition to the machinations of tyranny stares you in the face. Every friend to his country, to himself and posterity, is now called to meet at Faneuil Hall at 9 o'clock this day (at which time the bells will begin to ring) to make a united and successful resistance to this last, worst, and most destructive measure of administration.[33]

As predicted, bells across the city pealed at nine. What began as a crowd of several hundred swelled to nearly five thousand, and organizers moved the meeting from Faneuil Hall to the more spacious Old South Meeting House. Governor Hutchinson ordered Hancock to assemble the Corps of Cadets and disperse the crowd. Hancock refused. Adams called the meeting to order and moved that the tea be shipped back to England, duties unpaid. A radical supporter, Dr. Thomas Young, shouted above the cheers with a call to dump the tea overboard. After Adams restored order, the meeting rejected the Young proposal and unanimously approved the Adams resolution. Adams ordered a watch on the wharf to prevent the *Dartmouth* from tying up and unloading its tea. Hancock jumped onto his horse and led the Corps of Cadets to pierside to help Adams's men guard the wharf to prevent any tea from landing.

Patriots in other New England ports followed suit, and one by one, towns across New England banned the use of British tea, with some going a step farther with a ban on all tea drinking. With tea now a symbol of the tyranny of big-government taxation, four ports in New Hampshire— Portsmouth, Newcastle, Exeter, and Dover—refused to offload British tea ships, and in New York, Patriots succeeded in forcing East India Company agents to resign. Despite efforts by New York Royal Governor William

Faneuil Hall. This is where British troops first lodged when they arrived in Boston on October 1, 1768, to quell the mobs that had overrun the streets of Boston. (LIBRARY OF CONGRESS)

Tryon to land the tea at the British troop encampment, the captain decided to sail his cargo back to England. A British journalist covering events in Boston sensed a major story developing and sent this running dispatch:

Thursday, December 16, 1773. What a contention is going on far overseas at Boston, New England. The case is well known and still memorable to mankind. British Parliament, after nine years of the saddest haggling and baffling to and fro under constitutional stress . . . has made up its mind that America shall pay duty on their teas before infusing them, and America, Boston most especially, is tacitly determined that it will not, and that to avoid mistakes the teas shall not be landed at all. . . .

The Town Meeting resumed the following morning, with word that Hutchinson's sons and the Clarkes had fled to Castle William. The sheriff read a governor's order to disperse, but the crowd booed, cursed, and jeered until he fled the hall. The meeting voted again to block landing of the tea, and it agreed to send a report of its proceedings to other colonies and London. At five the next morning, Hancock sent an aide on horseback with copies for New York and Philadelphia. Governor Hutchinson responded to the extraordinary two-day meeting by ordering harbor authorities to bar the tea ships from leaving the harbor until their owners paid duties. He condemned Hancock for joining the rebel camp. "It is in everybody's mouth," he wrote, "that Hancock said at the close of this meeting he would be willing to spend his fortune and life itself in so good a cause."[34]

The *Dartmouth* remained at anchor for three days before docking at Griffin's Wharf, more than a half-mile south of Long Wharf (see map 1, page 12). A few days later, the second of the four Boston-bound tea ships tied up beside the *Dartmouth*. One of the two trailing ships sailed into port two days later, but the fourth ship, which carried Boston's precious new street lamps as well as tea, ran aground at Provincetown, on Cape Cod. Local workers joined the crew in salvaging the three hundred lamps—all undamaged—and fifty-eight chests of tea. As wagons carried the lamps off to Boston, one of the Clarkes sneaked into Provincetown, put the tea aboard a fishing schooner, and brought it safely to Castle William—the only tea that slipped through Patriot hands into consumer teapots.

But the tea ships in Boston had sailed into the worst type of legal trap—subject to government seizure, both ships and cargoes, if they did not land their cargo and pay the appropriate duties within twenty days. Nor could the ships turn around and return to England. By law, once the ships entered the harbor, they would not be able to return to sea without landing their cargo, but armed members of the Sons of Liberty stood on the wharves day and night to prevent the ships' crews from doing so.

At 10 A.M. on Thursday, December 16, more than five thousand people from Boston and the surrounding area pushed their way into Old South Meeting House and demanded that Francis Rotch, a part-owner of one of the tea ships, order his vessel back to England. Rotch said the British guns at Castle William would not let him pass without paying duties on the ship's cargo. After sending him to demand safe passage for his ship from the governor, the meeting adjourned until three that afternoon. Hancock, Adams, and the other leaders huddled in conference to decide their next move. When the meeting resumed, Rotch was nowhere to be found. Patriot leaders kept the crowd under control with a few rousing, albeit repetitive, speeches. After several hours, the crowd grew tired and the meeting was about to adjourn when Rotch returned. It was 5:45, with only a spark of candlelight piercing the winter's eerie early-evening darkness. Rotch said the governor had rejected Boston's demands, refusing to let the ship return to England and asserting that the Boston meeting had no legal standing. The governor issued this declaration: "I warn, exhort and require you and each of you thus unlawfully assembled, forthwith to disperse and surcease all further unlawful proceedings at your utmost peril."

An angry wail filled the hall. Some in the crowd said they heard Hancock call out, "Let every man do what is right in his own eyes."[35] Adams adjourned the meeting with an angry cry, "This meeting can do no more to save the country."[36] The English journalist reported hearing "a terrific war-whoop . . . almost on the instant, in front of the Old South Meeting House, and about fifty Mohawk Indians, with whom Adams seems to be acquainted and speaks without interpreter." Some at the scene believed the war whoop was a prearranged signal for the Mohawks to march to Griffin's Wharf. In the hall, there were cries of "Boston harbor a tea-pot tonight!" "Hurrah for Griffin's Wharf!" and "The Mohawks are come!"[37]

"And sure enough," wrote the British reporter,

before the stroke of seven, these fifty painted Mohawks are forward without noise to Griffin's Wharf, have put sentries all around them, and in a great silence of the neighborhood, are busy in three gangs upon the dormant tea ships, opening their chests and punctually shaking them out into the sea. Listening from a distance you could hear distinctly the ripping open of the chests and no other sound.[38]

The crowd had poured out of the meeting house and followed the Mohawks to Griffin's Wharf, but remained a discreet distance behind, marching silently, eventually stopping at a safe distance to watch the spectacle—still silent, almost in mourning for an era it sensed had come to an end.

Accounts vary as to just how many Mohawks worked the tea ships. Members of Hancock's Corps of Cadets stood on guard when the Mohawks arrived, and corps members waved them aboard the ships and joined in facilitating their travails. Most witnesses put the number of Mohawks at more than fifty; together with Hancock's men, the number of Tea Party participants probably totaled at least eighty. All pledged to keep their exact number and identities secret. Although the notorious Ebenezer Mackintosh of the South End Gang claimed that his "chickens did the job," there is no evidence that many street toughs participated. Hancock had warned Adams sternly that any repetition of the violence, plundering, and wanton destruction of property that accompanied the Massacre would forever alienate large numbers of merchants and other moderates, and Adams was careful to make the "Tea Party" an orderly affair conducted by responsible citizens— evidently skilled craftsmen by the way they worked.

After escorting customs officers and ships' crews to safety, they began working methodically, almost artfully, lifting tea chests from the hold with blocks and tackles, carefully splitting each open with hatchets and axes, then dumping the tea and splintered chests into the water. "The night was clear, the moon shone brilliantly," making the work easier, swifter. The *Massachusetts Gazette* reported that "the town was very quiet during the whole evening."

"Depend on it," John Adams wrote years later. "These were no ordinary Mohawks. The profound secrecy in which they have held their names, and the total abstinence of plunder, are proofs of the character of the men."[39]

The men worked steadily, silently, until they had dumped all the tea in the harbor—342 chests in all, valued as £9,659[40] or $1 million in today's currency[41]—without damaging any other cargo, stores, or materiel. There were no fights, no brutality, no injuries—nothing but calm, orderly, disciplined discharging of tea. It did not take long—less than three hours. A crowd of about one thousand watched silently, whispering occasional comments to each other, always looking over their shoulders for the approach of British troops.

> About ten P.M. all was finished . . . the Mohawks gone like a dream, and Boston sleeping more silently even than usual.[42]

The Boston Tea Party. Here, it is as imagined by artist/engraver Nathaniel Currier in 1846.
(LIBRARY OF CONGRESS)

By morning, wind and tidal flows had washed a thick blanket of tea leaves and splintered tea chests over the bay from Boston to the Dorchester flats to the south. According to the *Massachusetts Gazette*, "Those who were from the country went home with a merry heart, and . . . joy appeared in almost every countenance, some on account of the destruction of the tea, others on account of the quietness with which it was effected."[43]

On the morning after the Tea Party, Sam Adams sent this letter on behalf of the Committee of Correspondence of Boston to other committees:

Yesterday, we had a greater meeting of the body than ever, the country coming in from twenty miles around, and every step was taken that was practicable for returning the tea. The moment it was known out of doors that Mr. Rotch could not obtain a pass for his ship by the castle, a number of people huzza'd in the street, and in a very little time, every ounce of the teas on board . . . was immersed in the bay. . . . The spirit of the people on this occasion surprised all parties who viewed the scene.[44]

Adams was more ebullient in a letter he sent to Arthur Lee, Richard Henry Lee's younger brother, who was serving as the Massachusetts agent in London. "You cannot imagine the height of joy that sparkles in the eyes and animated the countenance as well as the hearts of all we meet on this occasion; excepting the disappointed, disconcerted Hutchinson and his tools." And in a subsequent letter to Lee, Adams insisted that

> the people of Boston and the other adjacent towns endeavored to have the tea sent back to the place from whence it came. . . . Governor Hutchinson and other crown officers . . . made use of [their] powers to defeat the intentions of the people and succeeded; in short, the governor, who for art and cunning as well as inveterate hatred of the people was inferior to no one . . . both encouraged and provoked the people to destroy the tea. . . . In this view of the matter, the question is easily decided who ought in justice to pay for the tea if it ought to be paid for at all.[45]

In the end, both Americans and British would all pay for the tea dumped on Boston Harbor with the blood of thousands of their countrymen.

Chapter 12

"We Will Never Be Taxed!"

From the isolation of Castle William, the angry Royal Governor Thomas Hutchinson lamented over the Boston Tea Party, calling it "the boldest stroke that had been struck against British rule in America." A royalist pamphleteer agreed:

> Now the crime of the Bostonians was a compound of the grossest injury and insult. It was an act of the highest insolence towards government, such as mildness itself cannot overlook or forgive. The injustice of the deed was also most atrocious, as it was the destruction of property to a vast amount, when it was known that the nation was obliged in honor to protect.[1]

Just who participated in the Tea Party and who witnessed it from shore remains one of the tantalizing mysteries in American history (see Appendix B). Whoever they were, most kept their names secret for many years thereafter—largely because they realized that even after the United States had become independent, they remained liable for destruction of private property and faced civil as well as criminal charges and damages.

The skills of the original Tea Party Patriots point to craftsmen, whereas the discipline they displayed and the quickness and ease with which they boarded and moved about the ships indicate participation by members of

Hancock's Corps of Cadets, who had stood watch the previous nights. The *Massachusetts Spy* reported that John Hancock "was the first man that went aboard the vessel, to destroy the tea," but most historians discount the possibility that a man as wealthy and recognizable, not to mention as cautious, as Hancock would have risked arrest, trial, and imprisonment in England along with a huge lawsuit. Moreover, Hancock's huge, gilt-trimmed coach and liveried servants never stood far from their master, and he seldom moved about without them. He was also beginning to suffer attacks of gout, an extremely painful disease that would probably not have allowed him to bound aboard and about a cargo ship.

As the Tea Party entered the legends of American history, descriptions—most of them contradictory—continued surfacing for years. Governor Hutchinson, who was out of town at the time, claimed that most of the crowd at the Old South Meeting House had marched to the wharves and watched while the "Mohawks" dumped the tea. The *Dartmouth* log of December 16 claims the crowd numbered only about one thousand, including men "dressed and whooping like Indians."[2] One Boston merchant said the meeting at Old South did not end until "the candles were lit" and that those who boarded the tea ships were "cloathed in blankets with the head muffled, and copper colored countenances, being each armed with a hatchet or axe, and pair of pistols . . . before nine o'clock . . . every chest . . . was knocked to pieces and flung over the sides."[3]

Tens of thousands later claimed they were at the meeting at Old South and participated in or witnessed the Tea Party. All four ships would have sunk under the weight of such a crowd. In 1835, more than sixty years later, one such "witness" produced a list of fifty-eight participants, whose number included silversmith Paul Revere, merchant William Molyneux, and the leatherworker/shoemaker and mob leader Mackintosh. A subsequent list of fifty-five more names were culled from interviews with Bostonians who claimed they had participated in or witnessed the Tea Party or were members of the immediate families of participants (see Appendix B for both lists). The majority were skilled craftsmen—including eight carpenter/house builders, four coopers, three leatherworkers, and eight other craftsmen in a variety of trades, including Paul Revere, the silversmith. The list showed fourteen merchants having participated in the Tea Party, but only two shopkeepers—one a bookseller, the other a butcher. The list also includes six civil servants and midlevel politicians as having boarded the tea ships, along with five farmers, two physicians, one printer/newspaper publisher, one engineer, one schoolteacher, and one clergyman. Only about half the names on the list—thirty-five—are known to have served later in the Revolutionary War. As for Mackintosh's "chickens," only six men with various ties to the waterfront might possibly have qualified as one of Mackintosh's toughs. Clearly, the majority of Tea Party Patriots emerged from a moderate segment of Boston society—literate, skilled, often well educated, and nonviolent. Typical of many, Thomas Melvill—a grandfather of author Herman Melville—was a young businessman with a bachelor's degree and master's degree from the College of New Jersey (later Princeton), who joined the Tea Party motivated by sheer idealism and the belief that taxes filled the pockets of corrupt politicians while generating few benefits for ordinary citizens.

One witness claimed to have recognized Hancock "not only by his ruffles" but "by his figure and gait . . . his features . . . and by his voice, also, for he exchanged . . . an Indian grunt. . . ."[4] Years later, a teamster claimed he "loaded at John Hancock's warehouse and was about to leave town when Mr. Hancock requested me to be on Long Wharf at 2 o'clock P.M. [the very time Hancock and the others sat in Old South!] and informed me what was to be done. I went accordingly [and] joined the band. . . . We mounted the ships and made tea in a trice. This done, I took my team and went home, as an honest man should."[5] Still another unlikely witness cited Dr. Joseph Warren and Paul Revere as participants, and a popular street ballad about the Tea Party opened with the words,

> Rally Mohawks! Bring out your axes,
> And tell King George we'll pay no taxes
> On his foreign tea.

Another verse included the lines

> Our Warren's there and bold Revere,
> With hands to do and words to cheer,
> For Liberty and laws.[6]

On December 17, the day after the Tea Party, Revere began his legendary ride to Philadelphia, spreading news of the Tea Party everywhere, believing—as did Boston Patriots—that the Tea Party would unite Americans. Some colonists did indeed stop drinking tea, and bands of Tea Party Patriots began forming in other cities. As they had done with stamp agents in the 1760s, tax protesters in major cities such as Philadelphia, New York, and Charleston forced East India Company tea agents to resign.[7] New York Governor William Tryon warned the British Board of Trade that it would require "the protection of the point of the bayonet and muzzle of the cannon" to land tea in New York.[8] A newspaper reported that "a vast number of the inhabitants, including most of the principal lawyers, merchants, landowners, masters of ships and mechanics" had joined the "Sons of Liberty of New York" and pledged to turn back tea ships. Outside Philadelphia, a crowd of eight thousand tax protesters greeted the ship *Polly*, carrying 697 chests of tea as it prepared to sail up the Delaware on Christmas Day. It put about and sailed out to sea.

In all his breathless rides and many descriptions of the Tea Party, Paul Revere never said he participated in dumping tea into Boston Harbor, and, indeed, there is not a shred of evidence to show who did or did not participate. The sheriff arrested a barber named Eckley, but released him for lack of evidence. John Adams, who had been in court in Plymouth for a week and rode back into Boston the morning after the Tea Party, said he did not know any Tea Party participants. As he rode into town, he saw splintered tea chests and huge clots of tea leaves covering the water as far as his eyes could see. They washed ashore along a fifty-mile stretch of coastline as well as on the offshore islands.

"This," he entered in his diary when he reached his home, "is the most magnificent movement of all.

> There is a dignity, a majesty, a sublimity in this last effort of the Patriots I greatly admire. The people should never rise without doing something to be remembered—something notable. And striking. This destruction of the tea is so bold, so daring, so firm, intrepid and inflexible, and it must have so important consequences, and so lasting, that I cannot but consider it as an epocha [sic] in history.[9]

Three days later, on December 21, John Hancock wrote to his London agent:

> We have been much agitated in consequence of the arrival of tea ships by the East India Company, and after every effort was made to induce the consignees to return it from whence it came and all proving ineffectual, in a very few hours the whole of the tea on board . . . was thrown into the salt water. The particulars I must refer you to Captain Scott for indeed I am not acquainted with them myself, so as to give a detail. Philadelphia and New York are determined the tea shall not land. No one circumstance could possibly have taken place more effectively to unite the colonies than this maneuver of the tea.[10]

Hancock shipped all his stocks of tea back to England at his own expense. The *London Chronicle* published a long, grisly account of the Boston Tea Party and a portrait of a city in open rebellion against the crown. The report infuriated the king, his cabinet, Parliament, and most Londoners, who called it vandalism. England's attorney general formally charged Boston's most outspoken political leaders—John Hancock and Samuel Adams, among others—with "the Crime of High Treason" and "High Misdemeanors" and ordered them brought to justice in England, where British law dictated hanging by the neck and "while you are still living your bodies are to be taken down, your bowels torn out . . . your head then cut off, and your bodies divided each into four quarters."[11]

Not many American leaders in the South rallied to the defense of Boston's Tea Party Patriots. Far from uniting colonists, the Tea Party had alienated many property owners, who held private property to be sacrosanct and did not tolerate its destruction or violation. George Washington concluded that Bostonians were mad, and like other Virginians and most Britons, he condemned the Boston Tea Party as vandalism and wanton destruction of private property—an unholy disregard for property rights. After the repeal of the Townshend Acts, Virginians saw no reason to persist in boycotting their British countrymen, and they resumed drinking tea, consuming eighty thousand pounds of tea in 1773, with plans to drink even more in 1774. In Charleston, South Carolina, importers of East India

Company tea protested against local boycotts that discriminated against them while allowing other merchants to smuggle cheap Dutch tea at will.

Although winter snows and bitter cold dampened Boston's enthusiasm for street protests, Sam Adams kept anti-British passions burning with fiery newspaper articles—all signed with pseudonyms. One article asserted that Chinese peasants packed East India Company tea into chests in Canton by stomping on it with dirty, bare, disease-infected feet. Consumers by the thousands discarded whatever tea they had in their homes, while students at the College of New Jersey ran amok, destroying all the tea they could find in the college commissary. By the end of the eighteenth century, coffee would supplant tea as America's most popular hot beverage, in part because of nonimportation agreements but also because of Adams's relentless propaganda equating tea with disease and tea duties with runaway British taxation.

The new year brought a resumption of disorders, with Boston Patriots tarring and feathering two customs commissioners. One of the mobs broke down the door of Commissioner John Malcolm's house. Although he repelled the first attackers with his sword as he backed up the stairway, the mob overwhelmed him as he reached the second floor landing. They then tied him up and lowered him through a window into the tumbrel, where "they stripped him, tarred and feathered and haltered him," according to Chief Justice Peter Oliver. After rolling Malcolm to the Liberty Tree, they hung him from a branch "and whipped him with great barbarity in the presence of thousands—and some of them members of the General Court."[12] They beat him with sticks and clubs until he shrieked, at the behest of his torturers, that he deserved to die and *thanked* the mob for their *mercy* in beating instead of killing him. As he lapsed into unconsciousness, onlookers grew bored and drifted away; the remnants of the mob dropped Malcolm back into the cart, rolled him back to his house, and dumped his limp body by the door. Amazingly, he survived.

Early in March sixty Boston Mohawks reprised the Tea Party by boarding the *Fortune*, forcing the crew below, and dumping nearly thirty chests of tea (about one hundred pounds per chest) into the bay. The second Boston Tea Party combined with the arrival of fine spring weather to infect Americans with Tea Party fever. In town after town, ordinarily law-abiding citizens—

Customs Commissioner John Malcolm on the scaffold. Here, he is being lowered from his home into the cart for tarring and feathering by the Boston mob. (LIBRARY OF CONGRESS)

some dressed as Indians, others as Redcoats—marched merrily through the streets, mocking, flaunting, and taunting British authorities and soldiers and, wherever they could, dumping or burning tea. A mob disguised as Indians boarded a tea ship in New York in March and dumped its entire cargo into the water. In April a tea ship tied up in Annapolis with two thousand pounds of tea aboard, only to a have a mob set fire to it and destroy its cargo.

"I think, sir, I went to Annapolis yesterday to see my liberty destroyed," declared Joseph Galloway, the thoughtful speaker of the Maryland Assembly. Although he sided with protesters who claimed that Parliament had no constitutional right to tax colonists, he believed deeply that Britain had a lawful right to legislate for the American colonies and refused to countenance breaking the law or consider any but peaceful solutions to the conflict over taxation.

A ship attempting to land tea in Greenwich, New Jersey, met the same fate as the one in Annapolis. In June the *Grosvenor* sailed into Portsmouth, New Hampshire, with twenty-seven chests of tea. A mob of less strident

Joseph Galloway. Speaker of the Maryland Assembly, he condemned Tea Party Patriots for destroying a tea ship in Annapolis. A firm believer in Britain's legitimate rule over the colonies, he sought compromise in the dispute over taxation. (LIBRARY OF CONGRESS)

Patriots convinced the owner to order the ship to come about and head for Halifax. But when the same ship owner tried to land another thirty chests in September, the mob lost patience and all but destroyed his house.

Unfortunately, England's leaders continued to miscalculate the depth of colonial resentment toward British attempts to tax them—and the growing unity that the Tea Party was slowly provoking beyond Boston. Misinterpreting the Tea Party as an isolated criminal enterprise, the British ministry focused its efforts on crushing Boston and bringing its rebel chiefs to the gallows. Although formal arrest orders for Hancock and Adams would not reach Massachusetts for several weeks, Adams acted in kind by demanding that the Massachusetts House of Representatives impeach Chief Justice Peter Oliver for accepting his salary from King George instead of the Massachusetts House of Representatives. The House voted overwhelmingly in favor of impeachment, ninety-two to eight, but before the trial could begin, Governor Hutchinson adjourned the General Court. Uncertain how to respond, the Boston Town Meeting turned to John Hancock, inviting him to address them as Massacre Day orator on March 4.

On the eve of Hancock's speech, Andrew Oliver, the chief justice's older brother and the merchant whom the mob had twice humiliated at the Liberty Tree, died—a broken man. "The indignities offered him," his friend Governor Thomas Hutchinson lamented, "sunk his spirits, and he . . . at last left us suddenly. . . . The lieutenant governor is out of the reach of the malice of his enemies. They followed him, however, to the grave; a part of the mob . . . upon the relations coming out of the burying ground, giving three huzzas, and yet few better men have lived."[13]

Mob threats prevented Andrew's brother Peter Oliver from making a

> final visit to the death bed of an only living brother. . . . The risk of his life was too great for him . . . and his friends advised him not to pay his fraternal respect to his brother's obsequies. The advice was just, for it afterwards appeared that had he done so, it was not probable that he ever would have returned to his own home. Never did cannibals thirst stronger for human blood than the adherents to this faction. Humanity seemed abhorrent to their nature.

Mourners at the funeral later confirmed that a mob had indeed insulted them and interrupted the solemnity of the services.[14]

Massacre Day fell on a Saturday—Market Day—and the crowds were larger than expected. For most Americans, oratory was a principal form of entertainment, and the Market Day crowds and the curious joined Patriots from Boston and outlying areas flocking to Faneuil Hall to hear the merchant-king-turned-Patriot. The larger-than-expected crowd forced organizers to move the meeting to Old South Meeting House. Still, they filled every pew, every inch of space along the aisles, in the galleries and stairways, and even the outer hall. Hancock's coach arrived, and dressed, as always, in princely scarlet velvet, he made his way to the great pulpit, climbed the stairs, and waited for silence.

"He looked every inch an aristocrat," according to one observer, "from his dress and powdered wig to his smart pumps of grained leather . . . sturdily built . . . dashing good looks . . . his dark eyes were penetrating,

Old South Meeting House. This is where John Hancock told Bostonians, "Let every man do what is right!"—a signal that sent the "Mohawks" off to the "Tea Party" at Griffin's Wharf. (LIBRARY OF CONGRESS)

his mouth was firm, his chin determined."[15] Another called Hancock's facial expression "beautiful, manly, expressive." His delivery could excite audiences to "the highest pitch of frenzy" or "sooth them into tears."[16] On Massacre Day, 1774, Hancock did both as he delivered the most important speech of his life—in effect, seizing leadership of the American Revolution in Massachusetts. He began humbly, almost inaudibly:

Men, brethren, fathers and fellow-countrymen; The attentive gravity, the venerable appearance of this crowded audience; the dignity which I behold in the countenances of so many in this great assembly; the solemnity of the occasion upon which we have met together . . . fill me with an awe hitherto unknown; and heighten the sense which I have ever had, of my unworthiness to fill this sacred desk. . . . I pray, that my sincere attachment to the interest of my country, and hearty detestation of every design formed against her liberties, may be admired as some form of apology for my appearance in this place.

Hancock raised his voice a bit:

I have always, from my earliest youth . . . considered it as the indispensable duty of every member of society . . . as a faithful subject of the state, to use his utmost endeavors . . . to oppose every traitorous plot which its enemies may devise for its destruction.

His voice grew stronger, reaching a crescendo:

I glory in publicly avowing my eternal enmity to tyranny! Is the present system, which the British administration have adopted for the government of the colonies, a righteous government, or is it tyranny?

"Tyranny!" the audience roared in response.

"Tell me, ye bloody butchers!" Hancock thundered. "Ye dark designing knaves, ye murderers, parricides! How dare you tread upon the earth, which drank the blood of the slaughtered innocents, shed by your wicked hands! How dare you breathe the air which wafted to the ear of heaven, the groans of those who fell a sacrifice to your accursed ambition!"

The crowd was his to command. Referring to the Tea Party, he charged that if Boston had not acted, "We soon should have found our trade in the hands of foreigners, and taxes imposed on every thing which we consumed." He demanded "total disuse of tea in this country . . . to free ourselves from those unmannerly pillagers who impudently tell us that they are licensed by an act of the British parliament to thrust their dirty hands into the pockets of every American." He called on all Patriots to arm themselves and prepare to "fight for your houses, lands, wives, children . . . your liberty and your God" so that "those noxious vermin will be swept forever from the streets of Boston."

He then sounded the clarion call for national rebellion and independence, urging Americans to organize militias and "be ready to take the field whenever danger calls" and appealing for "a general union among us . . . and our sister colonies.

"Much has been done by committees of correspondence . . . for uniting the inhabitants of the whole continent," he declared, "but permit me here to suggest a general congress of deputies, from the several houses of assembly, on the continent, as the most effectual method of establishing such a union. . . .

> I conjure you by all that is dear, by all that is honorable, by all that is sacred, not only that ye pray, but that you act; that, if necessary, ye fight, and even die, for the prosperity of our Jerusalem. . . . I thank God that America abounds in men who are superior to all temptation, whom nothing can divert from a steady pursuit of the interest of their country. . . . Their revered names, in all succeeding times, shall grace the annals of America. From them, let us, my friends, take example; from them, let us catch the divine enthusiasm and feel, each for himself, the God-like pleasure of . . . delivering the oppressed from the iron grasp of tyranny.[17]

He finished with a passage from the Bible that left the immense crowd spellbound. As he descended the pulpit and shook hands with Sam Adams and other Patriot leaders, murmurs grew into applause, then erupted into cheers that swelled into a sustained roar as he made his way back to his coach to return to Hancock House. Old "Bishop" Hancock could not have stirred a congregation more than his grandson had just done. He had captured the hearts and minds of Boston's Patriot movement and become the undeniable leader of Massachusetts. John Adams called the oration "An elegant, a pathetic [in the sense of moving] and a spirited performance. A vast crowd, rainy eyes, etc. The composition, the pronunciation, the action—all exceeded the expectations of everybody. They exceeded even mine, which were very considerable. Many of the sentiments . . . came from him with a singular dignity and grace."[18]

After a month of debate and deliberations, during which the East India Company tried in vain to recoup its losses from its insurers, the British government agreed on a sweeping new policy "to secure the dependence of the colonies on the Mother Country." The new policy would punish not only the instigators of and participants in the Tea Party but the entire town of Boston for tolerating an atmosphere of indulgence that fostered the Tea Party. Declaring the Tea Party an act of high treason, the government equated it with "the levying of war against His Majesty" and "an attempt, concerted with much deliberation and made with open force . . . to obstruct the execution of an Act of Parliament."[19] To punish the town, the British government ordered Boston's port closed to all ships beginning on June 15, until the city repaid the East India Company for its losses—the first of several "Coercive Acts" to force Boston to submit unconditionally to Parliament's rule.

All England seemed to applaud the ministry's decisions, with a merchant in Bristol saying that the "clamor" in Britain against the Tea Party "is high and general," while another cited Boston—and Sam Adams in particular—as generators of all the discontent in America. "They are not only the worst subjects," he wrote of Bostonians, "but the most immoral men of any I have had to deal with." He called Bostonians "treacherous and seditious"—as bad "as Sodom itself was for a vice which ought not be named."[20]

The widespread anger provoked threats against Americans living in London, with Benjamin Franklin warning of "a great wrath" and Arthur Lee, Virginia's agent in London, warning that "active Americans here" might be in danger of assault. Some British newspapers published demands by irate readers that large bodies of troops be sent to keep colonists "in due subjection," while a more thoughtful reader suggested responding to the American boycott of British tea with a British boycott of American tobacco.

Although other American towns had held their own tea parties, the British government decided to make an example of Boston as the earliest and most outspoken antagonist of British colonial rule. "I think the town of Boston has deserved the animadversion of every part of this country," Lord North declared. Dismissing the charge that innocents would suffer as much as the guilty, North said the failure of the innocents to rein in the guilty made them equally guilty. "If they deny authority in one instance, it goes to all; we must control them or submit to them."[21]

When the government presented what it called the Boston Port Bill to Parliament, it found little opposition. Even Colonel Isaac Barré, who had fought with the American militia in the French and Indian War, agreed to punishing Boston and voted for the bill. Edmund Burke, another long-time champion of the colonists, also favored punishing the Tea Party Patriots but called it "devilish" to punish innocents in Boston for their failure to prevent the Tea Party.

"It looks to me to be narrow and pedantic to apply the ordinary ideas of criminal justice to this great public contest," he declared. "I do not know the method of drawing up an indictment against an whole people. . . . I really think that for wise men this is not judicious, for sober men not decent, for minds tinctured with humanity not mild and merciful."[22]

Burke's caution was of no avail. On March 25, the House of Commons passed the Boston Port Bill by a majority of five to one; three days later the House of Lords followed suit, and George III signed it into law on March 31, with the all-but-unanimous consent of the British people. Rather than uniting law-abiding Americans behind British rule, however, the Boston Port Bill united them against the Mother Country as never before. Parliament had changed direction. It was no longer enforcing tax collection; it was asserting unchecked, arbitrary authority over dissenting citizens, and Americans refused to submit.

Under the Port Bill, the British navy would shut Boston Harbor on June 1 until the city repaid both the East India Company for its Tea Party losses and the British government for the duties it would have collected on the tea. Except for military supplies and essential food and fuel, the law banned loading and unloading of all ships until "peace and obedience to the laws shall be . . . restored in the said town of Boston, that the trade of Great Britain may safely be carried on there and his Majesty's customs duly collected."[23] To ensure enforcement, the king replaced Governor Thomas Hutchinson with General Thomas Gage, commander in chief of British forces in North America, with orders "to repel force and violence by every means within his reach."[24] He responded by ordering four regiments of Redcoats in England and Ireland to sail to Boston immediately. To avoid humiliating Hutchinson, whom Sam Adams called "that damned arch traitor,"[25] the king granted Hutchinson temporary leave in England, with the understanding that he would return as governor after General Gage and the army succeeded in restoring peace.

"Tired with abuse," Hutchinson noted sadly, "I obtained leave to go to England. . . . I have the satisfaction of being assured that my conduct has been approved by my Sovereign. I wished for the approbation of my country also, but in the present state of this province they are not compatible."[26]

On May 13, Gage arrived at Castle William with instructions to move the General Court from Boston to Salem and prosecute Hancock, Adams, and the rest of the Patriot leaders for treason. Chief Justice Peter Oliver warned Gage that "the times are not favorable for prosecutions," and rather than provoke more riots, Gage deferred action. Four days later Gage sailed from Castle William to Boston to assume his office—just as a town meeting was about to meet to protest the Port Bill. Hancock ordered the Corps of Cadets to escort the new governor to Town House for his induction into office and from there to Province House, where, in a stunning act of public insolence, Hancock failed to order the cadets to salute the governor as he passed between their lines to his official residence.

The Town Meeting then acted on Hancock's Massacre Day proposal and invited other colonies to join a "Solemn League and Covenant" to end all business dealings with Britain and stop consumption of British imports after October 1. Paul Revere rode out again to distribute the request to other cities and carry Sam Adams's masterpiece of propaganda warning that the Boston Port Bill, "though made immediately upon us, is doubtless designed for every other colony. . . . Now therefore is the time, when all should be united in opposition to this violation of the liberties of all. . . . It is not the rights of Boston only, but of all America which are now struck at. Not the merchants only but the farmer, and every order of men who inhabit this noble continent."[27]

To the shock of Boston's Patriots, however, Revere's ride produced little unity—or sympathy for Boston's plight. While most New Yorkers and Philadelphians shrugged their shoulders in disinterest, Virginians debated the wording of a resolution to support the innocent people of Boston without condoning the Tea Party or provoking Parliament into closing Virginia's ports. George Washington was as indecisive as his colleagues, believing, on the one hand, that Americans should "never be taxed without their own consent" and that "the cause of Boston . . . [is] the cause of America." On the other hand, he strongly disapproved of the Boston mob's "conduct in destroying the tea" and disavowed all schemes to suspend all trade with Britain, which, he said, would only bankrupt planters and destroy Virginia's economy. He condemned the Bostonians who had destroyed private property and found it only just that they compensate the East India Company for damages.[28] Even the legalized quartering of British troops in taverns and empty buildings seemed reasonable enough to Washington and the rest of Virginia's planter-aristocracy as a necessary evil for maintaining law and order in rebellious Boston. As America's richest, most heavily populated, and largest state geographically, Virginia had much to lose from British taxes, but it had even more to lose from anarchy, with its consequent breakdown of public order and protections for life and property.

Ten days after Gage's arrival, more than one hundred Loyalists signed a farewell to Hutchinson, deploring the losses to the East India Company and pledging "to bear our share of those damages" in exchange for repeal of the Port Bill.[29]

Far from demonstrating any bitterness when he reached London, Hutchinson immediately set to work to repair the torn fabric of his beloved country by effecting a reconciliation between Bostonians and the crown. With supreme confidence, he began his quest at the palace. "The King received me in his closet and conversed near two hours with unusual freedom and confidence," Hutchinson exulted in a letter to his son Thomas back in Boston. "He surprised me that he was so intimately acquainted with the affairs of America." Although Parliament had "gone too far here to recede," he told his son, "there is all the disposition that can be wished, as well in the King . . . as in his ministers to afford the most speedy relief, and to comply with every reasonable request, and to forbear from any acts for taxation, provided the authority of Parliament be not denied or counteracted."[30]

Despite the evident pleasures of visiting the king and other exalted British personages, the Massachusetts governor longed for his native land. "Don't forget the cranberries," he ended his letter to his son, "at least six or eight bushels . . . get the largest and fairest and when they are come to their color and not too ripe." And he signed his letter, "Your affectionate father."[31]

Hutchinson also reported his conversation with the king to General Gage:

> The King asked me how the late acts of Parliament were received at Boston? That the first act was exceedingly severe, I did not presume to say, but it must bring the greatest distress upon the town . . . and that it would make me happy, if any way, consistent with His Majesty's honor, I might be instrumental, whilst I remained in England, in obtaining their relief. The King thereupon expressed his inclination and desire to grant it when they could put it in his power.

"I do assure you," Hutchinson concluded, "the greatest pleasure it gives me is from the prospect it affords of enabling me to serve my poor unhappy country, and in the long conference I had with the King, I made it my chief object to . . . obtain relief for the town of Boston on the easiest terms."[32]

Within a week of Gage's arrival in Boston, the intent of the Port Bill had become clear to all Bostonians, if not to Virginians and the rest of America. The British navy planned to divert all Boston-bound food supplies to Salem, where British troops would limit deliveries into Boston and starve the city into submission. Even a few members of Parliament who had voted for the bill expressed dismay.

"Reflect how you are to govern a people who think they ought to be free, and think they are not," Edmund Burke pleaded in Parliament. "Your scheme yields no revenue; it yields nothing but discontent, disorder, disobedience; and such is the state of America, that after wading up to your eyes in blood, you could only end just where you began; that is, to tax where no revenue is to be found."[33] Thomas Hutchinson agreed, calling the Boston Port Bill "extravagant," and expressing sympathies for the people of Boston, he pledged to continue his "constant endeavors among persons in high places in England to intercede for the purposes of relaxing or mitigating those distresses."[34]

The rest of the House of Commons ignored Burke, however, and went on to pass more acts to club Americans into submission. One of these annulled the Massachusetts Charter and colonial self-government and gave

Bostonians in distress. This cartoon depicts Bostonians suffering the effects of confinement and limited food supplies in Boston following the enactment of Britain's Boston Port Bill banning all ship traffic in Boston Harbor. (LIBRARY OF CONGRESS)

the king or royal governor sole power to appoint or remove colonial executive officers, judges, and law enforcement officers. To silence radicals, Parliament also banned town meetings without the consent of the governor and his approval of every item on the agenda. Virginians who had sanctimoniously approved the initial Coercive Act to punish Boston's Tea Party Patriots now had second thoughts. If Parliament could revoke the Massachusetts Charter, they realized it could revoke the Virginia Charter as well.

When word arrived of the new outbreak of tea parties in America, Parliament reacted with outrage, passing still another Coercive Act—the Quebec Act, which ended self-government in Canada and extended Canadian

Edmund Burke. A member of Parliament, he championed American colonists opposed to the Boston Port Bill, calling it "devilish" to punish thousands of innocent Bostonians for the acts of a few Tea Party Patriots. (LIBRARY OF CONGRESS)

boundaries to the Ohio River. In transferring the territory north of the Ohio River to Canada, the Quebec Act stripped Virginia and many of its wealthiest and most prominent citizens—George Washington, Patrick Henry, the legendary Lee family, and many others—of hundreds of thousands of acres and millions of pounds of investments in lands north of the Ohio River extending to the Great Lakes. Parliament had extended the punishment of Bostonians beyond the borders of Massachusetts to other colonies. The Quebec Act proved a colossal political error that now pushed Britain's largest, wealthiest, and most heavily populated American colony into the Patriot camp for the first time, along with wealthy and influential Pennsylvanians and Marylanders who had also invested in the Ohio Valley. Once fiercely loyal British subjects—most of them devout Anglicans as well—Virginia's planter aristocracy now faced the loss of properties accumulated over generations. With few exceptions, they agreed to pool their wealth and organize tens of thousands of Virginians who depended on them economically into an army to protect their property from the British government.

Facing the loss of his Ohio properties, Patrick Henry raced to the capital in Williamsburg to organize Virginia's collective response, urging the Assembly to support Massachusetts and railing at the king, his ministers, and Parliament for starving the people of Boston. Henry worked gallery spectators into such a frenzy that, according to one witness, "some . . . ran up into the cupola [of the capitol] and doused the royal flag which was there suspended."[35]

Outside the Assembly hall, Henry's words roused people to action. Farmers along the shores of Chesapeake Bay sent a huge supply of grain to Bostonians to ease the shortage created by the Boston Port Bill. The *Virginia Gazette* suggested a ban on horse racing and urged bettors to contribute moneys they would have spent on races to help relieve Boston. In Henry's native Hanover County, farmers and other freeholders rallied around him, declaring,

> We are free men; we have a right to be so. . . . *We will never be taxed but by our own representatives*; this is the great badge of freedom, and British America hath been hitherto distinguished by it. . . . Whether the people there [at Boston] were warranted by justice when they destroyed the tea we know not; but this we know, that the Parliament, by their proceedings, have made us and all North America parties . . . if our sister colony of Massachusetts Bay is enslaved we cannot long remain free. . . . We recommend . . . a hearty union of all our countrymen and sister colonies. UNITED WE STAND, DIVIDED WE FALL.[36]

With Virginia pledged to support Massachusetts Patriots, other colonial committees made plans for an intercolonial congress in Philadelphia in September 1774. In anticipation, the Massachusetts committee drew up another, more sweeping covenant under which delegates would bind their colonies to stop importing British goods and end all business dealings with Britain effective October 1—unless Parliament reopened the port of Boston and repealed the Coercive Acts.

Chapter 13

"We Must Fight!"

*J*n anticipation of the day when the Boston Port Bill would take effect, Patrick Henry, Thomas Jefferson, and other members of Virginia's committee of correspondence "cooked up a resolution . . . appointing the first day of June for a day of fasting, humiliation and prayer to implore heaven to avert the evils of civil war, to inspire us with firmness in support of our rights, and to turn the hearts of the King and Parliament to moderation and justice."[1]

More important than the prayers it generated, Henry's resolution served as a symbol of Virginia's unity with Massachusetts and the other American colonies in their opposition to the Coercive Acts. Without support from the powerful Virginians, the other colonies knew they would be unable to confront, let alone rebuff, the powerful British empire. With Virginia, they could now resist the British with confidence of success.

"The reception of the truly patriotic resolves of the House of Burgesses of Virginia gladdens the hearts of all who are friends to liberty," Samuel Adams exulted to Virginia's Richard Henry Lee. The *New Hampshire Gazette* was even more ecstatic: "Heaven itself seemed to have dictated it to the noble Virginians. O Americans, embrace this plan of union as your life. It will work out your political salvation."[2]

Patriots along the Atlantic Coast now heeded John Hancock's Massacre Day appeal to arm themselves. Town after town formed militias, and all the colonies but Georgia answered Hancock's call to meet at an intercolonial congress in September.

On June 1, Gage closed Boston Harbor to all trade except fuel and imposed virtual martial law on the city. Even ferries to Charlestown and Cambridge ceased operations. The following day Parliament passed still another Coercive Act that permitted quartering British troops in private homes. Somehow, Hancock got word to the captain of his last remaining ship in London to fill the hold with gunpowder to smuggle across the Atlantic to Salem.

On June 7, Gage convened the Massachusetts legislature in Salem, but instead of following Gage's agenda, the representatives barred the doors, pledged unanimous support for Boston, and appointed five delegates to go to Philadelphia to the Continental Congress the following September: Thomas Cushing, James Bowdoin, Robert Treat Paine, and John and Sam Adams—three merchants, a lawyer, and a bankrupt brewer. Hancock turned down the chance to go to Philadelphia, preferring to remain in Boston where, in the absence of Sam Adams and other Patriot leaders, he could consolidate his own power in Massachusetts as moderator of the Town Meeting, Speaker of the House of Representatives, and *de facto* leader of the Sons of Liberty and Tea Party Patriots. It was a brilliant political decision.

When Hancock got home to Beacon Hill, Gage sent him a message dismissing him as Colonel of the Corps of Cadets for failing to command them to salute on the day of the governor's arrival at Province House. To the governor's astonishment, the entire company responded by resigning. "The Governor appeared to be much agitated as the committee came upon him quite sudden and unexpectedly," said a Hancock aide. "Had he known our intention he would have prevented it by disbanding us before we would put it in execution. This we foresaw . . . and I was highly pleased to find that we had out-generaled the general."[3]

Within a few weeks the port closure created food shortages in Boston and sent prices soaring beyond the reach of the poor and unemployed. On June 28, however, a flock of more than two hundred sheep arrived at Boston Neck from Windham, Connecticut, with a letter: "This Town is very sensi-

General Thomas Gage hears the pleas of Boston's boys. The royal governor and commander in chief of British forces in Boston hears the pleas for food and other necessities from a group of boys suffering under the restrictions of the Boston Port Bill. (LIBRARY OF CONGRESS)

ble of the obligations we, and with us, all British America, are under to the Town of Boston who . . . are the generous defenders of our common rights and liberties."[4] On the same day, Groton, Connecticut, sent forty bushels of rye and corn, followed by more than one hundred sheep and some cattle a few weeks later. During the summer, a dozen more Connecticut towns sent similar gifts, and over the months that followed towns and cities throughout the colonies sent hundreds of sheep and thousands of bushels of grain and produce to try to feed the people of Boston. It was not enough, though, and as hunger spread across Boston, a group of mothers sent their boys to plead with General Gage to allow more food into the town.

Although the trade embargo left thousands out of work, Sam Adams formed a Committee of Ways and Means to organize public works and a Committee on Donations to collect money to pay for them. Unemployed men went to work repairing the town's pavements, operating the brickyard, digging a town well, and building a new town wharf. The committee set up looms for weavers to make clothes and a distribution center for wool, flax, cotton, leather, and other materials for producing clothes. Although the town's morale rose, tensions rose higher, with soldiers nervously patrolling every street. Even the sound of church bells signaling a fire sent soldiers running for cover.

Before the Boston delegation could leave for Philadelphia, James Bowdoin fell ill. Although the others pleaded with Hancock to fill his place, Hancock refused, insisting that Boston needed at least one leader at home to command the Sons of Liberty and represent the city at a forthcoming provincial congress. Hancock hosted a farewell dinner for the four remaining delegates, and the following morning they gathered at Cushing's mansion. In full view of British troops, they boarded Cushing's coach and four—its two drivers conspicuously armed—and trotted off on the six-day trip to Philadelphia.

Gage reacted to what he saw as an implicit threat of revolution by sending troops to Cambridge and Charlestown to seize the provincial militia's arms and ammunition. They found none. The Patriots had anticipated his move and rolled the Charlestown cannons to secret hiding places. Fearing attack, Gage began fortifying Boston Neck, the narrow strip of land connecting Boston to the mainland.

"The flames of sedition have spread universally throughout the country, with daily publications of determined resolutions not to obey the late acts of Parliament," Gage wrote to Lord Dartmouth, the king's counselor and secretary of state for colonial affairs. "The country people are exercising in arms in this province. Connecticut and Rhode Island are getting magazines of arms and ammunition . . . and such artillery as they can procure. . . . Sedition flows copiously from the pulpits." Gage reported that scattered mobs were roaming the countryside assaulting suspected Loyalists and that jurors refused to serve in court before the impeached Chief Justice Peter Oliver. In the face of near anarchy, Gage wrote, customs officials at other Massachusetts ports had fled to the safety of Boston, and he said he feared for his personal safety without the protection of his troops.[5]

On September 5, fifty-six delegates from all the colonies except Georgia assembled for the first time in colonial history at a gathering in Carpenter's Hall, Philadelphia, which the press dubbed the Continental Congress. All but seven delegates were or had been members of their own colonial assemblies, and nine were speakers or former speakers. All except Sam Adams ranged from relatively wealthy to incredibly so. There were five northern farmers, seven southern planters, thirty lawyers, and fourteen businessmen, of whom eleven were merchants, one a builder, one a miller, and another a wharf owner. By unanimous vote, they elected president Virginia's Peyton Randolph—a lawyer, owner of a large plantation, and head of the seven-man delegation from America's most powerful colony. With Randolph were three other lawyers, among them Patrick Henry, and three of the colony's largest planters—Benjamin Harrison, Richard Henry Lee, and George Washington. Like northern merchants, wealthy southern planters had been boycotting British imports to try to force repeal of duties. Washington summed up his motive for joining the boycott succinctly: "They have no right to put their hands in my pockets."[6] Washington, of course, had some of the deepest pockets in America, with a huge property of more than twenty thousand acres, including eight thousand acres of tobacco and wheat at Mount Vernon, about three hundred slaves, a fishery, a grist mill, and, until the Quebec Act, title to about one hundred thousand acres of wilderness in western Virginia and the Ohio Country.

As merchants, landowners, and lawyers were posturing in Philadelphia, Boston was preparing for rebellion, with the Loyalist *Boston Evening Post* listing Hancock, Sam Adams, Bowdoin, and Cushing as "authors . . . of all the misfortunes brought upon the province." The newspaper appealed to British troops, asking that "the instant rebellion happens—that you will put the above persons to the sword, destroy their houses, and plunder their effects. It is just that they should be the first victims to the evils they brought upon us."[7]

On September 20, Hancock's ship arrived safely in Salem Port with the shipload of gunpowder from London. With Patriot ammunition at the ready, Hancock ordered carpenters, who were building barracks for new contingents of British troops, to walk off their jobs. Gage demanded that Hancock order the men back to work. Hancock responded angrily that food shortages had made the men too hungry to work and that Gage was responsible for having "taken every possible measure to distress us."[8] Gage agreed to allow foodstuffs shipped to and from points within the harbor if the men went back to work, but Hancock refused, suspecting that Gage would close the harbor once the barracks were finished. Gage had to send to Halifax for carpenters to complete work on the barracks.

Three weeks later 250 self-appointed or nominally elected delegates from across Massachusetts met in Concord at the First Provincial Congress and staged a coup d'état, overthrowing royal rule and creating America's first independent government. It assumed all powers to rule the province, collect taxes, buy supplies, and raise a militia. It elected Hancock president, with far-reaching powers across the province—the first governor of the first independent state in the Americas. He immediately sent Paul Revere to the Continental Congress in Philadelphia with news of Massachusetts independence and the creation of the continent's first autonomous government.

After three days at Concord, the Provincial Congress moved to Cambridge, and after a few days there it moved again, continually changing locations every few days to prevent Gage from interfering in its deliberations. After two months, it agreed on a broad program of military preparedness. It authorized the Committee of Safety to organize a corps of "minute men" to "hold themselves in readiness [for battle] on the shortest notice." It agreed to provide each militiaman with "an effective fire arm, bayonet, pouch, knapsack, thirty rounds of cartridges and balls."[9] The Provincial Congress also ordered immediate procurement of twenty pieces of field artillery, carriages for twelve battering cannons, four mortars, twenty tons of grape and round shot, ten tons of bombshells, five tons of lead balls, one thousand barrels of powder, five thousand arms and bayonets, and seventy-five thousand flints. Total costs came to almost £21,000. To raise the money, Hancock ordered provincial tax collectors to turn over their receipts to a congressional receiver-general instead of the royal provincial treasurer. Those tax collectors who did not flee to British camps willingly complied with Hancock's order rather than risk Patriot tar and feathers, but the taxes they collected fell far short of the costs of arming the militia. Whenever he had to, Hancock solicited whatever resources he could from other merchants and used his own money to cover the difference.

Just as the Provincial Congress had achieved unity on military issues, a bitter debate broke out over a motion that "while we are attempting to preserve ourselves from slavery, that we also take into consideration the state and circumstances of Negro slaves in this province."[10] The motion was a response to a circular letter from Massachusetts slaves: "The efforts made by the legislature of this province in their last sessions to free themselves from slavery, . . . [we] cannot but expect your house will . . . take our deplorable case into serious consideration, and give us that ample relief, which, as men, we have a natural right to."[11] It was signed by Peter Bestes, Sambo Freeman, Felix Holbrook, and Chester Joie, all of them slaves.

The irony of Patriot slave owners protesting duties as a form of enslavement had undermined support of liberal thinkers in England and America for the colonist cause. Boston merchant Theophilus Lillie protested that "people who contend so much for civil and religious liberty should be so ready to deprive others of their natural liberty."[12] In London, Samuel Johnson expressed outrage at the Boston atrocities, asking, "How is it that we hear the loudest yelps for liberty among the drivers of Negroes?"[13]

The First Provincial Congress of Massachusetts rejected outright the motion to consider the slave issue.

In mid-October the Continental Congress in Philadelphia declared as unconstitutional thirteen parliamentary acts dating back to 1763. Calling the Coercive Acts cruel and unjust, it passed ten resolutions defining colonist rights, including individual rights to "life, liberty and property" and exclusive jurisdiction of elected provincial assemblies over taxation and internal legislation. The provinces pledged to stop importing British goods, to end the slave trade, to end consumption of British products and foreign luxury products, and to end all exports to Britain, Ireland, and the British West Indies. Congress also established the first "union" of sorts of the American colonies by forming the Continental Association. With establishment of that association, John Adams later argued, "the revolution was complete, in the minds of the people, and the union of the colonies, before the war commenced."[14]

After forming the Continental Association, Congress issued a proclamation to the king and the British and American peoples, reasserting the rights of colonists to govern themselves. Delegates agreed to reconvene on May 10, 1775, if Britain did not redress American grievances before then. In effect, the Congress rejected all authority of the British Parliament and declared the provinces independent, with only the British king retaining sovereignty in America.

When Samuel Adams and the other Massachusetts delegates returned from the Continental Congress to Boston, they found that in their absence, John Hancock had gathered the reins of power over the new Patriot government firmly in his hands—especially the powerful Committee of Safety. The Provincial Congress was still scurrying from town to town, with Gage unable to act against it without scattering his troops across the face of eastern Massachusetts and diluting his strength in Boston. At the beginning of November Hancock usurped the royal governor's prerogative of issuing the annual Thanksgiving Day proclamation in Massachusetts. He omitted the king's name from the document for the first time in colonial history. Two weeks later Hancock and the Provincial Congress called for twelve thousand volunteer Minutemen. Before it adjourned in December, the Provincial Congress elected Hancock to replace Bowdoin as delegate to the Second Continental Congress to be held the following May. Sensing the historic import of the Second Congress, Hancock accepted, adjourned the Provincial Congress until February 1, 1775, and returned to Boston.

Loyalist colonists and British soldiers were pouring into Boston from outlying areas, where armed Patriots had put Redcoats in fear for their lives. In Boston it was Loyalists' and soldiers' turn to bully Patriots who stood in their way, and Hancock's political prominence combined with his wealth put him in great personal danger. Rumors circulated that British troops were about to arrest, try, and hang Hancock and Adams. Other rumors insisted that British officers planned to assassinate Hancock, Adams, and Warren, but an officer vigorously denied the charges: "It would, indeed, have been a pity for them [Hancock and the others] to make their exit in that way, as I hope we shall have the pleasure of seeing them do it by the hands of the hangman."[15]

In London Governor Hutchinson pleaded with Lord Dartmouth to reverse the arrest orders for Hancock and Adams. "Lord Dartmouth . . . spake with great emotion that he was not the one that thirsted for blood," Hutchinson noted in his diary, "but he could not help saying that he wished to see Hancock and Adams brought to the punishment they deserved, and he feared peace would not be restored until some examples were made which would deter others."[16]

On February 27, 1775, Lord North succumbed to the arguments and pleas of Thomas Hutchinson to seek reconciliation with the American colonies. As Hutchinson had urged, North offered to recognize the Continental Congress and pledge that Parliament would no longer impose any taxes on the colonies other than customs duties without the consent of the provincial assemblies. In return, he asked that the Continental Congress recognize Parliament's "supreme legislative authority and superintending power." As petitions from merchants in London, Bristol, Birmingham, Liverpool, Manchester, and almost every other trading city demanded restoration of normal commercial relations with the colonies, the House of Commons agreed to adopt the principles of Lord North's reconciliation scheme by pledging to "forbear" laying taxes on any colony whose assembly agreed to tax itself to pay the costs of defense and support the civil government and judiciary within the province.

The king, however, would have none of it and demanded that the troops crush the rebellion in Massachusetts before England made any concessions. Lord Dartmouth, still Britain's secretary of state for colonial affairs, responded with blanket orders to royal governors and commanding generals in America to use whatever means necessary to enforce the Coercive Acts in Massachusetts and "arrest the principal actors and abettors."[17] Edmund Burke pleaded with his colleagues in Parliament to reconsider. "The use of force alone is but temporary," he protested. "It may subdue for a moment; but it does not remove the necessity of subduing again, and a nation is not governed which is perpetually being conquered."[18]

Parliament relented only slightly after Burke's speech by offering a blanket pardon to repentant rebels—with the exception of such "principal gentlemen who . . . are to be brought over to England . . . for an inquiry . . . into their conduct." Among them were George Washington, Patrick Henry, John Hancock, Samuel Adams, John Adams, and others. Then, in an all-but-inexplicable show of churlishness, the House of Commons not only declared Massachusetts in a state of rebellion, it proceeded to bar New England fishermen from the North Atlantic fisheries and forbid New England colonies from trading with any nation but Britain and the British West Indies. Nor was that enough. Two weeks later Parliament extended the trade restrictions to include New Jersey, Pennsylvania, Maryland, Virginia, and South Carolina.

With Dartmouth's blanket arrest orders, Thomas Hutchinson knew he had lost his quest to bridge the divisions among his countrymen. "You are contending for a phantom," he wrote to an old friend in Boston—possibly Thomas Cushing, the merchant who had remained the most moderate of Boston's Tea Party Patriots. "You say you are British subjects," he pleaded, "and you suppose you are constitutionally exempt from one of the obligations which British subjects are under. But if you are exempt from the one, you are exempt from all—and so, are not British subjects."

In writing to his friend, Hutchinson was wrestling with an important question, trying to analyze a problem that faced thousands of the most thoughtful American and British political and religious leaders and thinkers: When does disagreement over the principles of a government or religion cross the line between legitimate, beneficial reform and illegitimate subversion that infringes on the rights of other participants in that government or system. "Whilst you continue to deny the authority which made the laws," Hutchinson posited, "with what face can anybody apply for relief from them, either in whole or in part?

> If Parliament had no authority to make them, they are of no more force now than they will be after they are repealed. If you apply for an alteration in part only, it implies an acknowledgment of the authority of what remains, and consequently to the whole. Wherever I turn my thoughts to your relief, I find myself involved in absurdities so long as the denial of this authority is admitted. Cease to deny it, and the path is plain and easy.[19]

Despite his pessimism, Hutchinson promised to persevere in his efforts to seek reconciliation. "The prospect is so gloomy," he admitted, "that I am sometimes tempted to endeavor to forget that I am an American, and to turn my views to a provision for what remains of life in England. But the passion for my native country returns, and I will determine nothing until your case is absolutely desperate."[20]

When news of Parliament's trade embargo reached Virginia, the state assembly moved the capital inland to Richmond from Williamsburg, where

Patrick Henry. He called Americans to rebellion against British rule in his famous "liberty-or-death" speech in St. John's Church, Richmond, Virginia, on March 20, 1775. (LIBRARY OF CONGRESS)

a build-up of British naval strength in nearby waters raised the menace of the royal governor arresting Washington, Henry, and other Virginia political leaders. A town of only 600 residents and 150 homes, Richmond had no assembly hall as such. The largest seating area was in St. John's Anglican Church on Richmond Hill, with space in its pews for about 120 people.

On March 20, 1775, the delegates sidled into the pews—Washington, Jefferson, Richard Henry Lee, and other renowned Virginians. Henry took a seat in the third pew on the gospel, or left, side of the church facing the front. After the call to order, he stood to propose three resolutions. The first two echoed similar resolutions of the Maryland assembly: "That a well regulated militia, composed of gentlemen and yeomen, is the natural strength and only security of a free government; that such a militia . . . would forever render it unnecessary for the mother country to keep among us, for the purpose of our defense, any standing army of mercenary soldiers . . . and would obviate the pretext of taxing us for their support."[21]

Henry's third resolution, however, broke new ground, proposing, "That this colony be immediately put into a state of defense, and . . . prepare a plan for embodying, arming, and disciplining such a number of men, as may be sufficient for that purpose."[22] Spectators gasped—then began applauding as they realized Henry had called for armed rebellion. Richard Henry Lee seconded Henry, and in the debate that followed, many delegates insisted that Lord North's reconciliation plan had put peace within reach and that Henry's resolutions were premature. When debate ended, Henry rose again to speak, with what a clergyman at the scene called "an unearthly fire burning in his eye."

"Mr. President," Henry began, "it is natural to man to indulge in the illusions of hope.

> We are apt to shut our eyes against a painful truth—and listen to the song of that siren, till she transforms us into beasts. Is this the part of wise men engaged in a great and arduous struggle for liberty? . . . Let us not, I beseech you, sir, deceive ourselves longer . . . We have petitioned—we have remonstrated—we have supplicated—we have prostrated ourselves before the throne . . . we have been spurned, with contempt from the foot of the throne. There is no longer any room for hope. If we wish to be free . . . we must fight! I repeat it, sir: We must fight![23]

Henry paused, staring heavenward at the roof beams of the church, as if in prayer, as the tension in the audience increased.

> Gentlemen may cry peace, but there is no peace. . . . The war is actually begun! The next gale from the north will bring to our ears the clash of resounding arms! Our brethren are already in the field! Why stand we here idle? What is it the gentlemen wish? What would they have? Is life so dear, or peace so sweet, as to be purchased at the price of chains and slavery?

He raised his arms toward heaven. "Forbid it, Almighty God!" he cried out. "I know not what course others may take, but as for me, Give me liberty! Or give me death."[24]

After delegates had caught their collective breaths, the convention passed Henry's resolutions and appointed a committee to prepare a plan for "embodying, arming, and disciplining" the Virginia militia. Within weeks, men and boys in every county across the state had sewn the words "Liberty or death" on their shirt fronts and rode to their county courthouses to volunteer in local militias to fight the British.

In Boston, meanwhile, British troops, chafing under the constant, months-long barrage of epithets and missiles, seemed to snap. With no evident provocation, they seized a Patriot farmer at random in the marketplace and tarred and feathered him. Then, as the regimental band followed, its pipes and flutes squealing, the troops paraded their victim through town in a tumbrel while singing a tune that was new to Boston:

> *Yankee Doodle came to town*
> *For to buy a firelock;*
> *We will tar and feather him,*
> *And so we will John Hancock.*[25]

A second mob of troops then stomped across the Common to Beacon Hill, where they vandalized the fences and gardens of Patriot merchants.

"Colonel Hancock's elegant home . . . was attacked by a group of officers who, with their swords, cut and hacked the fence before his house in a most scandalous manner," merchant John Andrews wrote to his brother-in-law. Two days later "four sergeants and as many men were sent to insult John Hancock under pretense of seeing if his stables would do for barracks." Andrews said that when Hancock protested, the soldiers sneered and taunted the merchant, saying "his house, stables, etc., would soon be theirs, and then they would do as they pleased." Hancock raged at General Gage, who, rather than ignite an incendiary situation, sent "one of his aides-de-camp to the officer of the guard at the bottom of the Common to seize any officer or private who should molest Colonel Hancock or any inhabitant in their lawful calling." Gage issued an abject apology and promised to "redress him . . . if he was in any ways insulted again,"[26] but Hancock now recognized that he and his family were in great danger.

As Patrick Henry delivered his incendiary speech in Richmond, John Hancock left Boston for Concord, twenty miles away, where the Provincial Congress reconvened out of reach of Gage's forces. Hancock's Committee of Safety began purchasing medicines, canteens, "and all kinds of stores, sufficient for an army of fifteen thousand to take the field."[27] Some delegates worried that they had given Hancock and his committee too many war-making powers. They voted to restrict his authority to call out the militia until "the Army under command of General Gage, or any part thereof to the number of five hundred, shall march out of the town of Boston, with artillery and baggage."[28]

With Hancock's duties as Committee of Safety chairman requiring increasing amounts of his time, he yielded the presidency of the Provincial Congress to his friend Dr. Joseph Warren while he, Hancock, rode back to Boston to see to the arming of the proposed Massachusetts army. Recognizing the new army's need for artillery, he ordered men from the Sons of Liberty to recover the provincial militia's four mounted cannons then in the hands of British troops. Two each stood in the New and Old Gun Houses by a school at the bottom of the Common. While the sergeant usually on guard was at roll call, Patriots entered a side door of the Old Gun House, removed the barrels from their carriages and hid them in a large chest in the school next door. British soldiers who searched the school ignored the chest, on which the schoolmaster was posed, calmly resting his lame foot while listening to students recite their lessons. As the soldiers searched the school in vain, the patriots stole the two other cannons in the New Gun House and acquired the first artillery of what would grow into the American army. They immediately named the first two cannons "Hancock" and "Adams."[29]

On April 2, Hancock returned to the Provincial Congress at Concord, but recognizing the dangers of leaving his family in Boston, he arranged for his aunt and his fiancée and her father to flee to the manse in Lexington that had been his boyhood home and where he promised to join them. "I am not at liberty to say what I know," he wrote them, "but pray . . . remove immediately from Boston. . . . But pray do not make my name known abroad as to this advice. . . . Things will very soon be serious."[30]

Hancock's relatives and friends joined a growing stream of other panic-stricken families who fled Boston fearing an imminent outbreak of hostilities between the Minutemen and British troops. As they crossed Boston Neck to what they hoped was safer ground, they left behind a residue of scavengers—some of them members of Boston street mobs, others British soldiers—who plundered vacant homes and stripped them of their treasures. Although looters approached Hancock House, Redcoats now stood guard outside the palatial residency, waiting for British General Thomas Gage to take possession.

Hancock and his family did not reach Lexington a moment too soon. A week later, on April 14, General Gage received the official documents from the king "to arrest the principal actors and abettors in the Provincial Congress,"[31] and with additional troops on their way, Gage made plans to turn the trade war into an armed conflict.

Gage had planted enough spies within the various Patriot groups to learn that the Patriots had hidden their arsenal at Concord, that Hancock had fled to Lexington, and that Sam Adams had joined him. Gage ordered a two-stage assault, with the main force to march to Concord to destroy the Patriot arsenal while a detachment stopped in Lexington to capture the traitors Hancock and Adams. But the Patriots had spies of their own, along with so-called vigilance committees in almost every hamlet. In Boston, Dr. Joseph Warren had organized a spy network of thirty crafts-men such as Revere, whom the British troops allowed to move about the town freely with their apprentices, plying essential trades—and gathering intelligence on British troop movements. They learned that someone in the Patriot camp had alerted Gage to the secret arsenal at Concord and the whereabouts of Hancock and Sam Adams.

"We frequently took turns, two and two, to watch the soldiers patrolling the streets all night," Revere wrote. "The boats belonging to the transports were all launched and carried under the sterns of the men-of-war. . . . On Tuesday evening . . . a number of soldiers were marching

*Major General Dr. Joseph Warren. A renowned physician, he
became speaker of the Massachusetts House of Representatives
and, as a major general in the Massachusetts militia, fought
and died on Bunker's Hill.* (NATIONAL PORTRAIT GALLERY,
SMITHSONIAN INSTITUTION)

towards the bottom of the Common. About 10 o'clock, Dr Warren sent in
great haste for me and begged that I would immediately set off for Lexington, where Messrs. Hancock and Adams were, and acquaint them of the
movements and that it was thought they were the objects."[32]

Gage dispatched small bands of soldiers to intercept Patriot spies on the
Lexington and Concord road, but there were too few soldiers and too many

Patriots. Warren sent two of them—Revere and William Dawes—by different routes to warn Hancock and Adams. Revere set off on his famous midnight ride on Tuesday, April 18. Two friends rowed him across the Charles River to Charlestown, where he picked up a horse and rode toward Lexington, stopping at Medford to awaken the captain of the Minutemen. "I alarmed almost every house till I got to Lexington. I found Messrs. Hancock and Adams at the Reverend Mr. Clarke's. I told them my errand and inquired for Mr. Dawes. They said he had not been there. . . . After about half an hour Mr. Dawes came. We refreshed ourselves and set off for Concord to secure the stores."[33]

Revere gave Hancock and Adams a letter from Warren "stating that a large body of British troops . . . were on their march to Lexington."[34]

"Mr. Hancock gave the alarm immediately," said Dorothy Quincy, then Hancock's fiancée and later his wife.

> The Lexington bell was rung all night, and before light about 150 men were collected. Mr. H. was all night cleaning his gun and sword and putting his accouterments in order, and was determined to go out to the plain by the meetinghouse . . . to fight with the men . . . and it was with very great difficulty that he was dissuaded from it by Mr. Clarke and Mr. Adams, the latter clapping him on the shoulder, said to him, "that is not our business; we belong to the cabinet." It was not till break of day that Mr. H. could be persuaded that it was improper for him to expose himself against such a powerful force . . . that the enemy would indeed triumph if they could get him and Mr. Adams in their power.[35]

Revere and Dawes, meanwhile, rode off to warn Concord, joined by Dr. Samuel Prescott. On the way, a British patrol surprised them, but Prescott escaped and got through to Concord. The troops captured Revere, brought him back to Lexington, and released him.

The following day after nightfall, a force of seven hundred Redcoats began their march to Concord with orders "to seize and destroy . . . military stores." Gage ordered the commander to "take care that the soldiers do not plunder the inhabitants, or hurt private property."[36] He sent "a small party

Paul Revere. The Boston silversmith who warned John Hancock and Samuel Adams of the approach of British troops with arrest warrants, he carried news of the British attack at Concord and Lexington—and the success of the Minutemen—to the Continental Congress in Philadelphia. (LIBRARY OF CONGRESS)

on horseback" to ride ahead "to stop all advice of your march getting to Concord before you," but, of course, Revere, Dawes, and Prescott had already alerted the entire countryside.

After much discussion, Hancock and Adams rode away to safety at dawn, leaving Hancock's aunt and fiancée behind in the manse to face the British. In fact, they were far safer in the parsonage with the minister's family than they would have been with the fugitives. Except for a British shot that whizzed by her head as she watched the action on the green, Hancock's aunt was unharmed, as was his fiancée, who later helped care for two wounded Minutemen.

Years later, Elizabeth Clarke, the minister's daughter, described the scene:

Oh! I now can see from this window . . . in my mind just as plain—all the British troops marching off the common . . . how [Hancock's] aunt was crying and wringing her hands and helping mother dress the children. Dolly going round with father to hide money, watches, and anything down in the potatoes and up garret . . . and in the afternoon, father, mother, with me and the baby, went to the meeting-house. There was the eight men that was killed . . . all in boxes made of four large boards nailed up, and, after Pa had prayed, they were put into two horse carts and took into the graveyard.[37]

The following day, Patriot messengers galloped off in all directions with copies of a dispatch from the Massachusetts Committee of Safety:

Watertown, Wednesday Morning near 10 o'clock

To all the friends of American liberty. Be it known that the morning before break of day a brigade consisting of about 1000 or 1200 men landed at Phillips' Farm at Cambridge and marched to Lexington, where they found a company of our colony militia in arms, upon which they fired without any provocation and killed 6 men and wounded 4 others; by an express from Boston this moment we find another brigade are now upon the march from Boston, supposed to be about 1000.[38]

The revolutionary teapot had finally come to a boil—and turned into a tempest that would engulf the North American continent.

Chapter 14

Savage Barbarities and
Diabolical Cruelties

$\mathscr{H}$ancock's lightweight phaeton had just raced off the Lexington-Concord road when he and Samuel Adams heard the shots behind them in Lexington. They did not last long. As the British had approached Lexington, militia Captain John Parker positioned the Minutemen in two lines on the green, one behind the other. They ranged in age from sixteen to sixty-five—almost half the town's population—and included eight pairs of fathers and sons who stood together, side by side, to face the dreaded Redcoats.

Major John Pitcairn led the advance guard of some seven hundred troops of the crack British field artillery into town, convinced that "one active campaign, a smart action, and burning two or three of their towns, will set everything to rights."[1] Pitcairn ordered the Patriots to lay down their arms and surrender, but Parker ordered them to hold their ground. When Pitcairn saw some Minutemen break ranks and run to cover behind nearby stone walls, he commanded his men to move against the Minutemen. Amidst the confusion and shouting that followed, someone fired the "shot heard 'round the world."[2] No two accounts agree on the details of the engagement, and like so many events leading up to the Revolutionary War, the number who claimed to have witnessed the exchange at Lexington green far exceeded the actual number of people at the scene. Although the Massachusetts Provincial Congress heard many testimonials, only a handful of British accounts remain, including this written report by Pitcairn to General Gage:

> I gave directions to the troops to move forward, but on no account to fire, or even attempt it without orders; when I arrived at the end of the village, I observed drawn upon a green near 200 of the rebels; and when I came within about one hundred yards of them, they began to file off toward some stone walls on our right flank—the light infantry observing this, ran after them. I instantly called to the soldiers not to fire, but to surround and disarm them, and after several repetitions of those positive orders to the men not to fire etc., some of the rebels who had jumped over the wall, fired four or five shots at the soldiers, which wounded a man of the Tenth, and my horse was wounded in two places from some quarter or other and at the same time several shots were fired from a meeting house on our left—upon this, without any order or regularity, the light infantry began a scattered fire and continued in that situation for some little time, contrary to the repeated orders of both me and the officers that were present.
>
> Your most obedient humble servant,
> John Pitcairn[3]

When the firing ceased, eight Minutemen, including Parker, lay dead and ten lay wounded. Although Parker suffered only a musketball wound in the initial skirmish, a British soldier subsequently ran him through with a bayonet. The Minutemen wounded only one British soldier and Pitcairn's horse, but they ignited a revolution that would send the world's greatest empire into irreversible decline.

As the smoke of gunshot drifted across the silent wood, the British troops marched off to Concord, and Dr. Benjamin Church, the Whig leader, tended the wounded but ran out of medical supplies and rode off to Boston to find more.

While the British force searched in vain for Patriot arms at Concord, Minutemen attacked a platoon the British had posted to guard Concord's North Bridge. Realizing the Patriots had removed most of the arsenal, the

British commander ordered his men to return to Lexington. On the way, they met a growing rain of sniper fire. Minuteman ranks had swelled into the thousands. Musket barrels materialized behind every tree, every boulder, every stone wall. Facing annihilation unless they returned to Boston, they abandoned plans to search for Hancock and Adams and stepped up their pace to double time. Although General Lord Hugh Percy met Pitcairn's men in Lexington and added 1,000 more troops to the British contingent, the Minuteman force had grown to 4,000. They came from every direction, with town after town—Watertown, Roxbury, Needham, Danvers, and others—each sending one hundred, two hundred, or whatever number it could muster to join their fellow countrymen. Had there been a supreme commander to organize the growing force and plan the attack, the colonists would have wiped out the British force. Their relentless, albeit uncoordinated, assault nevertheless left 73 British soldiers dead, 174 wounded, and 26 missing before the expedition reached cover at Charlestown and boarded boats to Boston across the bay. The Patriots suffered 49 killed, 42 wounded, and 5 missing. The humiliated British troops had wreaked revenge in every town, looting and burning houses, bayoneting anyone who stood in their way, civilian or military. But in the end, a disorganized group of untrained, ill-equipped farmers had defeated crack troops from the world's most powerful, best trained, best equipped, professional army, leaving Boston's Patriots—and, indeed, the rest of America's Patriots—confident they could win the war against Britain and end Parliament's rule over America.

Before the British debacle on the retreat from Concord, Lord Percy had scoffed at colonists as "cowards—frightened out of their wits . . . whenever we appear." After the retreat from Lexington, he conceded,

> Whosoever looks upon them as an irregular mob, will find himself much mistaken. They have men amongst them who know very well what they are about, having been employed as rangers against the Indians and Canadians, and this country being much covered with wood and hill, is very advantageous for their method of fighting. . . . For my part, I never believed, I confess, that they would have attacked the King's troops, or have the perseverance I found in them yesterday.[4]

The Patriot propaganda machine that Sam Adams had built sent riders like Revere with word of victory throughout the colonies, along with reports of alleged British atrocities. Besides accusing the British of setting fire to homes, shops, and barns in Lexington, the Patriot dispatches claimed the British had "pillaged almost every house they passed by, breaking and destroying doors, windows, glasses, etc. and carrying off clothing and other valuable effects. It appeared to be their design to burn and destroy all before them. . . . But the savage barbarity exercised upon the bodies of our brethren who fell, is almost incredible; not contented with shooting down the unarmed, aged and infirm, they disregarded the cries of the wounded, killing them without mercy; and mangling their bodies in the most shocking manner."[5] The propaganda had its desired effect, inflaming passions across the colonies and provoking at first hundreds then thousands of colonists from farms and villages and cities to gather their arms and set off to Boston to rally to the side of the Minutemen.

The British countered with reports that Patriot soldiers had "scalped and otherwise ill-treated one or two of the men who were either killed or wounded." One report claimed that "the Rebels . . . scalped and cut off the ears of some of the wounded men who fell into their hands." And the sister of a Boston customs officer wrote a friend in England that British soldiers had "found two or three of their people lying in the agonies of death, scalped and their noses and ears cut off and eyes bored out."[6] As for who fired first, both sides tried to sway public opinion in England and America, with each side gathering as many depositions as possible to support its claim that the other side fired first.

As the Redcoats had marched into Lexington, Hancock and Adams had taken refuge at Woburn, less than five miles northeast of Lexington, off the Concord road. They left for Worcester, Massachusetts, the next morning to rendezvous with John Adams, Thomas Cushing, and Robert Treat Paine to begin the journey to Philadelphia together. Sam Adams, however, was not dressed to attend an intercolonial congress. His clothes—always the coarse cloth of workingmen—were soiled and torn. Despite Adams's angry protests, Hancock bought him a new suit, wig, shoes, and silk hose and gave him some pocket money.

Cushing and Paine arrived the next day with a military escort and breathless reports of seventy thousand Minutemen on the march to lay siege to Boston. Volunteers by the thousands were pouring into Cambridge from everywhere in New England. In addition, Connecticut's Benedict Arnold was raising a force in western Massachusetts to try to capture the huge cache of British artillery and military supplies at Fort Ticonderoga on Lake Champlain. Although Patriot leader Dr. Benjamin Church had been captured in Boston, General Gage issued a proclamation permitting inhabitants, including Church, to evacuate the city with all their belongings, except weapons. In an uncharacteristically generous move that puzzled Patriot leaders, Gage released Church with a wagon load of medical supplies and allowed him to return to Lexington to tend the wounded Minutemen.

On April 28, Hancock, Sam Adams, Cushing, and Paine set off for Philadelphia. John Adams caught up with them in Hartford, Connecticut, where, on April 29, they met with Governor Jonathan Trumbull, another Harvard graduate and former merchant—and the only royal governor in America to go over to the Patriot side. After the British defeat at Concord and the retreat to Boston, civil government in other colonies had disintegrated, with every royal governor except Trumbull fleeing to the safety of the nearest British military enclave.

After an overnight rest in Hartford, Hancock and the others resumed their journey along the dusty, rutted road to New York, where thousands turned out to cheer. As the city's church bells pealed, a marching band and hundreds of mounted militiamen and infantrymen awaited Hancock's carriage to lead him in triumph through the city to Wall Street. New York merchants hosted a dinner at Fraunces' Tavern at the southern tip of Manhattan Island overlooking New York Bay. Both the Adamses agreed it was the most elegant dinner either had ever seen.

The following morning, New York delegates joined those from Massachusetts and Connecticut at the North River Ferry to begin the trip to Philadelphia. Huge military and civilian groups hailed them on both sides of the river and at every city, town, and crossing—at Newark, Elizabethtown, Woodbridge, New Brunswick, Trenton, Princeton. . . . To ensure the safety of the procession, each town's militia turned over escort duties to the succeeding town.

On the morning of May 10, the huge procession reached Philadelphia, led by an escort of two to three hundred mounted militiamen with swords drawn. Philadelphia was larger than Boston, with a population of about twenty-five thousand squeezed into an area twenty-five blocks long but only twelve blocks wide. Squalid slums covered the western part of the city, but the area around the State House boasted wide, tree-lined streets with brick walkways lit by whale-oil lamps. Again, church bells pealed and crowds roared—somewhat to the envy of delegates from other colonies who were waiting impatiently for the Second Continental Congress to convene. But even they agreed that Hancock, more than anyone else there, had made enormous sacrifices for the Patriot cause and deserved public acclaim. He had lost his sloop *Liberty*, spent at least £100,000 of his own money on arms and ammunition, and risked the rest of his fortune on the success of the revolution. If arrested on the king's warrant, he faced trial on charges of treason, with the possible loss of both his honor and his life. Even as Hancock arrived in Philadelphia, British General Henry Clinton, who had come to assist General Gage, had comfortably settled into Hancock House on Beacon Hill and was drinking his fill of fine Madeira wine from Hancock's prized cellar.

The raucous procession for Hancock and the New Englanders notwithstanding, the Second Continental Congress convened as scheduled on May 10 at the Pennsylvania State House. Hancock was one of several important new faces—another being the venerable Benjamin Franklin. Although not a new face, forty-three-year-old George Washington drew admiring stares from all the delegates. He looked superb, conspicuously dressed in the commander's striking blue-and-buff uniform of the Independent Regiment of Fairfax, Virginia—the only delegate who had come dressed for war.

From the beginning, Congress had little opportunity for quiet reflection. Outside the State House windows, twenty-eight Philadelphia infantry companies drilled twice a day to the incessant squeal of fifes and the roll of drums. Inside, regional antagonisms delayed some of the most basic organizational proceedings. The southern provinces had longstanding disputes with New England colonies over territorial claims in the West. Moreover, the South, which had no intention of arming its slave majority, had far smaller militias than the North, and some southern delegates feared that the huge Massachusetts militia might take advantage of a colonist victory over Britain to replace British rule in America with rule by New England.

Although delegates reelected Virginia's Peyton Randolph as president, North-South frictions surfaced when Randolph resigned abruptly and returned home after only two weeks. In the debate over a possible replacement, northern delegates grew as annoyed by Virginia's preponderant influence in Congress as southern delegates were by Massachusetts influence in military affairs. John Adams and George Washington, however, stepped forward with a solution.

They had developed one of the few truly collegial relationships that crossed the North-South barrier. Physically, they were an incongruous pair. Washington was the most visible delegate. At six feet, four inches, he towered over most of the others. Although forty-three, he was fit and strong. In contrast, the forty-year-old Adams was one of the least imposing delegates. As his wife conceded, he was "short, thick and fat."[7] Although some delegates considered Washington aloof and unfriendly, Adams found "something charming . . . in [his] conduct," and he admired Washington's willingness to risk his enormous fortune by supporting the rebellion.[8]

As northerners accused southerners of slighting them in the presidential selection process, Adams and his new friend Washington acted to ease tensions and convinced Benjamin Harrison, another Virginia planter, to support them. Without Georgia, Congress was evenly divided between north and south, with the North consisting of New York, New Jersey, and the four New England colonies, whereas the South encompassed all the other colonies—and Pennsylvania.

With the support of Washington, Harrison, and the other Virginians, John Adams nominated John Hancock for the presidency—not just because of his personal sacrifices but, as Adams accurately stated, because of his years of experience as a moderator—at Boston town meetings, in the Massachusetts House of Representatives, and, most recently, at the Massachusetts Provincial Congress. In all three, he had often reconciled Loyalists, moderates, and radicals—even rural interests with urban interests. At the urging of Virginians, other southern delegates joined the rest of Congress in electing John Hancock unanimously. Amidst "general acclamation," the southerner Benjamin Harrison led the northerner Hancock to the chair and proclaimed, "We will show Great Britain how much we value her proscriptions."[9]

In addition to North-South divisions, Hancock faced a second, three-way political divide in Congress between radicals, moderates, and conservatives, whose membership had little to do with geography. Congressional radicals led by Sam Adams demanded nothing less than a declaration of independence from Britain. Philadelphia's John Dickinson, whose "Farmer's Letters" had brought him international renown, led the conservatives, with Boston's Thomas Cushing abandoning Sam Adams and supporting Dickinson. Dickinson, Cushing, and other conservatives sought nothing more than a redress of grievances and a return to the normalcy of pre–Stamp Act days. They found an effective voice to enunciate their amorphous goals in a new delegate who arrived late and took his seat just as Hancock took over the presidency of Congress: thirty-two-year-old Virginia legislator Thomas Jefferson. Jefferson had written a widely circulated essay "A Summary View of the Rights of British America," which accepted the king's sovereignty in America but insisted that provincial legislatures held all legislative authority, including authority over taxation, and that "British parliament has no right to exercise authority over us."

As moderator, Hancock had to remain impartial—and did. Although his neutral stance incurred the growing enmity of Sam Adams, he won the respect of all other delegates. No longer the fiery Tea Party Patriot of Massacre Day, he metamorphosed into the perfect president, with some appeal to all factions and favoritism for none. He understood everyone's point of view. His experience as moderator and legislator appealed to moderates; his wealth, business position, and education appealed to conservatives; and his defiance of British authority in Boston appealed to radicals. And what appealed to all was his vast experience directing a large organization, namely the House of Hancock.

His broad appeal cannot be overstated for a body made up not of *united states*, but of twelve separate and independent colonies with no ties to each other. Indeed, they had seldom communicated with each other until Adams and Henry established the network of committees of corres-

Thomas Jefferson. A Virginia delegate to the second session of the Continental Congress, he was a principal author of the Declaration of Independence.
(LIBRARY OF CONGRESS)

pondence a year earlier, and few had ever met face to face as a group until six months earlier at the First Continental Congress. Although all were powerful leaders in their individual states, all were equals in Congress, with each state delegation, no matter how large, able to cast but one vote.

For the first month Hancock tried to pick men from these disparate delegations to work together in committees and to keep the larger body intact, focused and moving forward in pursuit of a common agenda. Along the way, he had to prevent defections, soothe injured feelings, and calm any anger over perceived slights or oversights.

"Such a vast multitude of objects, civil, political, commercial and military, press and crowd upon us so fast that we know not what to do first," said John Adams about the opening days of the Continental Congress. "Our unwieldy body moves very slow. We shall do something in time."[10]

On June 2, Dr. Benjamin Church arrived from Boston with a letter from Dr. Joseph Warren, the new president of the Massachusetts Provincial Congress, urging the Continental Congress to assume control of the disorganized intercolonial army laying siege to Boston and appoint a commander in chief.

"The army now collecting from different colonies is for the general defense," Warren wrote. "The sword should, in all free states, be subservient to the civil powers . . . we tremble at having an Army (although consisting of our own countrymen) established here without a civil power to provide for and control them. . . . We would beg leave to suggest to your consideration the propriety of your taking the regulation and general direction of it."[11]

In a separate, more dire letter to Samuel Adams, Warren warned, "The continent must strengthen and support with all its weight the civil authority here; otherwise our soldiery will lose the ideas of right and wrong, and will plunder, instead of protecting the inhabitants."[12] A week later John Adams proposed, and the Continental Congress agreed, to make the Patriot forces besieging Boston a national "Continental Army," and it appropriated £6,000 for supplies.

Two days later General Thomas Gage imposed tightened martial law over Boston and declared all Americans in arms and those siding with them to be rebels and traitors. To avoid unnecessary bloodshed, however, he issued a general amnesty in Massachusetts—to all but two men: John Hancock and Samuel Adams.

"In this exigency of complicated calamities," Gage wrote in the amnesty, "I avail myself of the last effort . . . to spare the effusion of blood; to offer . . . in His Majesty's name . . . his most gracious pardon to all persons who shall forthwith lay down their arms and return to their duties of peaceable subjects; excepting only . . . Samuel Adams and John Hancock, whose offenses are of too flagitious a nature to admit of any other consideration than that of condign punishment."[13]

Gage's amnesty made it official: Hancock and Adams were now fugitives from justice, wanted by the British government for treason and subject to arrest on sight—with all-but-certain death to follow. Gage offered a reward of £500 each for their capture.

Infuriated by Gage's assault on its president, Congress resolved to raise six companies of riflemen in Pennsylvania, Maryland, and Virginia to march to New England, and Hancock appointed a five-man committee to draft rules for the administration of the army and name a commanding general. With each delegation eager to name a worthy patriot from his state, the committee decided to give the top position to the most qualified man they could find. Hancock had become enamored of his gold-braided colonel's uniform and had come to believe that his service on the Boston Common with the Corps of Cadets qualified him to be commander in chief. He all but grinned as he recognized his Massachusetts colleague John Adams to nominate the commander in chief of the Continental Army.

When John Adams rose, however, he had a different perspective from Hancock's. Adams had mingled discreetly among the delegates for several days—southerners as well as northerners—listening to and trying to understand every view and sentiment. There was little doubt that delegates from middle and southern colonies harbored "a jealousy against a New England Army under the Command of a New England General." Connecticut delegate Eliphalet Dyer suggested that selecting a non–New Englander "removes all jealousies, more firmly cements the southern to the northern, and takes away the fear of the former lest an enterprising eastern New England gentleman, proving successful, might with his victorious army give law to the southern or western gentry."[14]

It was evident to all that George Washington had the most "skill and experience as an officer" of any candidate.[15] He had commanded the Virginia Regiment for nearly five years during the French and Indian War and acquired an intimate knowledge of both conventional and unconventional battle tactics. On June 10, John Adams of Massachusetts helped unite the North and the South by proposing Virginia's Washington as commander in chief of the Continental Army. His interminable preamble, however, wearied all but President Hancock, who beamed approvingly with the certainty that he would hear his own name called when Adams reached the end of his oration. "I had no hesitation to declare," John Adams later wrote, "that I had but one gentleman in mind for that important command, and that

Commander in Chief George Washington. A Virginia delegate to the Continental Congress, he was named commander in chief of the Continental Army in 1775. He is seen here in his general's uniform in 1785. (LIBRARY OF CONGRESS)

was a gentleman from Virginia who was among us and very well known to all of us, a gentleman, whose skill and experience as an officer, whose independent fortune, great talents, and excellent universal character, would command the approbation of all the colonies better than any other person in the Union."[16]

When Adams pronounced the name George Washington, Hancock's face fell. "Mortification and resentment were expressed as forcibly as his face could exhibit them," according to John Adams. Sam Adams, still piqued at Hancock for having seized political power in Boston, sprang up to second the Washington nomination—a move that did not "soften the President's physiognomy."[17] Hancock was furious and broke completely with Sam Adams, whose outspoken radicalism had already alienated northern moderates and most of the southerners. Hancock had developed increasingly warm friendships with "southerners," who, like him, were wealthy, well-educated, cultured men who appreciated fine clothes, foods, wines, and other luxuries. Ever bitter about Hancock's wealth and good fortune, Sam Adams tried to undermine Hancock's reputation in Philadelphia, calling him, alternatively, "an oriental prince," "King Hancock," and a victim of "southern manners and the parade of courtly living."[18]

Adams's attacks only convinced Dickinson, John Jay of New York, and other "aristocrats" in Congress that New England was a land of "Goths and Vandals." Hancock responded by keeping Sam Adams off committees while investing his own office with all the trappings of a sovereign nation's chief executive.

The day of the Tea Party Patriot had ended, with its indiscriminate attacks on persons and properties of Americans who espoused law, order, and moderation. The day of the American statesman had dawned. John Hancock was determined to be—and look the part of—the statesman.

As he had done at the House of Hancock, Hancock dressed magnificently, traveled in an "elegant chariot"—again, Sam Adams's bitter description—attended by four liveried servants mounted on richly ornamented horses, escorted by fifty horsemen, half ahead and half trailing, their swords drawn. Sam Adams muttered bitterly about Hancock's "unrepublican ostentation,"[19] but Hancock was, after all, spending his own money, and in his mind, he was honoring and personifying the office he held.

Although some New England delegates argued that a New England army required a New Englander to lead them, John Adams and other moderates convinced the delegates to vote unanimously for Washington as a figure who not only had the most military experience but whose popularity in the South would ensure participation by southern militias. Washington accepted the post, and in a grand gesture aimed at uniting disparate elements in the Congress, he refused the $500 monthly salary, declaring it his solemn obligation to serve his country without remuneration. He asked only that Congress reimburse him for his expenses.

Two days later Hancock wrote to Dr. Joseph Warren in Watertown, Massachusetts, where the Third Provincial Congress had convened. His letter bore no trace of disappointment: "The Congress here have appointed George Washington, Esq., General and Commander-in-Chief, of the Continental Army. His commission is made out, and I shall sign it tomorrow. He is a gentleman you will all like. I submit to you the propriety of providing a suitable place for his residence and the mode of his reception . . . such as to do . . . the Commander-in-Chief great honor."[20] As Hancock penned his inimitable signature, however, Warren already lay dead on the field of battle at Breed's Hill on the Charlestown peninsula opposite Boston. Like Boston, Charlestown sat on what was nearly an island across the bay, connected to the mainland by a narrow neck (see map 2, page 82). Two hills dominated the peninsula—Bunker's Hill, as it was then called, near the neck, and the far smaller Breed's Hill, near the water, overlooking Boston. Warren had gone to Bunker's Hill to warn the commander of ammunition shortages and then joined the troops at a makeshift fortification on Breed's Hill. He thus became the only leader of the Tea Party Patriots to jump into the trenches and fire at the enemy alongside the men he had incited to go to war.

At dawn on June 17, 1775, British warships all but surrounded the head of land and fired relentlessly on Breed's Hill. When the tide ebbed, an assault force of 2,400 landed and charged up the hill, only to be repelled by a rain of rifle-fire from the 1,600-man Patriot force. Again the British charged; again they fell back. With the third charge, however, the Patriots ran out of powder and fell back to Bunker's Hill. The British seized Breed's Hill, then quickly overran Bunker's Hill. Somehow, the madman James Otis managed to flee his brother's home with a rifle, charge up Bunker's Hill through a hail of British shot, and emerge unharmed. Patriot soldiers finally subdued him and carried him to safety. One hundred other Patriots died, however. One of them was Dr. Joseph Warren. The British wounded 267 and took 30 prisoners. But the British paid a heavy price for their victory, with more than 1,000 casualties—many of them officers, whose bright red jackets made them all-too-easy targets for distant sharpshooters. Never before had Britain suffered so many casualties in a single day's battle.

On July 3, two weeks after the battle, George Washington arrived in Cambridge and took command of the Continental Army, which had grown to 14,500 men. Two days later John Hancock signed the so-called Olive Branch Petition, which John Dickinson had written reiterating the allegiance of the American people to George III and their sincere hopes for peace. There were many merchants and planters in Congress who were more loathe than Hancock to sacrifice their fortunes to the ill-defined, ephemeral concept of "liberty." They pleaded with the king to order an end to hostilities and initiate reconciliation. The following day, however, Hancock signed another Dickinson resolution, a "Declaration of the Causes and Necessities of Taking Up Arms." Although it rejected independence, it reasserted the resolve of Americans to die rather than submit to enslavement by the British Parliament.

At the beginning of August, Congress adjourned for a month, and when it reconvened, a delegation from Georgia arrived to transform it into a *de facto* national government, representative of all thirteen American colonies. In early November Congress learned that King George III had refused even to receive, let alone read, Dickinson's Olive Branch Petition and proclaimed *all* the American colonies to be in rebellion. By Christmas he ordered the colonies closed to all commerce, effective March 1. By then, however, hostilities between British and American troops had broken out in both the North and South, with American troops invading Canada and capturing Montreal before suffering defeat at Quebec. Patriots in the South were more successful, defeating British troops at Norfolk, Virginia. The war against Britain turned into a civil war in the spring of 1776 when North Carolina Patriots confronted—and crushed—a force of Loyalists at Moore's Creek Bridge near Wilmington. Farther south, a British fleet rained cannon fire on the fortifications of Sullivan's Island at the entrance to Charleston Bay. Instead of destroying the fort, however, the cannon balls embedded themselves in the soft palmetto logs of the fort's walls and strengthened them—indeed, made them all but impenetrable. When the fort's cannons returned fire, the British fleet had no choice but to sail away ingloriously, leaving the South free of British occupation.

Outside Boston, meanwhile, Henry Knox, a local bookseller whom Washington had appointed chief of artillery, had just completed an improbable three-hundred-mile journey with his men to Fort Ticonderoga, New York, and back, dragging forty-three cannons and sixteen mortars through deep snows to Cambridge. By the end of February, some two thousand American troops had captured Dorchester Heights overlooking Boston, allowing Knox to put his artillery in positions to rake the entire city and harbor with cannon fire. By then, nearly twelve hundred Loyalists—men, women, and children—had crowded into Boston seeking the protection of British forces. Among them were two hundred merchants, four hundred farmers, and hundreds of British civilian officials, including Chief Justice Peter Oliver.

On March 2, 1776, "the rebels, who had surrounded the town, began to bombard and cannonade it for three nights successively," according to Oliver. General William Howe, who had replaced Thomas Gage as military commander, had no choice but to evacuate Boston or allow patriot shells to slaughter thousands of British troops and loyal civilians. On March 17, he began an evacuation by sea, and the civilians in his protection joined a stream of eighty-five thousand other Loyalists who would choose exile over disloyalty to king and country. Many Loyalists were left behind and "were obliged to take their chances of ill usage," Oliver noted, "and some of them felt it severely.

> One, in particular, was used in a strictly diabolical manner. He was a Loyalist, but an inoffensive one in his behavior. He had an amiable wife and several amiable children. The Rebel Cart, in imitation of the Inquisition Coach, called at his door in the morning and they ordered him into the cart . . . his wife begging on her knees to spare her husband and his daughters crying with entreaties. This infernal crew were deaf to the cries of distress and drove on until they had got six in the cart, whom they carried to . . . the extreme part of the town and there tipped up the cart and tumbled them into a ditch . . . forbad their entering the town again and . . . forbad the people in the country to give them food or to shelter them . . . as to save these unhappy sufferers from meeting the cruel death assigned to them by their persecutors. . . . A colonel of a *rebel* regiment was so roused with a compassionate resentment that he succored them and declared to his employers that if such inhumanity was suffered, he would resign his commission and quit their cause.[21]

In a spree of sadism during the days and nights that followed, gangs of thugs broke into Loyalist homes, looting and burning, terrorizing and

The Tory's Day of Judgment. This newspaper engraving shows the fate of Loyalists after British troops evacuated Boston in March 1776. (LIBRARY OF CONGRESS)

mistreating occupants, and, as often as not, dragging off the men to be tarred, feathered, and hung from tree limbs or makeshift scaffolds, where they suffered endless hours of physical abuse. The mob had now regained control of the Tea Party movement and tarred its good works with terror.

On March 17, the last of the British troops in Boston boarded their ships and on the following day they began destroying Castle William—a process that took a week, according to Oliver, who watched from the flagship.

The conflagration was the most pleasingly dreadful that I ever beheld. Sometimes it appeared like the eruption of Mount Etna; and then a deluge of fire opened to the view; that nothing could reconcile the horror to the mind, but the prevention of such a fortress falling into the hands of rebels, who had already spread such a conflagration of diabolical fury throughout America.[22]

On March 26, the last of the British fleet sailed out of Boston Bay on its way to Halifax, Nova Scotia, leaving Massachusetts an independent state in the hands of the Americans and their forces. Deep sadness overwhelmed Peter Oliver as his native land faded from view:

Here I took my leave of that once happy country, where peace and plenty reigned uncontrolled, till that infernal hydra rebellion with its hundred heads had devoured its happiness, spread desolation over its fertile fields and ravaged the peaceful mansions of its inhabitants . . . [with] savage barbarities and diabolical cruelties which . . . were instigated by leaders who were desperate in their fortunes, unbounded in their ambition and malice, and infernal in their dictates. Here I drop the filial tear into the urn of my country. And here I bid adieu to that shore, which I never wish to tread again till that greatest of social blessings, *a firm established British Government*, precedes or accompanies me thither.[23]

As Oliver sailed off, a rebel mob attacked Oliver Hall, his magnificent home in Middleborough, and burned it to the ground. His nephew, Reverend Andrew Oliver, remained behind and revisited the site. After the fire, he reported, "the ruins gradually fell to decay, and it is difficult now to discover any traces of what once stood there."[24]

As Howe was evacuating Boston, Patriot General Alexander Lord Stirling's forces put down a Loyalist counter-revolution in New Jersey and arrested its leader, Royal Governor William Franklin, the illegitimate son of Benjamin Franklin. "I have provided good, genteel, private lodgings for him," Lord Stirling wrote to President Hancock from Elizabethtown. "I intend he shall remain until I have directions from Congress what to do with him."[25] After discreet discussions with his father, Hancock ordered William

Franklin imprisoned in Litchfield, Connecticut, where he remained for two years before being exchanged for Patriot prisoners. He eventually went into exile in England.

A few days later President Hancock heard from Washington:

> It is with great pleasure I inform you that, on Sunday last, the 17th March, 1776, about 9 o'clock in the forenoon, the ministerial army evacuated the town of Boston and that the forces of the United Colonies are now in actual possession thereof. I beg leave to congratulate you sir and the honorable Congress on this happy event, and particularly as it was effected without endangering the lives and property of the remaining unhappy inhabitants.[26]

Earlier, on March 3, Congress had sent Connecticut's Silas Deane to Paris to purchase war materiel and recruit officers to help train American militiamen, and word soon arrived that France had guaranteed the safety of American ships sailing into French harbors and would provide clandestine material support for the Continental Army. Congress announced that all American ports would now be open to trade with all nations but Britain.

On April 12, a North Carolina convention joined Massachusetts in declaring its independence from Britain, and Virginia followed suit on May 15. On June 7, after a year had passed since the appointment of Washington as commander in chief, Congress looked back on an extraordinary number of American triumphs. Confident that the British would withdraw rather than submit to further humiliations, Virginia Congressman Richard Henry Lee stood in the Continental Congress to resolve that "the United Colonies are, and of right ought to be, free and independent states." In the debate that followed, Congress voted to postpone a decision on the resolution until July 1, but nonetheless appointed a committee consisting of Thomas Jefferson, Benjamin Franklin, John Adams, Robert Livingston (New York), and Roger Sherman (Connecticut) to prepare a formal Declaration of Independence. Members of the committee then assigned to Jefferson the task of writing the document. On July 2, twelve of the thirteen states voted in favor of Richard Henry Lee's resolution, with New York abstaining until it could obtain the consent of the New York Provincial

*King George III. His refusal to read, let alone sign, John
Dickinson's Olive Branch Petition motivated the
Continental Congress to issue and sign the Declaration of
Independence and end the king's sovereignty over the richest
jewel of the English empire.* (LIBRARY OF CONGRESS)

Congress. Boston's Thomas Cushing joined John Dickinson in voting
against the resolution.

After a few changes by Adams and Franklin, the committee presented
Jefferson's Declaration of Independence to the Congress on July 4, 1776.
Congress approved the document—without dissent—and President Hancock signed it, with Pennsylvania's Charles Thomson, the secretary of the
Congress, witnessing Hancock's signature. None of the other members of
Congress could sign it without the approval of each of their state legislatures. Hancock ordered copies made and, after it had been read to the
public on July 8, he sent copies to all the states for their legislatures' approval (see Appendix A for text).

Silence reigned over the State House in Philadelphia on August 2, 1776, as each of fifty-five signatories affixed their names to the document that severed the ties of Britain's thirteen American colonies with the motherland. Although Thomas Cushing and John Dickinson again refused to sign, for them and all the framers and signers of the Declaration of Independence, the tempest had ended.

Chapter 15

The Forgotten Patriots

*A*s experienced statesmen like John Hancock, John Adams, Benjamin Franklin, and Thomas Jefferson assumed leadership of Congress, the most bellicose Tea Party Patriots like Samuel Adams slipped to the rear of national leadership. The time for tearing down government had ended; the time had come to build a new government—and a new nation. The fiery words of Sam Adams and the original Tea Party Patriots had roused Americans to rebellion, but proved of little value devising military strategy or negotiating complex agreements between state leaders or foreign rulers and military commanders. Nor were they of any help raising money for arms, ammunition, clothes, shoes, blankets, and tents for the troops. And they proved counterproductive for guiding the American people to productive peacetime pursuits.

To the consternation of many Tea Party leaders, the revolution they had helped foment not only failed to end taxation, it forced the new, independent state governments to tax more heavily than the British had proposed or would ever have conceived of proposing. Like other colonies, Massachusetts had to support its own government and an armed militia on its own—without British help. In addition, the states collectively had to support a central national government and a national military force—two entities the British government had previously financed without colonist help. For a while, the Continental Army and state militias could rely on materiel captured or stolen from the British, but they soon learned they would have to buy the arms and ammunition they needed at a steep price, borrowing much of the money but eventually taxing citizens to raise the rest.

Of the original Tea Party Patriots, only John Hancock had the genius to rise to national prominence—as President of the Continental Congress and, indeed, first President of the United States of America under the Articles of Confederation that Congress approved in 1777. He spent nearly two, often heroic years in that post before returning to Massachusetts to assume command of the state militia and lead it into action at the battle of Newport, Rhode Island, in 1778. In 1780 the people of Massachusetts elected him the state's first governor by an overwhelming majority. He held the post for five years, resigning suddenly in February 1785 after disingenuously pleading exhaustion and allowing Lieutenant Governor Thomas Cushing to finish his term. In fact, the state was facing bankruptcy, and Hancock saw no way out of the financial morass without imposing the very taxes that he and his fellow Tea Party leaders had so vehemently opposed under British rule. His successor James Bowdoin had no choice but to raise property taxes, and in doing so, he set off widespread antitax rioting. Bowdoin raised private moneys to send an armed militia to crush the rebellion and leave the state's farmers seething with discontent and anger that they misdirected at Bowdoin.

Recovering from his convenient bout with fatigue, Hancock won reelection to the governorship with grand promises to ease the plight of farmers. Reducing his own salary as a sop to protesters, he cajoled the legislature into declaring a one-year tax holiday, obtained full pardons for farmer protesters, and forced through legislation ending the self-defeating practice of seizing tools from debtors and sending them to prison, with no means of ever repaying their debts. He and Lieutenant Governor Thomas Cushing helped finance Boston's recovery, turning it into America's most beautiful city—with Hancock claiming most of the credit while the modest Cushing stood silently in Hancock's shadow. The people of Massachusetts reelected Hancock to the governorship until his death in 1793.

Despite his bluster, Sam Adams, unlike Dr. Joseph Warren, spent the war without firing a shot at the British—or contributing perceptibly to the

Boston rebuilt, 1789. View of Boston from Breed's Hill after Governor John Hancock and Lieutenant Governor Thomas Cushing led and helped finance Boston's recovery from the war and turned it into America's most beautiful city. (BOSTONIAN SOCIETY)

deliberations of the Continental Congress. He returned to Boston in 1781 but never recovered his influence or popularity. As the hugely popular Hancock was contributing every moment of his time and every penny of his personal wealth rebuilding Boston, Adams all but disappeared from public life after the war, unable or unwilling to contribute to reconstruction. After a failed attempt to win election to Congress, he resigned himself to oblivion until Hancock invited him to serve as lieutenant governor after Cushing's death in 1788. Adams remained in that obscure post until Hancock's death in 1793, when he automatically acceded to the governorship. He won reelection in 1794 and served until 1797. In acceding to the governorship, the one-time leader of the Tea Party Patriots—and arch foe of British taxation—now warned would-be tax protesters, "The man who dares to rebel against the laws of a republic ought to suffer death."[1] Samuel Adams died on October 2, 1803, one of the most puzzling figures in early American history.

James Otis, Jr. drifted in and out of sanity after his beating in the British Coffee House. By September 1771 he added heavy drinking to his erratic behavior, and three months later the probate court declared James *non compos mentis* and appointed his younger brother Samuel A. Otis his guardian. Although watched most of the time, James nonetheless managed to slip away with a rifle on June 17, 1775 and ran off to Bunker's Hill, where he rushed into battle amidst a hail of bullets. Amazingly, he escaped unharmed—one of the few to do so. He spent the rest of his days in quietude until lightning struck him dead as he stood in the rain to watch a thunderstorm near a farmhouse in Andover on May 23, 1783.

Thomas Cushing, the most moderate of the Tea Party Patriot leadership and an opponent of independence, remained in John Hancock's shadow at the Continental Congress as he had in Boston's revolutionary government and after independence as Hancock's lieutenant governor—a post he held until his death on February 28, 1788.

Dr. Benjamin Church, the radical who had shared quarters with Hancock when they were boys in Harvard, was arrested in October 1775 for spying for the British army. According to a report by George Washington to President Hancock, Church had been divulging Minuteman and Continental Army plans to General Thomas Gage for at least a year. Contrary to his claim, he had not been arrested in Boston after the Battle of Lexington but had gone straight to Gage's headquarters to report Minuteman activities, allowing the majority of the Redcoats on the Lexington road to escape capture after the battle at Concord Bridge. After assuming administration of the Continental Army Hospital in Cambridge, Church had shown a remarkable ability to slip in and out of Boston—always returning with surprisingly large amounts of medical supplies. During the summer he had sent his mistress with a coded message to one of Gage's aides, but she delivered it to someone who turned out to be a Patriot who reported her. She was arrested and confessed. The Massachusetts General Court, perhaps out of consideration for the past services of their longtime colleague, sent Church to jail in Norwich, Connecticut, where he remained until the end of the Revolution, "debarred the use of pen, ink and paper." After the war, he sailed to exile in the West Indies, but the ship never arrived, and he was never seen or heard from again.

James Bowdoin, who joined the Tea Party movement after the Boston Massacre, remained on the fringes of the political picture during and immediately after the Revolution because of an ongoing struggle with tuberculosis. In 1785, when the ever-popular John Hancock resigned as governor and allowed his lieutenant governor Thomas Cushing to finish out his term, Bowdoin decided to run against Cushing for the governorship and won. Faced with enormous state debts from the Revolutionary War, Bowdoin raised taxes—as Hancock had stubbornly refused to do. The popular response mirrored that of Boston Patriots after the British had tried raising taxes in the 1760s and 1770s. Farmers across the state rebelled. In western Massachusetts, former Captain Daniel Shays, a struggling farmer like the others, convinced neighbors that Boston legislators were colluding with judges and lawyers across the state to raise taxes to exorbitantly high levels and foreclose on properties when farmers found it impossible to pay. With that, he shouted what some feared would provoke a second American Revolution: "Close down the courts!"

Echoing his call, farmers marched to courthouses in Cambridge, Concord, Worcester, Northampton, Taunton, and Great Barrington—and shut down the civil courts. Hailed by farmers across the nation, the shutdowns frightened courts into ending foreclosures in Massachusetts. Determined to expand his success, Shays led a force of five hundred men to Springfield, where one thousand more farmers joined him. After shutting down the State Supreme Court, they marched to the federal arsenal, intent on seizing arms, ammunition, and artillery. In Boston, meanwhile, Bowdoin raised money privately and recruited a force of four thousand troops to march to Springfield to crush Shays and his rebels. Before they arrived at Springfield, however, soldiers at the arsenal unleashed a few artillery blasts that fell short of the approaching farmers but amply demonstrated the advantages of cannonballs over pitchforks. The troops from Boston chased the farmers to their homes and captured most of their leaders, although Shays fled to safety in what was then the independent republic of Vermont. In defeat, however, Shays's army scored a resounding victory when farmers across the state went to the polls and voted Governor Bowdoin and three-fourths of the legislature out of office. Recalled to power by popular demand, John Hancock and a new, pro-farmer legislature declared a tax holiday for a year, reduced taxes thereafter, released imprisoned debtors to go back to work, and exempted clothing, household possessions, and tools of trade from seizure in future debt proceedings. Bowdoin retired from politics and died in relative obscurity on November 6, 1790.

The irony of Bowdoin's ruthless suppression of Shays's tax protesters was not lost on other Tea Party leaders such as John Hancock or, indeed, on Revolutionary War leaders such as George Washington, Patrick Henry, and Richard Henry Lee. Only twenty years earlier, they had protested Britain's imposition of the all-but-miniscule stamp tax to help pay war debts incurred defending Americans in the French and Indian War. Although all British subjects *except* Americans paid the stamp tax, Patrick Henry branded anyone who supported Parliament's efforts to tax Virginians "AN ENEMY TO THIS HIS MAJESTY'S COLONY."[2] When he assumed the reins of government as Virginia's first governor, Patrick Henry not only taxed Virginians, he did so without their consent. Contrary to the promises of liberty and representation in government that American Patriot leaders had made to rouse the citizenry to rebellion, the state constitutions they wrote after the war limited voting and the right to stand for office to white, male property owners. As each state defined the minimum amount of tangible assets that qualified a man as a property owner, it further limited those who could vote to the same men of wealth and influence who had governed the states under royal governors before the Revolution. South Carolina, for example, required voters and candidates for governor to have assets of at least £10,000; Pennsylvania levied a hefty poll tax; Virginia limited voting to owners of at least five hundred acres of land. The qualifications disenfranchised many shopkeepers, craftsmen, farmers, and other hard-working, productive earners with small properties who had fought in the Revolution to get the vote and have a say in government.

For them—and, indeed, for most Americans—the Revolutionary War and independence from Britain produced few immediate benefits or changes in their way of life—except to free the wealthy elite in each state, America's "aristocracy" of sorts, to govern without oversight by British authorities. In effect, independence left those in power in each state free to exploit the land and the less fortunate without having to share their profits with the crown. Those who served the wealthy before the Revolution continued to serve them afterward, having gained no benefits. At the urging of John Hancock, Sam Adams, and other Tea Party Patriots, John Russell, a Boston stone mason, had smeared his face with lampblack and red ochre to board the *Dartmouth* on the night of December 16, 1773. Promised liberty, the right to vote, and no taxation without representation if he joined the Tea Party, he helped dump tea in Boston Harbor and went to fight for independence in the Revolutionary War. After he had done as they asked and raised them to political power, he remained a stone mason with no more individual rights or liberties than he had enjoyed under British rule. Only three of the newly independent states guaranteed the right of free speech, and although every state protected freedom of religion, five established state religions that taxed all citizens to support them, whether or not they practiced those faiths. Only eleven states guaranteed freedom of the press, and only eight protected the right to peaceful assembly. The Articles of Confederation that united the new states in "a firm league of friendship" did not guarantee any individual freedoms or even trial by a jury of one's peers—a right that had been guaranteed to British subjects since King John's signing of the Magna Carta in 1215. Contrary to the promise of the Declaration of Independence, Americans would have to wait more than a decade for a new constitution to grant them "certain inalienable rights."

More than eighty-five thousand Americans out of a population of about 2.5 million quit their native land during and after the American Revolution, stripped by savage mobs of their properties, their citizenship, and their birthrights. But the number is far more significant than it appears at first. Most of the émigrés were New Englanders—well over sixty thousand, or more than 10 percent of the population of that region. Thousands more Loyalists who refused to quit their native land fled westward into the wilderness, abandoning valuable properties their families had owned for generations and starting anew—often under assumed names and identities. Many of those who fled could trace their family roots in America to the time of the landing of the *Mayflower* at Plymouth. All had come seeking individual liberty and economic opportunity—the right to free speech, freedom to worship as they chose, freedom of the press, and freedom to reap the riches of their labors. For as many as 150 years, they had helped transform a savage land into a thriving country of productive farms, forests, mines, villages, towns, and ports. Most had obeyed the laws of the land, more or less scrupulously, and worked to better its economy and government. And for their loyalty to their country and its legal government, their countrymen expelled them. Most Loyalists were patriots who loved America; they and their forebears had fought for America in countless conflicts with Indians, in one war with the Spanish in the Florida area, and in three wars with the French, culminating with the French and Indian War.

After arriving in London in 1774, Thomas Hutchinson argued in vain with the king and his ministry to repeal the Coercive Acts. A year later Massachusetts officials sold his Boston townhouse and the rest of his estate and proscribed him—in effect stripping him of his birthright and the nationality he and his forebears had embraced for 150 years.

As the Massachusetts uprising turned into a full-scale revolutionary war, Hutchinson resigned himself to exile, writing the third volume of his *History of the Province of Massachusetts* and mixing in London's political and literary circles with such luminaries as Edward Gibbon, author of *The History of the Decline and Fall of the Roman Empire*. The premature deaths of his daughter Peggy and his son Billy, however, crushed him emotionally, and he died on June 3, 1780 at the age of sixty-nine, a broken man without a family or a country.

> I am sometimes tempted to endeavor to forget that I am an American, and to turn my views to a provision for what remains of life in England. But the passion for my native country returns . . . and though I know not how to reason upon it, I feel a fondness to lay my bones in my native soil and to carry those of my dear daughter with me.[3]

As screaming Boston mobs hounded the Oliver family day and night, Peter Oliver's wife collapsed and died in 1775. Oliver himself sailed out of Boston with the British army on March, 17, 1776, as the Redcoats finished destroying Castle William. Oliver reached Halifax, then sailed to London, where he was reunited with his brother-in-law Thomas Hutchinson. In the spring of 1778 he moved into the country near Birmingham, where members of the Oliver-Hutchinson clan gathered and settled after fleeing Massachusetts. By then, Oliver had arranged for his son and his son's wife to come to England. While there, he wrote his remarkable memoir, *Peter Oliver's Origin & Progress of the American Rebellion: A Tory View.* "We have seen a set of men," he wrote, "favored with the liberty . . . under the auspices of the English government and protected by it, but under an obligation to conform to such regulations as should be made by its authority.

> We have seen these new settlers, for a long series of years, paying all deference to those regulations . . . [but] they will sacrifice everything for money [and] for many years past . . . have been deeply immersed in the smuggling business—an importation of goods contrary to the laws of society to which we belong. . . . Libertinism, riot and robbery soon became the effects of this sort of public spirit; houses were plundered and demolished, persons were beaten, abused, tarred and feathered; courts of justice were insulted; the pillars of government were destroyed; and no way to escape the torrent of savage barbarity but by paying obeisance to the sovereign mandates of a mob.[4]

Peter Oliver died in Birmingham on October 13, 1791 at the age of 78. His son and daughter, who had followed him to England, died of tuberculosis within five years. His last son, Thomas, lived to be ninety-two, but died without issue, thus ending his line of the family, whose ancestors had arrived in America in 1630.

> Here I drop the filial tear into the urn of my country. And here I bid adieu to that shore, which I never wish to tread again till that greatest of social blessings, a firm established British government, precedes or accompanies me thither.[5]—Peter Oliver.

Like Thomas Hutchinson and Peter Oliver, tens of thousands of Loyalist Americans died in exile after the American Revolutionary War, never quite understanding why their fellow countrymen had driven them from their native homes. Indeed, one of the ironies of the American Revolution—of the Tea Party tempest—is that it cost the new nation some of America's most brilliant people—men that Patrick Henry described as "an enterprising, moneyed people" who would have made enormous contributions to the new nation's political, economic, and social evolution.

Even more ironic was that a decade after independence the American government seemed to mirror the very British government that Tea Party Patriots had fought to shatter. Virginia's Patrick Henry railed that the American Constitution had created "a great and mighty president with . . . the powers of a king" and given Congress the powers of Parliament to impose "unlimited . . . direct taxation." The Revolution from Britain, it seemed, had been for nought.

Elected Virginia's first governor, Henry became the only American Patriot leader to seek reconciliation by inviting exiled Loyalists to return to their native land with the promise to restore their property and citizenship rights. "The quarrel is over," he boomed.

> Peace hath returned and found us a free people. Let us have the magnanimity to lay aside our antipathies and prejudices. . . . Let . . . liberty stretch forth her fair hand . . . and bid them welcome.[6]

Appendix A:
The Declaration of Independence and Its Signatories

When in the course of human events, it becomes necessary for one people to dissolve the political bands which have connected them with another, and to assume among the Powers of the earth, the separate and equal station to which the Laws of Nature and of Nature's God entitles them, a decent respect to the opinions of mankind requires that they should declare the causes which impel them to the separation.

We hold these truths to be self-evident, that all men are created equal, that they are endowed by their Creator with certain inalienable Rights, that among these are Life, Liberty, and the pursuit of Happiness. That to secure these rights, Governments are instituted among Men, deriving their just powers from the consent of the governed. That whenever any form of Government becomes destructive of these ends, it is the Right of the People to alter or to abolish it, and to institute a new Government, having its foundation on such principles and organizing its powers in such form, as to them shall seem most likely to effect their Safety and Happiness. Prudence, indeed, will dictate that Governments long established should not be changed for light and transient causes; and accordingly all experience hath shown that mankind are more disposed to suffer, while evils are sufferable, than to right themselves by abolishing the forms to which they are accustomed. But when a long train of abuses and usurpations pursuing invariably the same Object evinces a design to reduce them under absolute Despotism, it is their right, it is their duty, to throw off such Government, and to provide new Guards for their future security. Such has been the patient sufferance of these Colonies; and such is now the necessity which constrains them to alter their former Systems of Government. The history of the present King of Great Britain is a history of repeated injuries and usurpations, all have in direct object the establishment of an absolute Tyranny over these States. To prove this, let Facts be submitted to a candid world.

He has refused his Assent to Laws, the most wholesome and necessary for the public good.

He has forbidden his Governors to pass laws of immediate and pressing importance, unless suspended in their operation till his Assent should be obtained; and when so suspended, he has utterly neglected to attend to them.

He has refused to pass other Laws for the accommodation of large districts of people, unless those people would relinquish the right of Representation in the Legislature, a right inestimable to them and formidable to tyrants only.

He has called together legislative bodies at places unusual, uncomfortable, and distant from the depositor of their Public Records, for the sole purpose of fatiguing them into compliance with his measures.

He has dissolved Representative Houses repeatedly, for opposing with manly firmness his invasions of the rights of the people.

He has refused for a long time, after such dissolutions, to cause others to be elected; whereby the Legislative Powers, incapable of Annihilation, have returned to the People at large for their exercise; the State remaining in the meantime exposed to all the dangers of invasion from without, and convulsions within.

He has endeavored to prevent the populations of these States; for that purpose obtaining the Laws of Naturalization of Foreigners; refusing to pass others to encourage their migration hither, and raising the conditions of new Appropriations of Lands.

He has obstructed the Administration of Justice, by refusing his Assent to Laws for establishing Judiciary Powers.

He has made judges dependent on his Will alone, for the tenure of their offices, and the amount and payment of their salaries.

He has erected a multitude of New Offices, and sent hither swarms of Officers to harass our people, and eat out their substance.

He has kept among us, in times of peace, Standing Armies without the Consent of our legislatures.

The Declaration of Independence. Engrossed (handwritten) copy of the Declaration of Independence, issued in early 1777. The original document of July 4, 1776, bore but one signature—that of John Hancock—for more than a month until the various state legislatures approved it and authorized their delegates to the Continental Congress to sign it. (LIBRARY OF CONGRESS)

He has affected to render the military independent of and superior to the Civil Power.

He has combined with others to subject us to a jurisdiction foreign to our constitution, and unacknowledged by our laws; giving his Assent to their acts of pretended legislation.

For quartering large bodies of armed troops among us.

For protecting them, by a mock Trial, from Punishment for any Murders which they should commit on the Inhabitants of these States.

For cutting off our Trade with all parts of the world.

For imposing taxes on us without our consent.

For depriving us in many cases, of the benefits of Trial by Jury.

For transporting us beyond Seas to be tried for pretended offenses.

For abolishing the free System of English Laws in a neighboring Province, establishing therein an Arbitrary government, and enlarging boundaries so as to render it at once an example and fit instrument for introducing the same absolute rule into these colonies.

For taking away our Charters, abolishing our most valuable Laws, and altering fundamentally, the Forms of our Government.

For suspending our own Legislatures, and declaring themselves invested with Power to legislate for us in all cases whatsoever:

He has abdicated Government here, by declaring us out of his Protection and waging War against us.

He has plundered our seas, ravaged our Coasts, burnt our towns, and destroyed the lives of our people.

He is at this time transporting large armies of foreign mercenaries to compleat the works of death, desolation and tyranny, already begun with circumstances of Cruelty & perfidy scarcely paralleled in the most barbarous ages, and totally unworthy the Head of a civilized nation.

He has constrained our fellow Citizens taken Captive on the high Seas to bear Arms against their Country, to become the executioners of their friends and Brethren, or to fall themselves by their Hands.

He has excited domestic insurrections amongst us, and has endeavored to bring on the inhabitants of our frontiers, the merciless Indian Savages, whose known rule of warfare, is an undistinguished destruction of all ages, sexes and conditions.

In every stage of these Oppressions We have Petitioned for Redress in the most humble terms: Our repeated Petitions have been answered only by repeated injury. A Prince, whose character is thus marked by every act which may define a Tyrant, is unfit to be the ruler of a free people.

Nor have We been wanting attention to our British brethren. We have warned them from time to time of attempts by their legislature to extend an unwarrantable jurisdiction over us. We have reminded them of the circumstances of our emigration and settlement here. We have appealed to their native justice and magnanimity, and we have conjured them by the ties of our common kindred to disavow these usurpations, which would inevitably interrupt our connection and correspondence. They too have been deaf to the voice of justice and of consanguinity. We must, therefore, acquiesce in the necessity, which denounces our Separation, and hold them, as hold the rest of mankind, Enemies in War, in Peace Friends.

We, therefore, the Representatives of the United States of America, in General Congress, assembled, appealing to the Supreme Judge of the world for the rectitude of our intentions, do, in the name, and by authority of the good People of these Colonies, solemnly publish and declare, That these United Colonies are, and of Right ought to be Free and Independent States; that they are Absolved from all Allegiance to the British Crown, and that all political connection between them and the State of Great Britain, is and ought to be totally dissolved; and that as Free and Independent States, they have full power to levy War, conclude Peace, contract Alliances, establish Commerce, and to do all other Acts and Things which Independent States may of right do. And for the support of this Declaration, with a firm reliance on the Protection of Divine Providence, we mutually pledge to each other our Lives, our Fortunes and our sacred Honor.

Signers of the Declaration of Independence

Connecticut
Samuel Huntington
Roger Sherman
William Williams
Oliver Wolcott

Delaware
Thomas McKean
George Read
Caesar Rodney

Georgia
Button Gwinnett
Lyman Hall
George Walton

Maryland
Charles Carroll
Samuel Chase
William Paca
Thomas Stone

Massachusetts
  John Adams
  Samuel Adams
  Elbridge Gerry
  John Hancock
  Robert Treat Payne
New Hampshire
  Josiah Bartlett
  Matthew Thornton
  William Whipple
New Jersey
  Abraham Clark
  John Hart
  Francis Hopkinson
  Richard Stockton
  John Witherspoon
New York
  William Floyd
  Francis Lewis
  Philip Livingston
  Lewis Morris
North Carolina
  Joseph Hewes
  William Hooper
  John Penn

Pennsylvania
  George Clymer
  Benjamin Franklin
  Robert Morris
  John Morton
  George Ross
  Benjamin Rush
  James Smith
  George Taylor
  James Wilson
Rhode Island
  William Ellery
  Stephen Hopkins
South Carolina
  Thomas Heyward
  Thomas Lynch
  Arthur Middleton
  Edward Rutledge
Virginia
  Carter Braxton
  Benjamin Harrison
  Thomas Jefferson
  Francis Lightfoot Lee
  Richard Henry Lee
  Thomas Nelson
  George Wythe

Appendix B:
The First Tea Party Patriots

*T*he following names appeared on a list of Boston Tea Party participants said to have been compiled by printer/publisher Benjamin Edes.[1]

(Where a name lacks information, such as age at time of Tea Party, occupation, etc., it was unavailable.)

Thomas Bolter, 38. Housewright (home builder).

James Brewer. Pump and blockmaker [as in block and tackle, pulleys], Freemason and Hancock's Corps of Cadets.

Nicholas Campbell, 56. Native of Malta; served on unspecified ship during war.

Thomas Chase. Distiller, Freemason, Hancock's Corps of Cadets.

Benjamin Clarke, 23. Cooper; served in artillery during Revolutionary War.

Adam Collson, 35. Leather worker, Freemason, Hancock's Corps of Cadets.

S. Coolidge.

John Crane, 19. House carpenter, Freemason, colonel, then brigadier general in Continental Army artillery.

Edward Dolbear. Cooper.

Joseph Eayers.

Nathaniel Frothingham, 27. Coachmaker.

John Gammell, 24. Carpenter; construction department of Continental Army during the war.

Thomas Gerrish.

Samuel Gore, 22. Painter, Freemason. Helped capture cannons from Boston gunhouse.

Moses Grant, 30. Upholsterer. Helped capture cannons from Boston gunhouse.

Nathaniel Green. Register of deeds.

William Hendley, 25. Mason.

George R. T. Hewes, 31. Farmer, fisherman, shoemaker.

John Hooton. Oar maker, wharf manager.

Samuel Howard, 21. Shipwright.

Edward C. Howe, 31. Rope maker.

Jonathan Hunnewell, 14. Mason. Son of Richard Hunnewell (see below), he became a Boston selectman and state legislator after the war.

Richard Hunnewell. Mason.

Daniel Ingoldson.

Joseph Lee, 28. Merchant, Freemason.

Matthew Loring, 23. Shoemaker.

————Martin.

Ebenezer Mackintosh, 31. Shoemaker, street tough, leader of street rioters. No known service in war; died in poverty at 82.

Thomas Melvill, 22. B.A., Princeton College; merchant; captain, then major in artillery during the war; U.S. government inspector; naval officer in War of 1812; state legislator, Boston fire warden. Herman Melville's grandfather.

William Molyneux, 57. Hardware merchant, cofounder "Manufactury House," to train Boston women to spin and weave textiles.

Thomas Moore, 20. Wharf manager.

Joseph Payson.

Samuel Peck. Cooper, Freemason.

William Pierce, 29. Barber.

Lendall Pitts, 26. Merchant, Corps of Cadets.

Dr. John Prince, Pastor, First Church, Salem, from 1779 to 1836.

Thomas Porter. Merchant.

Edward Proctor, 40. Importer of West Indian goods. Freemason, colonel in artillery during war.

Henry Purkitt, 18. Cooper. Fought at Trenton, Brandywine in Revolutionary War; joined Pulaski's Cavalry as sergeant, rose to colonel.

Paul Revere, 18. Goldsmith, silversmith, Freemason. Fought in French and Indian War, joined militia in Revolutionary War.

Benjamin Rice.

John Russell. Mason.

William Russell, 25. Schoolteacher. Served as sergeant-major in war, before signing on as a captain's clerk on a privateer. Captured and jailed on board notorious prison ship *Jersey*.

Joseph Shed, 41. Carpenter, grocer.

Benjamin Simpson. Bricklayer. Served in Continental Army.

Peter Slater, 24. Ropemaker. Served five years in Continental Army.

Samuel Sloper.

Thomas Spear.

Samuel Sprague, 20. Mason.

John Spurr, 25. Fought in Revolutionary War; captured and held captive in Halifax for fourteen months.

James Starr, 32.

Ebenezer Stevens, 22. Carpenter. Successively a first lieutenant, captain, and lieutenant colonel in artillery; fought at Saratoga and later in Lafayette's Virginia campaign. Leading New York merchant after war.

Abraham Tower.

Thomas Urann. Ship joiner, and surveyor of boards (forest lumber), Freemason.

Josiah Wheeler, 30. House builder.

Joshua Wyeth, 15. Served in Revolutionary army.

Dr. Thomas Young, physician, early follower of Samuel Adams. Became Samuel Adams's personal physician; was army surgeon in Revolutionary War.

The families and descendants claim that the following men participated in the Boston Tea Party:

Nathaniel Barber, 45. Merchant, insurance sales, Freemason.

Samuel Bernard, 26. Major in the Revolutionary War.

Henry Bass, 34. Merchant.

Edward Bates.

David Bradlee, 31. One of four Bradlee brothers; no other facts available on any of them.

Josiah Bradlee, 19.

Nathaniel Bradlee, 27.

Thomas Bradlee, 29.

Seth Ingersoll Brown, 23. House carpenter; wounded at Bunker Hill; fought during the rest of the war.

Stephen Bruce. Merchant, Freemason.

Benjamin Burton, 24. Officer in Revolutionary War; magistrate and state legislator post-war.

George Carleton.

John Cochran, 23.

Gilbert Colesworthy, 29.

Gershom Collier.

James Foster Condy. Bookseller.

Samuel Cooper, 18. Second lieutenant in artillery; later, quartermaster.

Thomas Dana, Jr.

Robert Davis, 26. Merchant, importer of groceries, wines, liquors; Freemason; artillery officer in war.

Joseph Eaton. Hatter, fought in artillery during the war.

————Eckley. Barber. Jailed after informer reported him to British.

William Etheridge. Mason.

Samuel Fenno. Housewright.

Samuel Foster. Minuteman at Lexington; captain during Revolutionary War.

John Fulton.

Samuel Hammond, 24. Farmer.

John Hicks, 18. Killed near Lexington.

Samuel Hobbs, 23. Farmer, tanner, leather worker.

Thomas Hunstsble, 20.

Abraham Hunt, 25. Wine-shop keeper, Freemason. Lieutenant, then captain during war.

David Kinnison, 27. Farmer; fought in Revolutionary War, War of 1812.

Amos Lincoln. 20. Housewright; Freemason; fought at Bunker Hill; served as artillery captain during war; supervised woodwork of Massachusetts State House; married a daughter of Paul Revere.

Thomas Machin, 29. Engineer, canal design and construction; surveyor. Wounded at Bunker Hill; served as lieutenant in artillery during war; laid out fortifications for defense of Boston and Boston Harbor.

Archibald MacNeil, 23.

John May, 25. Colonel in the Revolutionary War, Boston selectman and fire warden.

——Mead.

Anthony Morse. Lieutenant in Revolutionary War.

Joseph Mountford, 23. Cooper.

Eliphalet Newell. Freemason.

Joseph Pearse Palmer. Merchant of hardware, West Indian goods. Brigade major, then quartermaster-general in Revolutionary War.

Jonathan Parker. Helped capture cannon from gunhouse.

John Peters, 41. Born in Portugal; fought at Lexington, Bunker Hill, Saratoga, Yorktown. Moved to Philadelphia after war.

Samuel Pitts, 28. Merchant, Corps of Cadets.

Henry Prentiss, 24. Captain in artillery, then sea captain, then Boston merchant.

John Randall, 23.

Joseph Roby.

Robert Sessions, 21. Town official, South Wilbraham.

Phineas Stearns, 37. Farmer, blacksmith. Fought in French and Indian War and Revolutionary War.

Elisha Story, 30. Surgeon. Fought at Bunker Hill; served as doctor at Long Island, White Plains, and Trenton. Helped capture Boston cannons.

James Swan, 19. Merchant, politician, soldier, author.

John Truman.

Isaac Williams.

David Williams.

Jeremiah Williams, blacksmith.

Thomas Williams, 19. Minuteman at Lexington.

Nathaniel Willis, 18. Printer, publisher of *Independent Chronicle*.

Notes

Abbreviations:
Boston Public Library: BPL
Massachusetts Historical Society: MHS

Notes to Introduction

1. Herbert S. Allan, *John Hancock, Patriot in Purple* (New York: Beechurst Press, 1953), 136.

2. Douglass Adair and John A. Schutz, eds., *Peter Oliver's Origin & Progress of the American Rebellion: A Tory View* (Stanford, CA: Stanford University Press, 1961; original ms. written in 1781), 3.

3. Rodris Roth, "Tea Drinking in 18th-Century America: Its Etiquette and Equipage," in *United States National Museum Bulletin*, 61–91 (Washington, DC: Smithsonian Institution, 1961), 64.

4. Adair and Schutz, 28n.

5. Ibid., 143–44.

6. Ibid., 105.

7. Ibid.

8. Ibid., 162–63.

9. Lyman H. Butterfield, ed., *Diary and Autobiography of John Adams*, 4 vols. (Cambridge, MA: Harvard University Press, 1961), II:85–86.

Notes to Chapter 1

1. Adair and Schutz, 102.

2. Attributed to Adams by Francis Rotch, part owner of the *Dartmouth*, in Bernhard Knollenberg, *Growth of the American Revolution: 1766–1775* (New York: Free Press, 1975), 100.

3. Benjamin Woods Labaree, *The Boston Tea Party* (New York: Oxford University Press, 1964), 141.

4. Francis S. Drake, *Tea Leaves: Being a Collection of Documents Relating to the Shipment of Tea to the American Colonies in 1773 by the East India Company* (Boston: A. O. Crane, 1884), LXXI–LXXII.

5. Drake, LXVIII.

6. Adair and Schutz, 102–03.

7. Samuel Adams, *The Writings of Samuel Adams: 1764–1802, Collected and Edited by Harry Alonzo Cushing*, 4 vols. (New York: G. P. Putnam's Sons, 1908), I:5. [hereafter Adams, *Writings*]

8. Adair and Schutz, 28 (emphasis original).

9. Ibid.

10. John Adams to William Tudor, December 18, 1816; March 29, 1817; Charles Francis Adams, ed., *The Works of John Adams, Second President of the United States*, 10 vols. (Boston: Little, Brown and Company, 1856), X:232–34; 244–49. [hereafter Adams, *Works*]

11. Lawrence Henry Gipson, *The Coming of the Revolution, 1763–1775* (New York: Harper & Brothers, 1954), 38, citing William Tudor, *The Life of James Otis of Massachusetts* (Boston, 1823), 68–69.

12. A. B. Benson, ed., *Peter Kalm's Travels in North America*, 2 vols. (New York: Dover Publications, 1966), I:131, as cited in Gipson, 20.

13. *Boston News-Letter*, July 16, 1764, Boston Public Library [hereafter BPL].

14. Ibid.

15. W. T. Baxter, *The House of Hancock: Business in Boston, 1724–1775* (New York: Russell & Russell, 1965), 22.

16. Adair and Schutz, 39.

Notes to Chapter 2

1. Allan, 155.

2. *Boston Evening Post*, July 8, 1765, BPL.

3. Adair and Schutz, 162–63.

4. Samuel Eliot Morison, *Three Centuries of Harvard: 1636–1936* (Cambridge, MA: The Belknap Press of Harvard University Press, 1936), 144.

5. Donald Jackson and Dorothy Twohig, eds., *The Diaries of George Washington*, 6 vols. (Charlottesville: University Press of Virginia, 1976–79), I:195.

6. Adair and Schutz, 162.

Notes to Chapter 3

1. GW to Dinwiddie, June 3. 1754, in W. W. Abbot and Dorothy Twohig, eds., *The Papers of George Washington, Colonial Series: 1748–August 1755*, 10 vols. (Charlottesville: University Press of Virginia, 1983–1995), I:122–25.

2. Douglas Southall Freeman, *George Washington*, completed by John Alexander Carroll and Mary Wells Ashworth, 7 vols. (New York: Charles Scribner's Sons, 1957), II:21.

3. Ibid., II:64.

4. Gipson, 30.

5. Ibid., 34.

6. Arthur M. Schlesinger, *The Colonial Merchants and the American Revolution* (New York: Atheneum, 1968), 40–41.

7. G. S. Kimball, ed., *Correspondence of William Pitt*, 2 vols. (New York, 1906), II:320–21.

8. Adair and Schutz, 46.

9. Affidavit of Salem Custom House clerk Samuel Toovey, September 17, 1764, in Hiller B. Zobel, *The Boston Massacre* (New York: W. W. Norton & Company, 1970), 20.

10. Thomas Hutchinson, *The History of the Province of Massachusetts Bay, 1749–74*, 3 vols. (London: John Murray, 1828), 3:117–18.

11. James Truslow Adams, *Revolutionary New England, 1691–1776* (Boston: Atlantic Monthly Press, 1923), 269.

12. Hutchinson to Richard Jackson, May 5, 1765, in Zobel, 22.

13. *Boston Gazette*, January 31, 1763, BPL.

14. Peter Orlando Hutchinson, *The Diary and Letters of His Excellency Thomas Hutchinson, Esq., Captain-General and Governor-in-Chief of His Late Majesty's Province of Massachusetts Bay in North America*, 2 vols. (Boston: Houghton, Mifflin, & Co., 1884), I:6.

15. Gipson, 38.

16. Schlesinger, 54n.

17. Adams, I:32.

Notes to Chapter 4

1. Reverend Francis Thackeray, *A History of the Right Honorable William Pitt, Earl of Chatham* (London, 1827), 31.

2. Adams, *Revolutionary New England*, 293.

3. *Pennsylvania Journal*, August 17, 1774; *Boston Evening Post*, November 21, 1763, BPL.

4. Jean-Jacques Rousseau, *The Basic Political Writings: On the Social Contract*, trans. and ed. Donald A. Cress (Indianapolis, IN: Hackett Publishing Company, 1987), 141.

5. Ibid., 144–53.

6. Adair and Schutz, 4–5.

7. Bernhard Knollenberg, *Origin of the American Revolution: 1759–1766* (New York: Free Press, 1960), 142.

8. Production of local currencies had created shortages of British currency in both England and America, as colonists hoarded all the British pounds they could obtain and insisted on paying for goods and services with colonial rather than British pounds. The drain illustrated the economic principle that Sir Thomas Gresham would enunciate in 1858: that bad money drives out good money, that is, when two coins of equal face value have different intrinsic value—such as a copper penny vs. a gold penny—the coin with the lower intrinsic value will remain in circulation whereas the public hoards the more valuable coin, and it disappears from the market.

9. *Boston Gazette*, January 16, 1764, BPL.

10. James Otis, *The Rights of the British Colonies Asserted and Proved* (1763), quoted in Adams, *Writings*, X:293–94.

11. Ibid., 294.

12. To this day, members of Parliament do not necessarily live in the boroughs they represent, and in the eighteenth century many came from so-called rotten boroughs inhabited by fewer than fifty people, and pocket boroughs inhabited by a single noble family. As William Pitt charged in his demand for electoral reforms, "The House of Commons is not the representative of the people of Great Britain, but of nominal boroughs, ruined towns, noble families, wealthy individuals, and foreign potentates."

13. Soame Janyns, in Paul D. Brandes, *John Hancock's Life and Speeches* (Lanham, MD: Scarecrow Press, 1996), 45.

14. Johnson to Board of Trade, August 20, 1762, in Knollenberg, *Origin*, 89–90.

15. John Hancock to Bernard & Harrison, April 5, 1765, Hancock Papers, Massachusetts Historical Society [hereafter MHS].

16. Schlesinger, 67.

Notes to Chapter 5

1. Hutchinson, II:197–98.

2. Ibid., December 20, 1736.

3. Sears, 17.

4. Ibid.

5. Ibid.

6. Thomas Hancock to Christopher Kilby, June 12, 1755, in Baxter, 132.

7. Ibid.

Notes to Chapter 6

1. John Hancock to Barnard & Harrison, February 7, 1765, MHS.

2. "Proceedings of the House of Commons the resolution and the bill of February 7 and 13," *Journals of the House of Commons*, XXX:98–101.

3. Jackson Garth (agent for South Carolina) to South Carolina Committee of Correspondence, February 8, 1765, in Knollenberg, 207.

4. John Hancock to Barnard and Harrison, May 13, 1765, MHS.

5. John Hancock to Thomas Pownall, July 6, 1765, MHS.

6. Instructions of the Town of Braintree to their Representative, 1765, in Adams, *Works,* III:465–68.

7. Ibid.

8. William Wirt Henry, *Patrick Henry, Correspondence and Speeches*, 3 vols. (New York: Charles Scribner's Sons, 1891). Edmund Randolph recalled the speech differently, saying Henry actually retreated at the end of his attack. Here is how Randolph recalled this part of the speech: "'Caesar,' cried he, 'had his Brutus; Charles the first his Cromwell, and George the third . . . ' 'Treason, sir,' exclaimed the Speaker, to which Henry instantly replied, 'and George the third, may he never have either.'" Edmund Randolph, *History of Virginia*, ed. Arthur H. Shaffer (Charlottesville: The University Press of Virginia, published for the Virginia Historical Society, 1970), 169. But another burgess who heard Henry's speech rebuts Randolph: "If Henry did speak any apologetic words, they were doubtless uttered almost tongue in cheek to give him some legal protection." Randolph, 169 n.38–170n.

9. From Henry manuscript, in Moses Coit Tyler, *Patrick Henry* (Boston: Houghton Mifflin, 1887), 85.

10. Tyler, 85.

11. *Maryland Gazette*, July 4, 1765.

12. Letter from Fauquier, November 3, 1765, in Robert Douthat Meade, *Patrick Henry, Patriot in the Making* (Philadelphia: J. B. Lippincott Company, 1957), 184.

13. Tyler, 82.

14. *Boston Gazette*, April 4, 1763, BPL.

15. Adams, *Works*, II:178–79.

16. "Attack on Andrew Oliver of Massachusetts," Governor Bernard to Lord Halifax, August 15 and 16, 1765, Bernard Papers, cited in Knollenberg, *Origin*, 211.

17. Bernard to Board of Trade, August 15, 1765, in Gipson, 991.

Notes to Chapter 7

1. Hutchinson, I:18.

2. Adair and Schutz, 53–54.

3. Adams, *Writings*, II:201.

4. William M. Fowler, Jr., *The Baron of Beacon Hill: A Biography of John Hancock* (Boston: Houghton, Mifflin Company, 1980), 58–59.

5. Governor Bernard to Board of Trade, August 31, 1765, in Gipson, 93.

6. Adair and Schutz, 54.

7. Ibid., 52.

8. Ibid.

9. Governor Bernard to Board of Trade, August 31, 1765, in John C. Miller, *Samuel Adams: Pioneer in Propaganda* (Boston: Little, Brown and Company, 1936), 68.

10. Ibid.

11. Governor Bernard to Board of Trade, op. cit.

12. Adams, *Works*, II:259–61.

13. Ibid., II:144.

14. Adair and Schutz, 40.

15. Ibid.

16. John Hancock to Jonathan Barnard, September 11, 1765, Hancock Papers, MHS.

17. "A Petition to the King from the Stamp Act Congress, October 19, 1765," in Paul Leicester Ford, ed., *The Writings of John Dickinson, Volume I, Political Writings* (Philadelphia: The Historical Society of Pennsylvania, 1895), 193–96.

18. Francis Bernard to Thomas Pownall, November 5, 1765, Bernard Papers, Houghton Library, Harvard University, Cambridge, MA.

19. John Hancock to Jonathan Barnard, October 14, 1765, Hancock Papers, MHS.

20. John Hancock to Jonathan Barnard, December 1765, Hancock Papers, MHS.

21. John Hancock to Jonathan Barnard, January 18, 1766, Hancock Papers, MHS.

22. Francis Bernard to Thomas Pownall, November 6, 1765, Houghton Library.

23. Ibid.

24. John Hancock to Barnard & Harrison, December 21, 1765, MHS.

25. *Pennsylvania Gazette*, February 27, 1766.

26. George Washington to Francis Dandridge, September 20, 1765, in Abbot and Twohig, 7:395–96.

Notes to Chapter 8

1. Brandes, 53.

2. Grenville to House of Commons, December 17, 1765, in Knollenberg, *Origin*, 16.

3. Gipson, 110, citing *Parliamentary History of England* (London: T. C. Hansard, 1813), XVI.

4. English Merchants' Circular Letter, February 28, 1766, MHS.

5. *Parliamentary History of England*, XVI:181–88, as cited in Gipson, 115.

6. Ibid., XVI:172–76.

7. Customs Commissioners to Lords of the Treasury, March 27, 1766, in Public Record Office, cited in Baxter, 260.

8. Adams, *Works*, II:259–61.

9. *Massachusetts Gazette Extraordinary*, May 22, 1766, BPL.

10. Ibid.

11. Schlesinger, 92.

12. William V. Wells, *The Life and Public Services of Samuel Adams*, 3 vols. (Boston, 1865), I:124.

13. *Pennsylvania Gazette*, November 27, and December 11, 1766 (with datelines of September 20 and September 30, respectively).

14. Hutchinson, II:277.

15. Adams, *Works*, X:218.

16. *Boston Evening Post*, June 9, 1766, BPL.

17. John Hancock to William Reeve, September 3, 1767, New England Historical and Genealogical Society.

18. Adair and Schutz, 6.

19. *Boston Gazette*, October 3, 1768, BPL.

20. *Letters from a Farmer in Pennsylvania to the Inhabitants of the British Colonies by John Dickinson, 1768*, in Ford., *Writings of John Dickinson*, 307–406.

21. John Dickinson to James Otis, December 5, 1767, MHS.

22. *Boston Gazette*, March 14, 1768, BPL.

23. Customs Commissioners to Lord of the Treasury, May 12, 1768, in Knollenberg, *Growth*, 56.

24. Wells, I:186.

Notes to Chapter 9

1. Excerpt from a "Letter to a Loyalist Lady," cited in John C. Miller, *Samuel Adams: Pioneer in Propaganda* (Boston: Little, Brown and Company, 1936), 141.

2. Miller, 142.

3. Ibid., 144–45.

4. *Boston Gazette*, August 4, 1768, BPL.

5. *Boston Gazette*, July 3, 1767, BPL.

6. Ibid.

7. George Washington to George Mason, April 5, 1769, in Abbot and Twohig, *The Papers of George Washington, Colonial Series*, 8:177–81.

8. Sears, 114.

9. Miller, 153.

10. *New Hampshire Gazette*, November 1, 1768, BPL.

11. Hutchinson, *The Diary and Letters*, II:333.

12. Francis Bernard to Lord Hillsborough, October 1, 1768, and William Dalrymple to Thomas Gage, October 2, 1768, in Colonial Office Documents, cited in Zobel, 181.

13. David Hackett Fischer, *Paul Revere's Ride* (New York: Oxford University Press, 1994), 22.

14. *Boston Gazette*, October 26, 1768, BPL.

15. Thomas Gage to Lord Hillsborough, October 26, 1768, in Gipson, 191.

16. *Boston Evening Post*, July 24 and 31, 1769, BPL.

17. Francis Bernard to Lord Hillsborough, October 4, 1768, in Colonial Office Documents, in Zobel, 183.

18. Thomas Hutchinson to Thomas Whately, October 4, 1768, in Allan, 114.

19. Butterfield, III:306.

20. Ibid., 306n.

21. Roth, 68, citing Léon Chotteau, *Les Français en Amérique* (Paris, 1876).

22. Ibid.

23. *Boston Gazette*, August 29, 1768, in Schlesinger, 109.

24. *Boston News-Letter,* January 11, 1770.

25. Schlesinger, 173.

26. Unsigned, undated paper from America, c. 1769, "Liverpool Papers," in Labaree, 31.

27. Adair and Schutz, 72–73.

28. *Newport Mercury*, September 4, 1769, BPL.

29. *Boston Chronicle*, October 26, 1769, BPL.

30. Ibid., October 30, 1769, BPL.

31. Adair and Schutz, 105.

32. Article by Samuel Adams, signed "An Impartialist," in *Boston Gazette*, September 25, 1769, BPL.

33. Adams, *Works*, II:226–27.

34. Thomas Hutchinson to Francis Bernard, November 27, 1769, Bernard Papers, MHS.

35. Ibid., 227.

36. Miller, 220.

37. William Samuel Johnson to Jonathan Trumbull, February 3, 1771, MHS.

38. Ibid.

Notes to Chapter 10

1. Hutchinson, *Diary and Letters*, III:136.

2. Adair and Schutz, 42–43, 105.

3. Gipson, 197.

4. Zobel, 167.

5. Ibid., 171.

6. Roth, 66.

7. Ibid.

8. Ibid.

9. M. Jacquelin, York, Virginia, to John Norton, London, August 14, 1769, in Roth, 66.

10. *Boston Post-Boy*, November 16, 1767, in Schlesinger, 108.

11. Butterfield, I:349–50.

12. *Boston Gazette*, February 26, 1770, BPL.

13. Thomas Gage to Lord Hillsborough, April 10, 1770, in Zobel, 181.

14. Brandes, 83.

15. Zobel, 189.

16. Zobel, 189–294 and 346–56 cover these events in detail, minute by minute.

17. Ibid.

18. Ibid.

19. Ibid.

20. Ibid., 202.

21. Ibid., 203.

22. Adams, *Works*, II:229–30.

23. *New York Public Advertiser*, April 28, 1770, New York Public Library.

24. *Boston Gazette*, March 12, 1770, BPL.

25. Pelham sent Revere an angry letter accusing the silversmith of printing the Pelham drawing without permission and depriving the artist of his just revenues "as truly as if you had plundered me on the public highway." They eventually settled their differences. Fischer, 23n.

26. Committee to Pownall, March 12, 1770, in *Gentleman's Magazine* (London), April 1770.

27. Adams, *Works*, VIII:384.

Notes to Chapter 11

1. John Ferling, *John Adams, A Life* (New York: Henry Holt and Company, 1992), 70.

2. Harlow Giles Unger, *John Hancock, Merchant King and American Patriot* (New York: John Wiley & Sons, 2000), 150.

3. Adair and Schutz, 91–92.

4. Ibid., 88.

5. *Boston Gazette*, December 10, 1770–January 28, 1771, BPL.

6. Miller, 235–36.

7. Schlesinger, 240.

8. Ibid., 241.

9. Adams, *Works*, II:260.

10. Hutchinson to person unknown, June 5, 1771, in Allan, 123–24.

11. Hutchinson to Thomas Gage, December 1, 1771, Massachusetts Archives, XXVII, 258.

12. Hutchinson to Francis Bernard, January 29, 1772, ibid., 286.

13. *Journals of the House of Representatives of Massachusetts, 1772* (Boston), 15.

14. Samuel Adams to Arthur Lee, April 22, 1773, in Allan, *John Hancock*, 125, citing R. H. Lee, *Life of Arthur Lee* (Boston, 1829), 203.

15. *Boston Gazette*, May 12, 1772, BPL.

16. Hutchinson to Lord Hillsborough, June 15, 1772, in Allan, *John Hancock*, 127.

17. Adair and Schutz, 110.

18. Boston Town Records, 95–108, cited in Fowler, Jr., 148.

19. Ibid.

20. Ibid., 149.

21. Hutchinson, II:364–69.

22. *Boston Gazette*, January 11, 1773, BPL.

23. John Adams, "Two Replies of the Massachusetts House of Representatives to Governor Hutchinson," in George A. Peek, Jr., *The Revolutionary Writings of John Adams* (Indianapolis, IN: Liberty Fund, 2000), 117–45.

24. Hutchinson to Thomas Whately, October 4, 1768, and January 1769, in Fowler, 132–33.

25. Sears, 128–29.

26. Gipson, 219.

27. Brandes, 103.

28. Fowler, 158.

29. Brandes, 104, citing John Boyle's "Journal of Occurrences in Boston," *New England Historical and Genealogical Society Register* 84 (1930), 367–68.

30. Ibid., citing Anne Row Cunningham, ed., *Letters & Diary of John Rowe* (Boston, 1903).

31. Thomas Hutchinson to John Hancock, November 11, 1773, First Corps of Cadet Papers, Mugar Memorial Library, Boston, cited in Brandes, 106.

32. Brandes, 107.

33. Allan, 136.

34. Hutchinson to person unknown, December 3, 1773, in ibid., 138.

35. Ibid., 34.

36. Attributed to Adams by Francis Rotch, part owner of the *Dartmouth*, in Knollenberg, 100.

37. Labaree, 141.

38. Ibid.

39. Drake, XC.

40. Valuation determined by East India Company, in Knollenberg, *Growth*, 100. Another estimate in Drake, *Tea Leaves* (LXV) puts the value at twice that amount.

41. Ferling, 92.

42. Drake, LXXXVIII.

43. *Massachusetts Gazette*, December 23, 1773, BPL.

44. Adams, *Writings*, III:64.

45. Samuel Adams to Arthur Lee, December 31, 1773, and January 25, 1774, in ibid., III:66–68 and III:69–71.

Notes to Chapter 12

1. Drake, LXXXV, LXXXVII.

2. Knollenberg, *Growth*, 99–100.

3. Ibid., 100.

4. Allan, 140–41.

5. Zobel, 189–294 and 346–56 cover the events in minute-by-minute detail.

6. Fischer, 25–26.

7. The Boston Tea Party and the antipathy it produced for English tea ended consumption of tea as the primary hot beverage in the colonies and, later, the United States. Americans turned to hot chocolate and hot coffee instead. Ironically, Britain itself produced no tea.

8. Tryon to Lord Dartmouth, January 3, 1774, in Gipson, 221.

9. Butterfield, II:85–86.

10. Hancock to Jonathan Barnard, December 21, 1773, MHS.

11. Robert Douthat Meade, *Patrick Henry, Practical Revolutionary* (Philadelphia, PA: J. B. Lippincott Company, 1969), 3.

12. Adair and Schutz, 98.

13. Hutchinson, I:133.

14. Adair and Schutz, 112.

15. William Sullivan, *Familiar Letters on Public Characters and Public Events . . .* (Boston: Russell, Odiorne, and Metcalf, 1834), 10 (Letter of January 27, 1833), in BPL.

16. Ebenezer S. Thomas, *Reminiscences of the Last Sixty-five Years* (Boston: Case, Tiffany, and Barnham, 1840), I:244, BPL.

17. John Hancock, *An Oration Delivered, March 4, 1774, at the Request of the Inhabitants of the Town of Boston to Commemorate the Bloody Tragedy of the Fifth of March, 1770* (Boston: Edes & Gill, 1774), BPL.

18. Adams, *Works*, II:332.

19. Report of the British Attorney-General and Solicitor-General, February 11, 1774, in Labaree, 174–75.

20. *Remarks of a Merchant who makes an annual Progress through the Colonies . . . ,* February 1774, Dartmouth Papers, William Salt Library, Stafford, England; *Morning Chronicle,* February 23, 1774.

21. *Parliamentary History,* XVII, 1167–69.

22. Edmund Burke, *Speech on Conciliation with America,* in Louis I. Bredvold and Ralph G. Ross, *The Philosophy of Edmund Burke: A Selection from His Speeches and Writings* (Ann Arbor: The University of Michigan Press, 1967), 36–37.

23. Knollenberg, *Growth,* 105.

24. Ibid., 108.

25. Miller, 300.

26. Hutchinson, *Diary and Letters,* I:133.

27. Committee of Correspondence Papers, June 24, 1774, MHS.

28. George Washington to George William Fairfax, June 19, 1774, in Abbot and Twohig, *Papers of George Washington, Colonial Series,* 10:94–101.

29. Knollenberg, *Growth,* 163–64.

30. Thomas Hutchinson, Sr. to Thomas Hutchinson III, July 2, 1774, in ibid., 179–80.

31. Ibid.

32. Thomas Hutchinson to General Gage, July 4, 1774, in Hutchinson, *Diary and Letters,* 175–76.

33. Edmund Burke, *First Speech on the Conciliation with America and American Taxation* before Parliament, April 19, 1774, as cited in John Bartlett and Justin Kaplan, eds., *Familiar Quotations,* 16th ed. (Boston: Little, Brown and Company, 1992), 331.

34. Hutchinson, *Diary and Letters,* 188–89.

35. Henry, I:164.

36. *Virginia Gazette,* July 28, 1774.

Notes to Chapter 13

1. Ford, *Writings of John Dickinson,* I:9–10.

2. Samuel Adams to Richard Henry Lee, April 10, 1773 and *New Hampshire Gazette,* June 18, 1773, in Henry, I:167–68.

3. William Palfrey to Samuel Adams, September 1774, in First Corps Cadet Papers, cited by Allan, 175.

4. Allan, 164.

5. Knollenberg, *Growth,* 168.

6. Ferling, 126.

7. *Boston Evening Post,* September 19, 1774, BPL.

8. Allan, 164.

9. William Lincoln, ed., *The Journals of Each Provincial Congress of Massachusetts in 1774 and 1775 . . .* (Boston: 1838), 643–44, BPL.

10. Ibid., 629.

11. Circular letter of April 20, 1773, in Knollenberg, *Growth*, 261.

12. *Boston News-Letter,* January 11, 1770.

13. [Samuel Johnson], *Taxation No Tyranny* (London, 1775), cited in Knollenberg, *Origin*, 261.

14. Adams, *Works*, X:197.

15. Entry dated March 6, 1775, in Elizabeth E. Dana, ed., *The British in Boston: Being the Diary of Lieutenant John Barker* (Cambridge, MA, 1924), 25–26.

16. Hutchinson, *Diary and Letters*, I:203.

17. Unger, *Hancock*, 191.

18. Edmund Burke, *Second Speech on Conciliation with America. The Thirteen Resolutions*, March 12, 1775, in Bartlett and Kaplan, *Familiar Quotations*, 331.

19. Thomas Hutchinson to _____, August 8, 1774, Hutchinson, *Diary and Letters*, I:215.

20. Ibid.

21. Henry, I:257–58.

22. Ibid.

23. Ibid., I:262–64.

24. Ibid., I:266. (*Author's note*: No actual transcript of Henry's speech exists; the words shown here represent a reconstruction by Henry's first biographer William Wirt. A renowned attorney and historian, Wirt extrapolated its contents from recollections— forty years after the event—by those present at St. Paul's, including Judge John Tyler, an intimate of Henry's, Thomas Jefferson, Edmund Randolph, and Judge St. George Tucker, among others. Hardly a friend of Henry, Jefferson did not alter a word in Wirt's reconstruction of the speech and reiterated his appraisal of Henry as the greatest orator in history. As I stated previously, I believe that word-for-word accuracy is less important than an accurate presentation of Henry's meaning, his passion, and his eloquence.)

25. MHS *Proceedings*.

26. MHS *Proceedings*, 1st Series, V (1862):211.

27. MHS *Journals*, 509–12.

28. Ibid., 748–50.

29. All four guns served in the Revolutionary War, although two of them eventually fell into British hands, whereas the "Adams" exploded and left the Hancock as the only one to serve during the entire war. It stands today at the Bunker Hill Monument with this inscription attached:

THE HANCOCK

SACRED TO LIBERTY

This is one of four cannon which constituted the
whole train of Field Artillery possessed by the
British colonies of North America
at the commencement of the war on the

19th of April, 1775.

THIS CANNON

and its fellow, belonging to a number of citizens

of Boston, were used in many engagements

during the war. The other two, the

property of the Government of

Massachusetts, were taken by

the enemy.

By order of the United States Congress assembled, May 19, 1788.

30. John Hancock to Edmund Quincy, April 7, 1775, Houghton Library.

31. Fowler, Jr., 181.

32. Paul Revere to corresponding secretary of Massachusetts Historical Society in MHS *Collections*, 1st Series, V (1798):106–07, MHS.

33. Ibid., 107.

34. Ibid.

35. General William H. Sumner, "Reminiscences," in *New England Historical and Genealogical Register* VIII (1854):187–88.

36. Knollenberg, *Growth*, 189.

37. Elizabeth Clarke to Lucy W. Allen, April 19, 1841, in Lexington Historical Society *Proceedings* IV (1912):91–92.

38. Ibid., 91.

Notes to Chapter 14

1. G. R. Barnes and J. H. Owens, eds., *The Private Papers of John, Earl of Sandwich, First Lord of the Admiralty, 1771–1782* (Naval Records Society Publications 69, 71, 75, 78 (1932–1938), I:61, cited in Don Higginbotham, *The War of Independence: Military Attitudes, Policies and Practice, 1763–1789* (New York: Macmillan Company, 1971), 61.

2. Although romantics call the first shot fired at Lexington "the shot heard 'round the world," the phrase was actually created by Ralph Waldo Emerson for the first stanza of the "Hymn Sung at the Completion of the Battle Monument" at Concord, July 4, 1837, and it refers to the skirmish at Concord Bridge *after* Lexington—not the encounter at Lexington:

> *By the rude bridge that arched the flood,*
> *Their flag to April's breeze unfurled,*
> *Here once the embattled farmers stood,*
> *and fired the shot heard round the world.*

3. Pitcairn to Gage, April 1775, in Clarence E. Carter, ed., *The Correspondence of General Thomas Gage* (New Haven, CT: Yale University Press, 1931–1933), II:181,

cited in Bruce Lancaster, *From Lexington to Liberty, The Story of the American Revolution* (Garden City, NY: Doubleday & Company, 1955), 99.

4. Lord Percy to General Edward Harvey, April 20, 1775, in Charles K. Bolton, ed., *The Letters of Hugh Earl Percy . . . 1774–1776* (1902), cited in Knollenberg, *Growth*, 195.

5. *Essex Gazette*, April 25, 1775, BPL.

6. Knollenberg, *Growth*, 267.

7. Abigail Adams to Mary Cranch, October 6, 1766, in Ferling, 53.

8. Ferling, 124.

9. Sears, 178–79.

10. Higginbotham, 84.

11. Worthington C. Ford, ed., *Journals of the Continental Congress*, 34 vols. (Washington, DC, 1904–1936), II:77–78.

12. Richard Frothingham, *The Life and Times of Joseph Warren* (Boston: Little, Brown and Company, 1865), 495–96.

13. "Proscription of Thomas Gage," June 12, 1775, in Peter Force, ed., *American Archives . . .* , 4th ser., II (1839):969.

14. Higginbotham, 84–85.

15. Ferling, 124.

16. Adams, *Works*, II:416–17.

17. Miller, 336.

18. Ibid.

19. Ibid.

20. John Hancock to Joseph Warren, June 18, 1775, in Allan, 196.

21. Adair and Schutz, 143–44.

22. Ibid., 143, 143n.

23. Journal of Chief Justice Peter Oliver, in Hutchinson, *Diary and Letters*, II:48.

24. Rev. Andrew Oliver to Peter Oliver, July 27, 1787, in Hutchinson, *Diary and Letters*, II:423–24.

25. Lord Stirling to John Hancock, January 10, 1776, MHS.

26. George Washington to John Hancock, March 19, 1776, in W. W. Abbot, Dorothy Twohig, and Philander D. Chase, eds., *The Papers of George Washington, Revolutionary War Series, June 1775–April 1778*, 14 vols. (Charlottesville: University of Virginia Press, 1984–2004 [in progress]), 3:489–91.

Notes to Chapter 15

1. *Columbian Sentinel*, April 2, 1794.

2. *Maryland Gazette*, July 4, 1765.

3. Ibid.

4. Adair and Schutz, 144–51.
5. Journal of Chief Justice Peter Oliver, in Hutchinson, II:48.
6. Ibid., II:193–96.

Note to Appendix B

1. List taken from Drake.

Bibliography

Abbot, W. W., and Dorothy Twohig, eds. *The Papers of George Washington, Colonial Series: 1748–August 1755*. 10 vols. Charlottesville: University Press of Virginia, 1983–1995.

Abbot, W. W., Dorothy Twohig, and Philander D. Chase, eds. *The Papers of George Washington, Revolutionary War Series, June 1775–April 1778*. 14 vols. Charlottesville: University of Virginia Press, 1984–2004 [in progress].

Adair, Douglas, and John A. Schutz, eds. *Peter Oliver's Origin and Progress of the American Rebellion: A Tory View*. Stanford, CA: Stanford University Press, 1961.

Adams, Charles Francis, ed. *The Works of John Adams, Second President of the United States*. 10 vols. Boston: Little, Brown and Company, 1856.

Adams, James Truslow. *Revolutionary New England: 1691–1776*. Boston: The Atlantic Monthly Press, 1923.

Adams, Samuel. *The Writings of Samuel Adams: 1764–1802, Collected and Edited by Harry Alonzo Cushing*. 4 vols. New York: G. P. Putnam's Sons, 1908.

Alden, John R.. *History of the American Revolution*. New York: Alfred A. Knopf, 1969.

Allan, Herbert S. *John Hancock, Patriot in Purple*. New York: Beechurst Press, 1953.

Ayling, Stanley. *George the Third*. New York: Alfred A. Knopf, 1972.

Ballagh, James C., ed. *The Letters of Richard Henry Lee*. 2 vols. New York: The Macmillan Company, 1911–1914.

Baxter, W. T. *The House of Hancock: Business in Boston, 1724–1775*. New York: Russell & Russell, 1965.

Benson, A. B., ed. *Per Kalm's Travels in North America*. 2 vols. New York, 1937.

Brandes, Paul D. *John Hancock's Life and Speeches*. Lanham, MD: Scarecrow Press, 1996.

Bredvold, Louis I., and Ralph G. Ross. *The Philosophy of Edmund Burke: A Selection from His Speeches and Writings*. Ann Arbor: The University of Michigan Press, 1967.

Brooke, John. *King George III, America's Last Monarch*. New York: McGraw-Hill, 1972.

Burnett, Edmund C., ed. *Letters of Members of the Continental Congress*. 8 vols. Washington DC: U.S. Government Printing Office, 1921–1938.

Butterfield, Lyman H., ed. *Diary and Autobiography of John Adams*. 4 vols. Cambridge, MA: Harvard University Press, 1961.

Carter, Clarence E., ed. *The Correspondence of General Thomas Gage*. New Haven, CT: Yale University Press, 1931–1933.

Cary, John. *Joseph Warren: Physician, Politician, Patriot*. Urbana: University of Illinois Press, 1961.

Chotteau, Léon. *Les Français en Amérique*. Paris: G. Charpentier, 1879.

Cushing, Harry Alonzo, ed. *The Writings of Samuel Adams, 1764–1802*. 4 vols. New York: G. P. Putnam's Sons, 1904–1908.

Dana, Elizabeth E., ed. *The British in Boston: Being the Diary of Lieutenant John Barker*. Cambridge, MA: 1924.

Drake, Francis S. *Tea Leaves: Being a Collection of Documents Relating to the Shipment of Tea to the American Colonies in 1773 by the East India Company*. Boston: A. O. Crane, 1884.

Ferling, John. *John Adams, A Life*. New York: Henry Holt and Company, 1992.

Fitzpatrick, John C., ed. *The Writings of George Washington, from the Original Manuscript Sources, 1745–1799*. 39 vols. Washington, DC: U.S. Government Printing Office, 1931–1944.

Fischer, David Hackett. *Paul Revere's Ride*. New York: Oxford University Press, 1994.

Ford, Paul Leicester, ed., *The Writings of John Dickinson*. Philadelphia: The Historical Society of Pennsylvania, 1895.

Ford, Worthington C., ed. *Journals of the Continental Congress*. 34 vols. Washington, DC: Library of Congress, 1904–1936.

Fowler, William M., Jr. *The Baron of Beacon Hill: A Biography of John Hancock*. Boston: Houghton Mifflin, 1980.

Freeman, Douglas Southall. *George Washington*, completed by John Alexander Carroll and Mary Wells Ashworth. 7 vols. New York: Charles Scribner's Sons, 1957.

Frothingham, Richard. *Life and Times of Joseph Warren*. Boston: Little, Brown and Company, 1865.

Gipson, Lawrence Henry. *The Coming of the Revolution, 1763–1775*. New York: Harper & Brothers, 1954.

Henry, William Wirt. *Patrick Henry, Correspondence and Speeches*. 3 vols. New York: Charles Scribner's Sons, 1891.

Higgenbotham, Don. *The War of Independence: Military Attitudes, Policies and Practice, 1763–1789*. New York: Macmillan Company, 1971.

Hutchinson, Peter Orlando, ed. *The Diary and Letters of His Excellency Thomas Hutchinson, Esq. Captain-General and Governor-in-Chief of His Late Majesty's Province of Massachusetts Bay, in North America . . . compiled from the original documents still remaining in the possession of his descendants by Peter Orlando Hutchinson, one of his great grandsons.* 2 vols. Boston: Houghton Mifflin, 1884.

Hutchinson, Thomas. *The History of the Province of Massachusetts Bay, 1749–74*. 3 vols. London: John Murray, 1828.

Jackson, Donald, and Dorothy Twohig, eds. *The Diaries of George Washington*. 6 vols. Charlottesville: University Press of Virginia, 1976–79.

The Journals of Each Provincial Congress of Massachusetts in 1774 and 1775. . . . Boston, 1838.

Journals of the House of Representatives of Massachusetts, 1772. Boston.

Kalm, Peter, *The America of 1750: Peter Kalm's Travels in North America*. Edited and translated by Adolph B. Benson. New York: Dover Publications, 1966.

Kimball, G. S., ed. *Correspondence of William Pitt*. 2 vols. New York: Macmillan, 1906.

Knollenberg, Bernhard. *Growth of the American Revolution: 1766–1775*. New York: Free Press, 1975.

———. *Origin of the American Revolution: 1759–1766*. New York: The Free Press, 1960.

Labaree, Benjamin Woods. *The Boston Tea Party*. New York: Oxford University Press, 1964.

Lancaster, Bruce. *From Lexington to Liberty, The Story of the American Revolution*. Garden City, NY: Doubleday & Company, 1955.

Lee, R. H. *Life of Arthur Lee*. 2 vols. Boston: Wells and Lilly, 1829.

Lee, Richard Henry. *The Letters of Richard Henry Lee*. Danvers, MA: General Books, 2009.

Meade, Robert Douthat. *Patrick Henry, Patriot in the Making*. Philadelphia: J. B. Lippincott Company, 1957.

———. *Patrick Henry, Practical Revolutionary*. Philadelphia: J. B. Lippincott Company, 1969.

Miller, John C. *Samuel Adams: Pioneer in Propaganda*. Boston: Little, Brown and Company, 1936.

Morison, Samuel Eliot. *Three Centuries of Harvard, 1636–1936*. Cambridge, MA: The Belknap Press of Harvard University Press, 1936.

Parliamentary History of England. London: T. C. Hansard, 1813.

Peek, George A., Jr. *The Revolutionary Writings of John Adams*. Indianapolis, IN: Liberty Fund, 2000.

Randolph, Edmund. *History of Virginia*. Edited by Arthur H. Shaffer. Charlottesville: The University Press of Virginia, published for the Virginia Historical Society, 1970.

Rose, J. Holland. *The Life of William Pitt*. London: Bell & Sons, 1923.

Roth, Rodris. "Tea Drinking in 18th-Century America: Its Etiquette and Equipage." In *United States National Museum Bulletin*, 61–91. Washington, DC: Smithsonian Institution, 1961.

Rousseau, Jean-Jacques. *The Basic Political Writings: On the Social Contract*. Translated and edited by Donald A. Cress. Indianapolis, IN: Hackett Publishing Company, 1987.

Schlesinger, Arthur M. *The Colonial Merchants and the American Revolution*. New York: Atheneum, 1968.

Sears, Lorenzo. *John Hancock, the Picturesque Patriot*. Boston: Little, Brown and Company, 1913.

Smith, Page. *John Adams*. 2 vols. Garden City, NY: Doubleday & Company, 1962.

Stillé, Charles J., ed. *The Writings of John Dickinson*. 2 vols. Philadelphia: The Historical Society of Pennsylvania, 1895.

Sullivan, William. *Familiar Letters on Public Characters and Public Events. . . .* Boston: Russell, Odiorne, and Metcalf, 1834.

Sutherland, Lucy S., ed. *The Correspondence of Edmund Burke, 1768–1774*. Cambridge: Cambridge University Press, 1960.

Thackeray, Reverend Francis. *A History of the Right Honorable William Pitt, Earl of Chatham*. London, 1827.

Thatcher, Benjamin B. *Traits of the Tea Party: Being a Memoir of George R. T. Hewes*. New York: Harper Brothers, 1835.

Thomas, Ebenezer S. *Reminiscences of the Last Sixty-five Years*. Hartford, CT: Case, Tiffany and Burnham, 1840.

Tudor, William. *The Life of James Otis of Massachusetts*. Boston: Wells and Lilly, 1823.

Tyler, Moses Coit. *Patrick Henry*. Boston: Houghton Mifflin, 1887.

Unger, Harlow Giles. *America's Second Revolution*. Hoboken, NJ: John Wiley & Sons, 2007.

———. *John Hancock: Merchant King and American Patriot*. New York: John Wiley & Sons, 2000.

———. *Lafayette*. Hoboken, NJ: John Wiley & Sons, 2002.

———. *The Last Founding Father: James Monroe and a Nation's Call to Greatness*. Philadelphia, PA: Da Capo Press, Perseus Books Group, 2009.

———. *The Unexpected George Washington: His Private Life*. Hoboken, NJ: John Wiley & Sons, 2006.

Wells, William V. *The Life and Public Services of Samuel Adams*. 3 vols. Boston: Little, Brown and Company, 1865.

Zobel, Hiller B. *The Boston Massacre*. New York: W. W. Norton & Company, 1970.

Reference Works

Bartlett, John, and Justin Kaplan, eds. *Familiar Quotations*. 16th ed. Boston: Little, Brown and Company, 1992.

The New Encyclopedia Britannica. 15th ed. Chicago: Encyclopedia Britannica, 1985.

Morris, Richard B. *Encyclopedia of American History*. New York: Harper & Brothers, 1953.

Ploetz' Dictionary of Dates. New York: Halcyon House, 1925.

Unger, Harlow G. *Encyclopedia of American Education*. 3 vols. 3rd ed. New York: Facts On File, 2007.

van Doren, Charles, ed. *Webster's American Biographies*. Springfield, MA: Merriam-Webster, 1984.

Manuscript Collections

Bostonian Society
Boston Public Library
Houghton Library, Harvard University
Library of Congress
Massachusetts Historical Society, Boston
Massachusetts State Archives
New England Historical and Genealogical Society
New York Historical Society
New York Public Library

Newspapers

Boston Chronicle
Boston Evening Post
Boston Gazette
Boston News-Letter
Boston Post-Boy
Maryland Gazette
Massachusetts Gazette Extraordinary
New Hampshire Gazette
Newport Mercury
New York Public Advertiser
Pennsylvania Journal
Virginia Gazette

General References

Dictionary of American Biography
The Dictionary of National Biography
Encyclopedia Britannica
Encyclopedia of American History
Webster's American Biographies
Webster's New Biographical Dictionary

Index